Open Minds 1re

Anglais Toutes séries B1-B2

Sous la direction de
Jean-Louis HABERT

Auteurs

Eva BOUSSAGUET
Agrégée d'anglais, Lycée Dhuoda, Nîmes

Claire CHAUVET
Agrégée d'anglais, Internat de la Réussite, Montpellier

Nathalie DESTRUELS
Certifiée d'anglais, Lycée Jean-Baptiste-Dumas, Alès

Jean-Louis HABERT
Agrégé d'anglais, docteur en linguistique

Martine HOYET
Certifiée d'anglais, Lycée Albert-Camus, Nîmes

Florence ROUX
Certifiée d'anglais, Lycée Alphonse-Daudet, Nîmes

Joanna WISTREICH
Certifiée d'anglais, Lycée Alphonse-Daudet, Nîmes

Avec la collaboration de
Graham Bushnell, M. A. (Oxon), RSA (Dip. TEFL)
et de Martine Roux-Bee, académie de Montpellier.

Belin: ÉDITEUR INDÉPENDANT DEPUIS 1777

8, RUE FÉROU 75278 PARIS CEDEX 06
WWW.EDITIONS-BELIN.COM

Illustrations et cartographie : Corédoc.
Iconographie : Any-claude Medioni.

Toutes les références à des sites Internet présentées dans cet ouvrage ont été vérifiées attentivement à la date d'impression. Compte tenu de la volatilité des sites et du détournement possible de leur adresse, les éditions Belin ne peuvent en aucun cas être tenues pour responsables de leur évolution. Nous appelons donc chaque utilisateur à rester vigilant quant à leur utilisation.

ISBN 978-2-7011-9274-1

Avant-propos

Les contenus de ***Open Minds 1re*** et les outils pédagogiques qui l'accompagnent ont été conçus et organisés pour répondre à plusieurs exigences :
– **appliquer le programme du cycle terminal**, tant pour ce qui est des savoirs que des savoir-faire (compétences) ;
– permettre une mise en place efficace de l'**approche actionnelle** ;
– commencer à entraîner les élèves aux nouvelles formes de l'examen final, à l'écrit comme à l'oral, et les aider à **acquérir la méthodologie** la mieux adaptée à leur réussite ;
– ouvrir l'esprit des élèves aux divers aspects de la civilisation anglo-saxonne, tout en les aidant à développer leur esprit critique envers le monde contemporain.

Ce manuel compte douze chapitres, répartis dans quatre parties correspondant aux grands **thèmes culturels du programme** (notions) : *Espaces et échanges, Mythes et héros, L'idée de progrès* et *Lieux et formes du pouvoir*.
Les divers aspects d'une notion sont étudiés sous la forme d'une **problématique**. Les deux premiers chapitres de chaque notion sont divisés en huit doubles pages ; le troisième contient deux doubles pages dédiées à la lecture cursive, tournées vers **l'étude littéraire**.

• La 1re double page pose la **thématique générale du chapitre**, à l'aide d'images qui en résument les différentes composantes et invitent les élèves à réagir.

• Les 2e, 3e et 4e doubles pages sont consacrées à l'**apprentissage de la langue**, de la **civilisation** et à la maîtrise des **compétences**. Les **supports** choisis, courts et variés, permettent la construction d'un projet pédagogique personnalisé. Une insistance particulière est mise sur **l'enrichissement lexical**. Chaque double page de leçon se termine par une **mini-tâche actionnelle (Your task)** préparant à la **tâche finale (Final task)**.

• La 5e double page vise des **aspects civilisationnels**, reliés à la thématique de chaque chapitre.

• La 6e est dédiée à la **réflexion sur la langue** et à la grammaire de l'anglais.

• La 7e contient des exercices d'**enrichissement** du vocabulaire et la **Final task**, projet **actionnel** en relation avec les contenus des pages qui précèdent.

• La 8e double page est consacrée à l'entraînement à l'examen (épreuves écrites et orales) ; les sujets types proposés sont accompagnés d'une **méthode appliquée**. Pour la classe de 1re, l'épreuve écrite est abordée avec un texte unique.

• Les 9e et 10e doubles pages proposent des extraits tirés de la littérature anglo-saxonne contemporaine et accompagnés d'une didactisation spécifique.

Les fiches du **Workbook téléchargeable** sont de trois sortes : aide à la compréhension du lexique des supports proposés (écrits ou audio) ; aide à la compréhension détaillée du contenu desdits supports ; entraînement à la maîtrise des faits de langues les plus courants.

Bonne réussite à tous !

LES AUTEURS

Les clés du manuel

L'OUVERTURE DE CHAPITRE

Trois **documents iconographiques** illustrant les thèmes traités dans les chapitres.

Des questions pour introduire les **problématiques**.

LES LEÇONS

La ou les **activités langagières** travaillées dans le document.

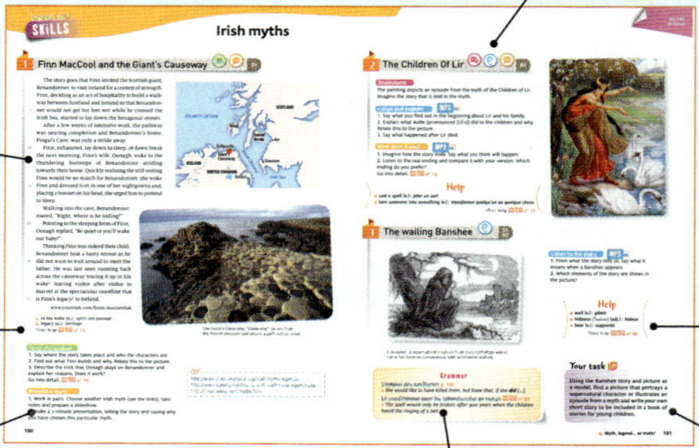

Des documents variés sur **différents supports**.

Le renvoi au **Workbook** téléchargeable.

Une **aide lexicale** pour les documents audio.

Les questions et les activités : un travail équilibré sur les **cinq compétences**.

À la fin de chaque leçon, une **tâche intermédiaire** pour préparer la tâche finale.

Des **faits de langue** soulevés dans les doubles pages de documents.

CROSS CULTURE

Des documents iconographiques sur des **thèmes variés** (art, histoire, société…).

Des activités en lien avec les thèmes des chapitres, pour développer la **culture générale**.

LOGOS

Compréhension de l'écrit — Expression écrite — Compréhension orale — Expression orale — Expression orale en interaction

DVD Renvoi au DVD classe — MP3 9 Renvoi au fichier MP3 — WBT n° 42 Renvoi au Workbook téléchargeable

Les fichiers MP3 et le WBT sont téléchargeables gratuitement sur le site **www.libtheque.fr/anglaislycee**

GRAMMAIRE

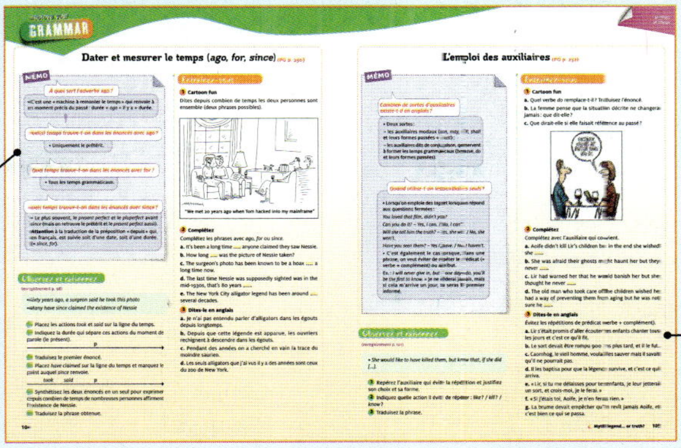

Une **fiche Mémo**
Des réponses aux questions les plus courantes que se posent les élèves. L'essentiel à retenir.

Des exercices de **réflexion** sur la langue.

VOCABULAIRE

FINAL TASK

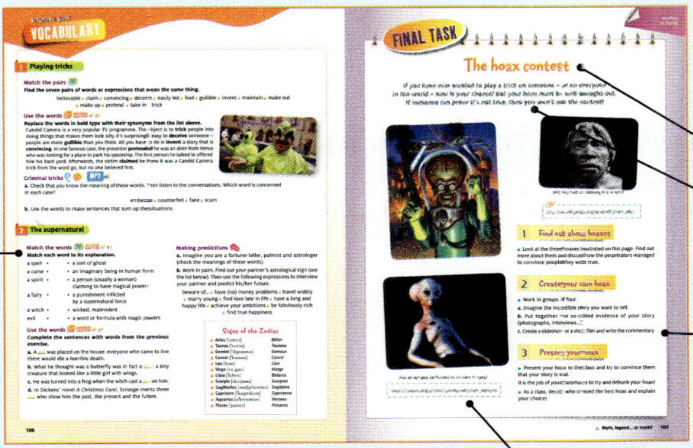

Des exercices reprenant les champs lexicaux des leçons pour **enrichir son vocabulaire**.

Le sujet de la **tâche finale**.

Une introduction pour annoncer le **sujet** et le **contexte**.

Une **mise en œuvre** de la tâche, avec étapes guidées.

Des **liens Internet** et des documents servant à la réalisation de la tâche.

PREPARE FOR THE BAC

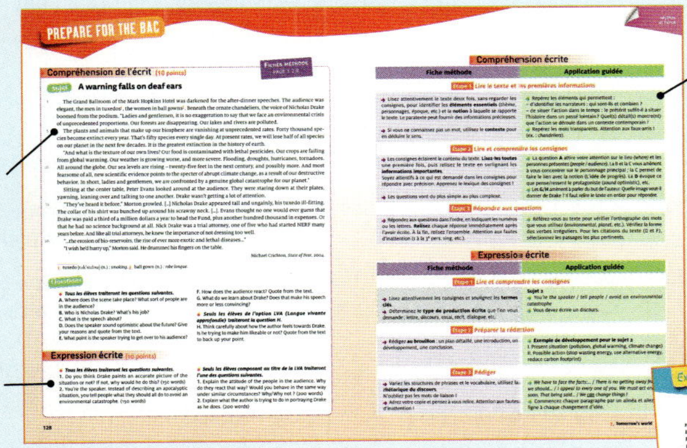

Une **Fiche méthode** avec une application guidée pour s'entraîner.

Le **sujet** de l'épreuve et les consignes.

Les **consignes**.

EXTENDED READING

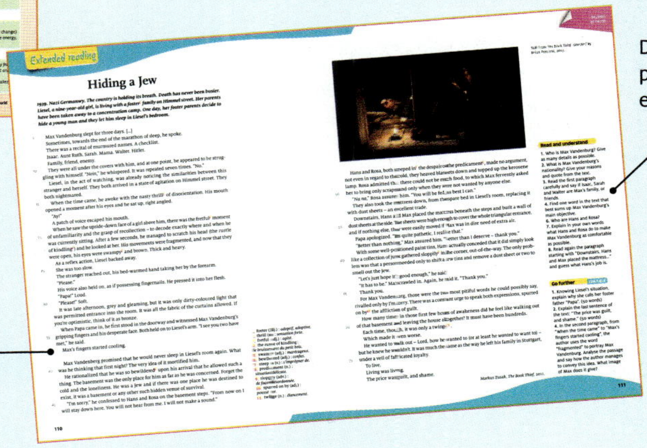

Des questions pour la série **LVA** et l'option **LELE**.

Des textes complémentaires de **lecture cursive**, orientés vers l'**étude littéraire**.

SKILLS

Espaces et échanges

Mythes et héros

SKILLS

L'idée de progrès

Lieux et formes du pouvoir

Chapter 1

Interconnections

Improve your skills

Cross culture

Improve your grammar

Improve your vocabulary

Final task

Prepare for the Bac

1 A phone box... full of books!

2 A jumble sale.

3 Angelina Jolie in Africa.

React !

1. How are the books in the phone box related to the items on sale at the jumble sale? Think about where the things came from.
2. Do the three photos illustrate something positive or negative about the world we live in?

Holidays:

1 Car pooling: not just for commuters B1

Car pooling is not just for commuters. Finding someone who is going your way and catching a lift is an increasingly common way to save some cash while travelling. If you're lucky, you might even find a driver willing to share some local insight along the way.

Although sometimes referred to as virtual hitchhiking, lift-sharing sites offer more than just the equivalent of raising a thumb in the air. Many allow readers to leave references for one another, or view social networking profiles to see if you have interests (or maybe even friends) in common. Other sites insist on checking members' driving licenses for added security, and a few have launched their own apps to make them more compatible with life on the road.

CoSeats.com, Australia

CoSeats has a rather rudimentary set up, where users do the groundwork. With no whistles or bells, it's more like a honed[1] Craigslist[2]: you simply post your route, add your contact details (phone or email) and other users contact you directly. Drivers and riders can link the profile to Facebook, and there's a "girls only" filter for women who want to travel together.

Interestingly (and handy in a country of this size), there is also a subsection, where you can pick up your own campervan for a bargain price (often with prepaid fuel). How? The site teams[3] with rental companies that need quick relocation to other parts of the country. A sample deal would be Brisbane to Cairns for £54.

Vicky Baker, *The Guardian*, April 12, 2013.

1. honed (adj.) : *(fig.) peaufiné.* 2. Craigslist : *plateforme mondiale de petites annonces et de forums.* 3. team (v.) : *faire équipe.*

More help WBT n° 1

A campervan driving near Uluru in Australia.

Explain and guess

1. Explain what car pooling is and why it is usually associated with commuters.
2. The photo illustrates a different sort of car pooling. Can you guess what it is?

Read and explain

1. Say which specific type of car pooling is described in the article. Find the other names for it.
2. List the advantages of this sort of car pooling, as suggested in the text.
3. Explain how CoSeats works.

Go into detail. WBT n° 2

2 Couchsurfing B1

Help

- spare room (n.) : *chambre d'ami*
- pitch (v.) : *monter (une tente)*
- hang out (with someone) (v.) : *traîner avec/fréquenter quelqu'un*

More help WBT n° 3

Listen to the recording MP3 1

1. Say what you found out about couchsurfing and how it works.
2. Note down the tips given at the end.

Go into detail. WBT n° 4

Role play

1. Work in pairs: A and B.

A: You want to go to Australia this summer and have contacted B on a couchsurfing site. You need to find out more and to fix dates.

B: You live in Sydney and have provisionally agreed to let A sleep on your couch. You want to find out more about him/her and fix dates.

2. Imagine your conversation on Skype.

share, lend or give?

3 Big Apple Greeters

B2

"New York is a city of eight million finalists; God knows where the finishing line is."

Bette Midler's comment is a home-grown expression of the Big Apple's popular image – the definitively restless, edgy, unsentimental metropolis. But the hard-boiled city has a soft centre. Why else would it offer visitors the Big Apple Greeter Programme, the best bargain since Dutch settlers bought Manhattan Island for 24 dollars from the Indians in 1626. The only difference is that the Greeter Programme is completely free.

More than 400 volunteer 'greeters' belong to this generous scheme, which offers visitors a walking tour of neighbourhoods in any of New York's five boroughs. The volunteers, all carefully vetted[1] and trained, have specialist knowledge of different areas. The scheme, run by the New York Visitors Bureau, is aimed at those who want an alternative to gawping[2] at the Empire State Building and the Statue of Liberty.

New York is a city for walkers. It has 6,500 miles of streets, and its lively and contrasting neighbourhoods are best seen on foot because they change so dramatically from block to block. The greeter programme provides an experienced volunteer to accompany you on a three- to four-hour walk in any area you choose. The 'friends', as they are called, are companions as much as guides: no money changes hands and tipping is considered inappropriate. They prefer to take groups of no more than four, and children are welcome.

The most popular walks are on the Upper West Side, the financial district, SoHo, the East Village, Little Italy and Harlem. If you give 48-72 hours' notice and a rough idea of your interests and what you would like to see, the organisers will match you with a resident who will meet you at your hotel and escort you to see how the natives live, work and play.

Richard Gilbert, *The Independent*, September 11, 1994.

1. vetted (adj.) : *(ici) (soigneusement) sélectionnés.* 2. gawp [gɔːp] (v.) : *regarder bouche bée.*

More help WBT n° 5

Brainstorm

Work out what "Big Apple Greeter" means. The title and the pictures will help you.

Read, explain and imagine

1. Explain the quotation at the beginning of the article.

2. Say briefly what the Greeter programme consists of and who it is aimed at.

3. Imagine why the programme was set up. Go into detail. WBT n° 6

A "greeter" showing some tourists around New York.

Your task

You are a volunteer greeter in your city. Choose a part of the city (a building, a district...) that you know very well and record a guided tour of it on an mp3 file. Talk about the history of the place, recount any anecdotes you know about it, say what you particularly like about it, etc.

Grammar

Ellipses dans les subordonnées p. 21

- *Although sometimes referred to as virtual hitchhiking.*
- *An increasingly common way to save some cash while travelling.*

Alternatives

1 Read me! B1

If you are passing through London's Waterloo station next week and notice an abandoned book with a label saying "Read me", don't dismiss it as a hoax[1].

For the lonely paperback will probably be an example of bookcrossing, a reading movement reminiscent of Amsterdam's hippy, white bicycle scheme[2] of the 1960s, in which cycles were scattered across the city for anyone's use.

Under the scheme, which began in America, people leave books in public places to be picked up and read by others who in turn pass them on, with all readers logging on to a website that tracks progress of the books. According to bookcrossing.com there were some 3,000 books "in the wild" in the UK yesterday waiting to be claimed, including several on trains in and out of London.

The term "bookcrossing" has made it into the Oxford English Dictionary and according to the bookcrossing.com website, there were 2,847 books released in Britain in the past 30 days.

Ciar Byrne, *The Independent*, February 26, 2005.

1. hoax [həʊks] (n.) : *canular.* 2. scheme (n.) [ski:m] : *programme, dispositif.*
More help WBT n° 7

Deduce and read

1. From the illustrations, imagine what bookcrossing is all about.
2. Read the article and compare the facts with your answer to the first question.

Go into detail. WBT n° 8

Write a homepage

Think of another category of objects that could be "left in the wild" and imagine you are creating a website to promote your idea. Write the text that will appear on your homepage to explain your idea and encourage people to adopt it.

2 What's mine is yours! B2

SWAP_ABLE

Listen and explain MP3 2

1. Say what is wrong with traditional holiday options if you want to experience a different culture.
2. List the advantages of swapping your home.
3. Say why the peer-to-peer economy has developed in recent years.

Go into detail. WBT n° 9

Help

- settle for (v.) : *se contenter de*
- nondescript (n.) ['nɒndɪskrɪpt]: *quelconque*
- swap (v.) [swɒp]: *échanger*

to the market economy?

3 Waste not, want not! B2

If you're stuck with a half-eaten pizza and can't face throwing it away, a startup originally from Seattle has the solution. Leftoverswap's app lets you offer your leftovers to locals, who sign up to be notified when there's free food to be had in their area.

"Some people are shocked and find the concept absolutely disgusting while others love it and some wonder whether it's real", says co-founder Dan Newman. But with some 10,000 users in US cities like New York and San Francisco as well as in Europe, Australia and Asia, Leftoverswap is very real indeed. It is, in fact, part of a growing trend: the food-sharing economy.

With developed countries wasting up to 40% of their food – British households, for example, throw away 20% of the food they buy, and more has been thrown away before it even reached the shop – sharing what's in your fridge seems like a sensible solution.

Barbara Merhart, a Munich-based coordinator for Foodsharing.de [says] "Food waste and the sharing economy are a good combination. Personally, I don't buy groceries any more. Why would you spend money on it?"

Unlike Leftoverswap, Foodsharing.de is a non-profit organisation. But the two outfits' mission is the same: to connect those who have edible[1] goods to give away with those who want them. According to Merhart, many of Foodsharing.de's recipients[2] aren't just those on a tight budget: many are professionals like Merhart, who simply want to keep food away from the skip[3], and who don't see the point of paying for something that can be had for free.

In a way, food sharing is the most social aspect of the sharing economy. Because food is perishable, and because it doesn't make sense to criss-cross a city in pursuit of leftovers, donors and recipients often live close to each other. "You check on the website what's available in your neighbourhood," explains Merhart. "Then you agree with the donor on where to meet." Foodsharing.de calculates that its nearly 40,000 members – in 218 German cities, but also in Austria, Switzerland, Mexico, Israel and the UK – have saved 33 tonnes of food.

Elisabeth Braw, *The Guardian*, May 5, 2014

1. edible (adj.) : *comestible.* 2. recipients (n.) : *(faux-ami) bénéficiaires.*
3. skip (n.) : *benne (à ordures).*

More help WBT n° 10

Grammar

Les pronoms possessifs
What's ***mine*** *is* ***yours****.*
WBT n° 12

Le gérondif
• *[...]* ***sharing*** *what's in your fridge.* WBT n° 16

Brainstorm

1. As a class, work out what the title means (it's a proverb).
Decide collectively on an explanation that uses no more than 20 words.
2. Explain "leftovers" and say how the picture relates to the proverb.

Read and explain

1. Say what foodsharing apps are and how they work.
2. Explain who the donors and the recipients are.
Go into detail. WBT n° 11

Your task

Work in groups. You are a family. You have found someone in the USA who wants to exchange their home for yours during the summer. You now have to write a list of instructions that you will mail to them before they leave. For guidance, go to *http://www.planet-swap.com* and download the home information pack.

Improve your SKILLS

Can you help?

1 Putting fame to good use? B1

Can this man...

https://www.looktothestars.org/celebrity/matt-damon

Look and explain

1. Describe the photomontage and explain what it illustrates.
2. What's your answer to the question posed? If your answer is yes, explain how. If your answer is no, explain why it can't be done.
3. What good can come out of celebrities getting involved in charities?
See the links.

...help this boy?

2 Crowdfunding B1 B2

Brainstorm

Say what you know about crowdfunding or guess (using the cartoon) what it might mean. Think about the two words that make it up.

Listen and explain MP3 3

1. Listen to the recording and explain how crowdfunding works.
2. What are the advantages of this system?
3. Explain what the cartoon is suggesting.
Go into detail. WBT n° 13

Help

- carry out (v.) : *(ici) réaliser*
- pledge (v.) : *promettre*
- pitch (n.) : *argumentaire de vente*

3 Wwoofing B2

It is a taste of the good life for the iPhone generation: more rewarding[1] than InterRailing, safer than kibbutzim. It even has a catchy name, wwoofing. Record numbers of environmentally-conscious young people are volunteering through the organisation Worldwide Opportunities on Organic Farms (Wwoof).

In the UK alone, volunteer numbers have doubled in the past three years, providing a stream of free labour that is proving a godsend[2] for some of Britain's struggling organic farmers. At the moment 400 of the UK's 5,000 organic farms participate in the scheme – under which more than 3,000 volunteers work for up to 30 hours a week, weeding[3], planting and fruit-picking in exchange for board and lodging. But the organisation says more farms are needed. "We've had a surge[4] in people wanting placements, and quite a few branches around the world have been swamped and have stopped taking on new members," said Katherine Hallewell, a spokeswoman for Wwoof UK. [...]

Bethany Wells, 25, an MA student from London, chose wwoofing as a way of seeing Scandinavia on the cheap, but said it has left more of a lasting legacy than most holidays. "It expanded the time I could travel for. I worked on the farm for more than two weeks, and it was good to get out of the centre of places and into the middle of nowhere," she said. "It is a great way of meeting people and I'm still in touch with one of the friends I made there. I got completely eaten by mosquitoes but the food was good, the company was good, and there was a lake and a wood-fired sauna we'd spend our evenings in."

Rachel Shields, *The Independent*, May 9, 2010.

1. rewarding (adj.) : *gratifiant*. 2. godsend (n.) : *aubaine*.
3. weed (v.) : *arracher les mauvaises herbes*.
4. surge [sɜːdʒ] (n.) : *poussée*.

More help WBT n° 14

Grammar

Omission du pronom relatif
- *One of the friends I made there.*

Le gérondif
- *weeding, planting and fruit-picking.*

WBT n° 16

Read the article

Explain the concept of wwoofing. In what way is it similar to, or different from, the other schemes you have studied in this chapter (bookcrossing, homeswapping, crowdfunding...)? Go into detail. WBT n° 15

Write an ad

You are an organic farmer and you need volunteers to help you harvest your crops. Prepare an advertisement for a wwoofing site: it must be no longer than 10 lines.

Your task

You are an entrepreneur and have had a very original idea for a new product or service. However, you need money to develop and launch the product or service and no bank is interested. Create a short video and/or a short text for a crowdfunding platform to attract investors.

CROSS CULTURE

Giving it away: charity...

Charity shops in the UK

Walk down any English High Street and you are bound to see one ore more charity shops. **There are 10,000** of them in the UK and numbers are growing despite (or because of?) recent economic crises. Most of the items on sale are good-quality second-hand goods donated by members of the public.

The Salvation Army

Founded in London in 1865 by William Booth, this Christian charity is organised on military lines – complete with uniforms and brass bands – and is present in 126 countries. Although controversial because of its beliefs, it helps millions of people worldwide.

Jumble sales

Called rummage sales in the USA, these events are usually organised by churches or other local organisations such as the Women's Institute or the Boy Scouts. All **goods are donated** and sold at extremely low prices.

... and philanthropy

John D. Rockefeller (1839-1937)

At one time the richest man in the USA (and the richest person in history when he died!), Rockefeller made his fortune in oil production and used most of it to fund **research foundations.**

Bill Gates (b. 1955)

Microsoft billionaire Gates and his wife created a foundation in 2000 through which they plan to give 95% of their wealth to **charity**.

Warren Buffett (b. 1930)

One of the world's richest and most powerful men, Buffett has pledged to give away 99% of his wealth to **good causes.** He acquired his immense wealth through profitable investments and is famous for his frugal lifestyle.

Activities

Discuss the following.

1. Relate the rising number of charity shops in the UK to recent economic crises. Is there a paradox here, or not?
2. If you find yourself with an unwanted Christmas present, would you give it to a charity or sell it on eBay? If you gave it away, which charity would you choose and why?
3. What motivates the super-rich to give away their wealth? Find out more about one of the philanthropists on this page and discuss his motivations.

Omission du pronom relatif (PG p. 249)

MÉMO

Dans quelles conditions peut-on omettre un pronom relatif anglais ?

- Tout dépend de la fonction du relatif dans la proposition relative.
- Les relatifs sujets ou compléments de nom (génitif, comme *whose*) ne peuvent pas être supprimés sans dommage pour le sens.
- Quelle que soit sa fonction, un relatif ne peut être supprimé s'il introduit une relative non-définissante *voir p. 250* (la plupart du temps – mais pas toujours –, ce type de relatif est précédé d'une virgule).

Quelle autre particularité la suppression du relatif entraîne-t-elle ?

- Si le relatif est complément indirect ou complément circonstanciel, il est normalement précédé d'une préposition. Si on choisit de l'omettre, la préposition est rejetée en fin de proposition relative.

Ex. : *The person about whom you're talking* → *The person you're talking about...* (La personne dont vous parlez).

N.B. En anglais moderne courant, le premier de ces deux débuts de phrase a peu de chance d'être retenu.

En anglais peu soutenu, il est assez courant de supprimer un relatif sujet. Ceci reste totalement agrammatical.

Mais il faut savoir détecter cette incorrection pour comprendre certains énoncés. Ex. : *There's a man wants to talk to you.*

Observez et raisonnez

(texte p. 17)

- *I'm still in touch with one of the friends I made there.*
- *There was a lake and a wood-fired sauna we'd spend our evenings in.*

1 Repérez les endroits où le relatif a été supprimé.

2 Reformulez les énoncés en rétablissant les relatifs. Lesquels allez-vous employer ? Justifiez vos choix.

3 Traduisez les énoncés.

Entraînez-vous

1 Cartoon fun

Expliquez en une phrase contenant une relative :
– ce que les Indiens veulent faire ;
– ce dont le dessinateur se moque dans ce dessin.

2 Expression

Complétez les ébauches de phrases données en ajoutant une relative dont le pronom sera omis, sans oublier le rejet de la préposition donnée dans les phrases-amorces.

Ex. You want to hang out with someone. Spend some time to find that person. → *Spend some time to find the person you want to hang out with.*

a. You don't know much about a culture. Couchsurfing is a way to come into contact with it. *Couchsurfing is a way* ....

b. You want to go to a place. Choosing that place is the first part. *The first part is choosing* ....

c. You think you could be friends with somebody. You have several tries to find that person. *After several tries, you find* ....

3 Dites-le en anglais

Omettez le relatif à chaque fois que c'est possible et n'oubliez pas le rejet de la préposition.

a. Lenate est le nom de la tribu à laquelle les Hollandais ont acheté Manhattan en 1626.

b. Le bénévole avec qui nous avons visité New York vivait à Brooklyn.

c. Certains bénévoles peuvent même parler la langue du pays d'où viennent les touristes.

d. L'une des règles qu'il faut respecter est de ne pas donner de pourboire aux guides bénévoles.

Ellipses dans les subordonnées

MÉMO

Qu'est-ce qu'une ellipse ?

• C'est une figure de style par laquelle on retranche quelques mots dans une phrase sans dommage pour le sens.

Ex. : Enfant, je ne suis jamais allé à l'école. = Quand j'étais enfant, je ne suis jamais allé à l'école.

Dans quels cas rencontre-t-on des ellipses en anglais ?

• Les cas les plus courants se trouvent dans les subordonnées conjonctives.

Quels sont les mots qui sont le plus souvent retranchés et pourquoi ?

• Ce sont le sujet et le verbe de la subordonnée parce qu'ils sont évidents dans le contexte considéré ou ou qu'ils sont les mêmes que ceux de la proposition principale.

Qu'apporte l'ellipse à la phrase ?

• C'est une façon d'alléger le style (voir exemples ci-dessous).

Observez et raisonnez

(texte p. 12)

• *Finding someone who is going your way and catching a lift is an increasingly common way to save some cash while travelling.*

• *Although sometimes referred to as virtual hitchhiking, lift-sharing sites offer more than just the equivalent of raising a thumb in the air.*

1 Identifiez les différentes propositions dont ces deux phrases sont constituées.

2 Indiquez leur nature (principale, relative, conjonctive…).

3 Repérez l'ellipse.

4 Dites quels mots ont été supprimés.

5 Reformulez les énoncés en ajoutant les mots supprimés pour vérifier votre analyse.

6 Traduisez les deux énoncés et leurs reformulations et comparez le fonctionnement des deux langues.

Entraînez-vous

1 Cartoon fun

Étudiez la légende du dessin et transformez-la en y introduisant une ellipse.

"Although the tortoise beat the hare, the tortoise was later disqualified for taking anabolic steroids, so the hare was declared the winner."

2 Reformulez

Repérez les ellipses. Reformulez les énoncés sans l'ellipse.

a. If passing through London's Waterloo station next week you notice an abandoned book with a label saying "Read me", don't dismiss it as a hoax.

b. When stuck with a half-eaten pizza, don't throw it away, a startup originally from Seattle has the solution.

c. Before reaching the store, more than 20% of the food sold in Britain has been thrown away.

d. Although completely eaten by mosquitoes, I spent a wonderful summer wwoofing in Sweden.

3 Expression

Procédez à l'ellipse qui permettra d'alléger le style.

a. While this power-to-the-people movement has mobilised an army of microentrepreneurs, it has also resulted in traveller benefits ranging from money-saving to authentic experiences and real human connection.

b. If you're lucky, you might even find a driver willing to share some local insight along the way.

c. When people are in doubt, they can check members' driving licenses with the help of the site for added security.

d. Whether you're young or old, you'll find that couchsurfing is a cheap and sociable way to travel.

e. Although it is a hard-boiled city, New York does have a soft centre.

Improve your

VOCABULARY

1 Travelling cheaply

Complete and match MP3 4

a. Listen to the conversations and find the missing words to complete the verb expressions. WBT n° 17

b. Listen again and match the expressions to their translations.

1. take pot ...... •	• *héberger quelqu'un*
2. do something on a ...... •	• *tenter sa chance*
3. put someone ...... •	• *faire une bonne affaire*
4. get a good ...... on something •	• *faire quelque chose avec un budget dérisoire*

Complete

Use the following words to complete the paragraph. Use each word only once.

abroad • afford • air • backpacking • broke • budget • cut-price • resort

Mike wanted to go ...... for the summer but he was ...... He couldn't even ...... a week in a ...... hotel in the cheapest ...... on the Costa Brava. After looking at all the last-minute ...... offers on holidays on the internet, he finally decided to go ...... in the Highlands of Scotland: he loved walking and he could sleep in the open ...... if the weather was good.

2 Trust and honesty

Un- or *dis-*?

a. Check that you know the meaning of these adjectives, then use the right prefix (*un-* or *dis-*) to form their opposites.

b. Which three adjectives in the left-hand column are synonyms?

c. Choose three adjectives (from either column) and put each one in a sentence of at least ten words.

dependable	...dependable
faithful	...faithful
helpful	...helpful
honest	...honest
reliable [rɪ'laɪəbl]	...reliable
reputable ['repjʊtəbl]	...reputable
trustworthy	...trustworthy

3 Charity work

Match the expressions

Match each expression with its definition or explanation.
WBT n° 17

do relief work •	• give money to a charity
an aid worker •	• a place where they sell second-hand goods; all the takings go to charity
a charity •	• get money for a charity by asking for donations
a charity shop •	• a person who does humanitarian work
collect for a charity •	• help people in desperate need (after a natural disaster, for example)
a fundraiser •	• a person who works without wanting to be paid
a volunteer •	• a non-profit-making organisation that raises money for good causes
make a donation •	• a person who persuades people and organisations to give money to charity

Role play

Work in pairs. Look at the picture and imagine the conversation. The young woman is asking the man for money. The man has never heard of "Save the Children". Use at least two expressions from the previous exercise.

FINAL TASK

Plan a trip on a shoestring

Several groups of friends have decided they want to go to New Zealand for a month. But money is tight... Who can plan the cheapest and most interesting trip? The object is to explore the country and the culture for the lowest possible cost.

Rotorua is a region of lakes, geysers and hot springs on North Island, with a flourishing Maori culture.

Milford Sound is on South Island: amazing mountains and coastal scenery.

1 Plan your month's trip

- Work in groups of four.
- Find information about:
  – what you want to see;
  – cheap plane tickets;
  – cheap accommodation and travel (remember "couchsurfing" and "lift-sharing"?).

The links will help you.

- Work out your itinerary.

2 Present your trip

- Present your trip to the other groups.
- Decide which group has planned the best trip (comparing interest and cost).

http://www.nzherald.co.nz/travel/news/article.cfm?c_id=7&objectid=10846894

https://www.lonelyplanet.com/thorntree/forums/australasia-pacific-australia-new-zealand-antarctica/topics/hitch-hiking-couch-surfing-around-nz

http://www.jetstar.com/au/en/cheap-flights/new-zealand

http://www.tripadvisor.com/Flights-g255104-New_Zealand-Cheap_Discount_Airfares.html

http://www.independenttraveler.com/travel-tips/australia-new-zealand/top-25-ways-to-save-on-new-zealand-travel

http://www.newzealand.com/int/destinations/

PREPARE FOR THE BAC

Compréhension de l'oral (10 points)

FICHE MÉTHODE P. 24-25

Modalités de l'épreuve

- Un **enregistrement** audio ou vidéo en lien avec une notion du programme. **(1 min. 30)**
- Le **titre** vous est communiqué avant la première écoute.
- **Trois écoutes/visionnages** espacés chacun(e) d'une minute, durant lesquels vous pouvez prendre des **notes**.
- Un **compte-rendu** en français, par écrit. **(10 min)**

Attention *! Il ne vous est pas demandé d'écrire le script de l'enregistrement, ni de commenter ce qui est dit, ni de prendre parti mais uniquement de **rendre compte de ce que vous avez compris**.*

Sujet d'entraînement

"Together", the Dutch car-sharing app

DVD

Lisez attentivement la fiche méthode en cachant la partie « application guidée », puis reportez-vous à l'aide, au fur et à mesure des difficultés rencontrées.

Fiche méthode	Application guidée
Étape 1 Anticiper à partir du titre donné	
➔ **Analysez le titre** pour préparer votre écoute. Cela vous guidera dans la compréhension du texte. ➔ Mobilisez le **vocabulaire** utile à ce document. Vous serez ainsi plus apte à comprendre certains termes utilisés.	➔ Repérez le thème abordé et la notion à laquelle il se rattache (Espaces et échanges). ➔ Listez tous les mots et expressions que vous connaissez et que vous êtes susceptible d'entendre dans cette vidéo (*share / ride / car-pooling / save / help each other*, etc.).
Étape 2 Écouter et noter au brouillon	
➔ **Première écoute** • Valorisez une compréhension **globale** : – **repérez** le type de support, la nature du document, le nombre d'intervenants, etc ; – **relevez** quelques mots ou expressions sans noter de phrases entières. (Les images peuvent vous aider à comprendre, mais attention elles peuvent aussi n'avoir qu'un rôle illustratif.)	➔ **Première écoute** – Type de support : vidéo / nature du document : reportage / voix : un homme. – Mots et expressions : *car / share / Amsterdam / ride / cost / spend on travel / natural / meet people / business.*
➔ **2e écoute** : • **Notez un maximum** de mots et expressions compris, accentués et répétés.	➔ **Deuxième écoute** *share a ride / get to office, festival, other city / Amsterdam / friendly / not for cars / surprised / many cars / insurance / petrol / reduction / sharing economy.*
➔ **3e écoute** • Concentrez-vous sur les **informations manquantes**. Relevez des informations plus précises (noms, dates, lieux, données chiffrées, etc.).	➔ **Troisième écoute** *85% of vehicles have 1 person in them / develop an application / company of 7 people / grow really big / number two (cost) is travel (after rent or mortgage) / engage with each other, etc.*

Étape 3 Rédiger le compte-rendu

➔ Détachez-vous de l'anglais et pensez maintenant uniquement **en français**. Réutilisez toutes vos **notes** pour rédiger votre compte-rendu et n'oubliez pas de faire une **introduction**. Si le support est une vidéo, ne décrivez pas les images mais concentrez-vous sur ce que vous avez entendu.
➔ Écrivez des phrases courtes et simples, utilisez des verbes **introducteurs** et variez le vocabulaire.
➔ Aérez votre copie et pensez à vous relire !

➔ Pensez en français pour faire un compte-rendu cohérent. Utilisez vos notes (étapes 1 et 2) pour la rédaction. Dans l'introduction, présentez le type de support et le contexte : qui ? où ? quand ? quoi ? *(un Hollandais / Amsterdam / nouvelle application pour co-voiturage / interview).*
➔ Pensez aux verbes introducteurs *(l'interviewé explique... / il décrit... / affirme... / ajoute... / termine en...).*
➔ Commencez chaque paragraphe par un alinéa et allez à la ligne à chaque changement d'idée.

À votre tour !

Bike-share expansion DVD

À présent, appliquez la méthodologie à cette vidéo.

Voici une grille de notation sur 10 correspondant aux attentes du baccalauréat pour essayer de vous situer selon que vous êtes en LV1 ou LV2.

CONTENT	LEVEL	LV1	LV2
COMPRÉHENSION TRÈS INSUFFISANTE **Vous n'avez repéré que des mots isolés (peut-être uniquement basés sur les images ou le titre), mais sans établir de liens entre eux.**		1	2
COMPRÉHENSION SUPERFICIELLE **Vous avez relevé des mots isolés, des expressions courantes et des phrases simples. Votre compréhension reste superficielle.**	A1	3	4
COMPRÉHENSION PARTIELLE **Vous avez su identifier le thème majeur de la discussion et identifier chaque locuteur sans comprendre toutes les informations.**	A2	5	7
COMPRÉHENSION SATISFAISANTE **Vous avez su relever les points principaux (contexte, objet, sentiments des interlocuteurs, conclusion de l'échange) et les mettre en relation.**	B1	8	10
COMPRÉHENSION FINE **Vous avez su relever les points principaux et un nombre suffisant de détails significatifs vous permettant de rendre compte du point de vue.**	B2	10	

English: more

1 British vs American B1

American vs. British Spelling Differences

ENSE vs. ENCE

American	British
defense	defence
license	licence

ER vs. RE

American	British
center	centre
liter	litre

OR vs. OUR

American	British
color	colour
favorite	favourite

ED vs. T

American	British
dreamed	dreamt
learned	learnt

E vs. Æ

American	British
encyclopedia	encyclopædia
medieval	mediæval

IZE vs. ISE

American	British
analyze	analyse
criticize	criticise

LL vs. L

American	British
enrollment	enrolment
fulfill	fulfil

OG vs. OGUE

American	British
analog	analogue
catalog	catalogue

Adapted from The English Test : http://www.masterstudies.com/English-test/

Find more words

Read the words and try to memorise their British and American spellings. Find at least one more word to add to each category.

2 2b or not 2b? B1

As a new variety of language, texting has been condemned as "textese", "slanguage", a "digital virus". [...] An extraordinary number of doom-laden[1] prophecies have been made about the supposed linguistic evils unleashed[2] by texting. Sadly, its creative potential has been virtually ignored. But five years of research has at last begun to dispel the myths. The most important finding is that texting does not erode children's ability to read and write. On the contrary, literacy improves.

David Crystal, *The Guardian*, July 5, 2008.

1. doom-laden (adj) : *apocalyptique*.
2. unleash (v) : *libérer, déchaîner*.

Read and explain

Sum up the article, giving the negative and positive aspects of texting.

than one language?

3 HRU? OK? B1

Comment and find out

1. Explain the title and say what the teacher is teaching in the cartoon.
2. What is the cartoonist's message or intention? Use the links.

What do they mean?

Guess what these text messaging abbreviations mean, compare your answers and then find out what they really mean.

IMO, JK, FYI, IDC, NVM, GTG

http://pocho.com pocho-ocho-top-spanglish-text-message-abbreviations/
http://www.docstoc.com/docs/94683837/TEXTING-ACRONYMSxlsx

"Copy and study this list of text messaging spelling words. We will have a test tomorrow."

4 Hiya pupils, please avoid slang, ta B2

A secondary school has instructed its pupils to stop using slang words such as hiya, cheers and ta, to enhance their prospects of landing[1] a top job. Sheffield Springs academy, which is based in one of the most deprived parts of the city, asks students to use standard English inside the school gates. [...]

The school had an ethos[2] that "the street stops at the gate", said Kathy August, ULT's deputy chief executive. Pupils were told to replace hiya, cheers and ta with good morning and thank you.

"We want to make sure that our youngsters are not just leaving school with the necessary As to Cs in GCSEs, but that they also have a whole range of employability skills," August said. "Understanding when it is and is not acceptable to use slang or colloquial language is just one part of this."

August was previously a headteacher of Manchester Academy, where she forbade pupils from using the word "innit" when talking to teachers.

Jessica Shepherd, *The Guardian*, February 14, 2012.

1. land (v.) a job : *décrocher un emploi.*
2. ethos [ˈiːθɒs] (n.) : *philosophie, ligne de conduite.*

More help WBT n° 18

Grammar

Les structures infinitives p. 37

- *A secondary school has instructed its pupils* ***to stop*** *using slang words.*
- *Pupils were told* ***to replace*** *hiya, cheers and ta with good morning and thank you.*

Read and comment

1. Say what the basic rule at Sheffield Springs academy is, and why.
2. Do you think the policy will work or not? Give your reasons.

Go into detail. WBT n° 19

Compare and discuss

Do you feel you can use the same language with your friends and with adults/teachers. Why/Why not? Compare and discuss your reasons.

Your task MP3 5

1. Listen to someone talking about Cockney slang. Note down the details (geographical and historical origin, the way it works, examples).
2. Work in pairs. Imagine you have to explain *verlan* to an English friend. Follow the same pattern as the explanation of Cockney slang. Write a monologue and read it aloud.

Improve your SKILLS

Disappearing languages

1 British languages in danger! B1

A special 2008 issue of Guernsey stamps.

Tourists looking for sun and sea but keen for something extra from their holiday break can now help save an ancient language.

Four languages spoken on British territories feature on an new "endangered" list, with the numbers of people using them seriously dwindling. There are particular fears for the future of Jersey French and Guernsey French, which are marked as "severely endangered" on a list of 33 under-threat languages.

The at-risk list is based on data from the Unesco Languages in Danger project which was launched in 1993.

A new report, which highlights the threatened languages, believes "linguistic tourism" can help save them by stimulating greater inte-rest in learning them and helping them survive, if not thrive[1]. Naren Shaam, the chief executive of GoEuro, said the travel planning company wanted to promote a new "linguistic-based" ethical tourism "allowing people to choose to directly benefit regions in which centuries-old languages are on the cusp[2] of extinction."

Tony Scott Warren, the Jersey French language officer known as Offici du l'Jèrriais, said: "It is a worry. We're making efforts to educate as many people as possible. It's not surprising we are on the list. The numbers have been declining for a long time." He estimates that about 1,000 native speakers remain. "We are looking to develop the range of what we're doing to get more people involved," he said.

Nick Clark, *The Independent*, November 9, 2014.

1. thrive [ðraɪv] (v.) : *prospérer*. 2. on the cusp of : *(ici) au bord de.*

More help WBT n° 24

Comment and explain

Look at the stamps. Say what you know about their "country" of origin and imagine why they were issued.

Read the article

1. Say what problem Nick Clark is writing about.
2. What solutions are being proposed?
3. Say what you know about the case of Jersey French.

Go into detail. WBT n° 24

What do you think?

Work in groups, discuss the following questions and report back to the class. Do you all agree or not?

1. Is it important to preserve endangered languages?
2. Do you feel concerned by the problem? Perhaps there are endangered languages in your own region...
3. Is enough being done to solve the problem?

2 Too late to save Spokane? B1 B2

Listen to the recording MP3 7

1. Say what you know about the person who is speaking.
2. On what occasions did he hear his native language when he was young?
3. Comment on the attitude of the elders with regard to Spokane.
4. Say who speaks Spokane these days and explain why.

Make a speech

You are one of the last speakers of an endangered language. You have been allowed to speak for two minutes at UNESCO in order to put the case for the preservation of your native language and suggest measures to be taken. Prepare and deliver the speech.

Spokane Tribe of Indians

The logo of the Spokane tribe whose reservation is in the Pacific North-West of the USA.

Help

- **gathering** (n.) : *rassemblement, réunion*
- **converse** [kən'vɜːs] (v.) : *parler, discuter*
- **handful** (n.) : *poignée*

Grammar

Used to* vs *would p. 36

- *When I was a child [...] **I used to** attend cultural gatherings.*
- *All the elders **would** sit around the edge of the room.*

Condition *sine qua non* WBT n° 25

- ***Unless** something is done within a very short while, the language will be gone forever.*

3 The world picture B2

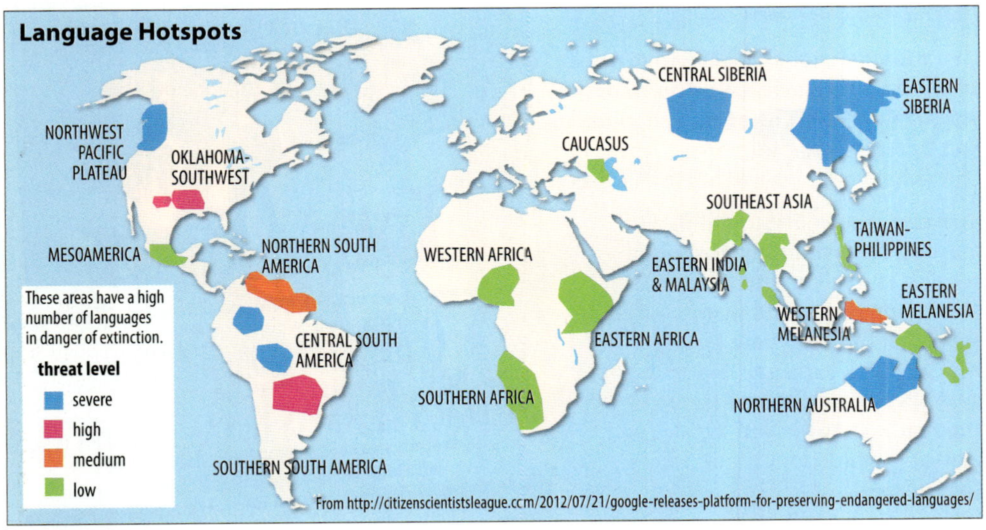

Look and explain

Study the map, say which parts of the world have a high number of endangered languages and discuss the possible reasons.

Your task

Work in groups. Choose an endangered language from one of the English-speaking regions on the map. Go on the Internet and find details (numbers of native speakers, programmes for the preservation of the language, etc.). Put together a slideshow (text and pictures) that sums up the situation.

Improve your

GRAMMAR

Used to vs would (PG p. 239)

MÉMO

***Used* est-il un modal au même titre que *would* ?**

• Le fait qu'il soit suivi de *to* répond à la question. *Used* + *to* est une forme figée qu'on ne trouve que dans un contexte passé. Ce n'est pas un modal, pas plus que *have* (+ *to*) ou *ought* (+ *to*) ne le sont.

Ex. : *I used to smoke a lot.* / *He didn't use to be so generous.*

Quelle nuance *used + to* apporte-t-il par rapport à un simple prétérit ?

• Il permet d'insister sur le fait que la situation décrite est révolue.

Ex. : *I used to be very shy when I was a child.* / *There used to be a bridge here.*

Comment rend-on cette nuance en français ?

• On ajoute souvent un adverbe à l'emploi de l'imparfait. Ex. : J'étais très timide quand j'étais enfant. / Il y avait un pont ici, autrefois.

Quelle différence existe-t-il entre *used to* et *would* ?

Lorsque les deux mots cohabitent au sein d'une même phrase, *used to* pose le caractère révolu des faits, et *would* indique le caractère répétitif d'une action (habitude).

Observez et raisonnez

(enregistrement p. 33)

• *I used to attend cultural gatherings in the long house on the reservation and I remember that all the elders would sit around the edge of the room.*

1 Repérez tous les mots qui, dans cet énoncé, renvoient à la notion de faits passés.

2 Vérifiez que ce qui est expliqué dans le « mémo » est bien illustré par cet exemple.

3 Traduisez l'énoncé.

Entraînez-vous

1 Cartoon fun

Expliquez en anglais ce que le père essaie de faire comprendre à son fils.

2 Choisissez entre *used to* et *would*.

a. I live in a place where, at one time, the dominant language ...... (be) Spokane.

b. Our tribe ...... (live) free, not on a reservation as they do today.

c. The meetings seemed endless; they ...... (go on) forever.

d. And during those meetings the elders ...... (talk) to one another in Spokane.

e. But when we children were there, they ...... (switch) to English.

3 Expression

Reconstruisez les énoncés à partir des éléments donnés dans l'ordre alphabétique. Une partie des phrases (en italique) est donnée pour vous aider.

1. a /and / and / at / backyard / be / end / go / I / in / it / lake / my / of / our / sister / swimming / the / There / to / used / would // *as soon as summer came. It's all dried up now.*

2. en deux phrases :

a. be / before / I / much / nights / remember / summer / the / to / used / war / warmer. //

b. difficult / find / it / So / warm / we / would // *to get to sleep.*

3. and / and / come / say / She / she / spend / summer / the / to / us / used / with / would // *we were her English family.*

4 Dites-le en anglais

a. Quand il se retrouvait dans une situation délicate *(get into a jam)*, il commençait à se ronger les ongles.

b. Autrefois, la basilique Sainte-Sophie était une mosquée, c'est maintenant un musée.

c. Je l'ai connue quand elle était enfant. C'était une fillette difficile.

d. À chaque fois que je prenais la parole à table, ils me disaient de me taire.

Les structures infinitives (PG p. 253)

MÉMO

De quelles constructions s'agit-il ?

• De celles du type :

– Il m'a dit de m'arrêter de fumer.

En d'autres termes, des structures qui suivent certains verbes et en particulier de ceux suivis des prépositions « à » et « de » ou « pour ».

La traduction de l'énoncé ci-dessus pose-t-elle problème ?

• Oui, car le groupe « de + infinitif » n'est pas toujours traduit par la même structure anglaise.

De quoi dépend la structure anglaise ?

• Du sémantisme du verbe qui précède la préposition :

– s'il renvoie vers l'avenir, la structure anglaise sera V + *to* + BV : *He told me to stop*. L'action *stop* n'a pas encore eu lieu au moment où l'on parle.

– s'il renvoie au passé, la structure sera V + BV-*ing* : *(he told me to) stop smoking*. Il faut avoir commencé pour pouvoir s'arrêter. L'action *smoke* précède l'action *stop*.

On peut symboliser sous la forme suivante :
He told me to stop smoking.
→ ←

N.B. Un grand nombre de verbes (*like*, *remember*, *stop*, *try*, etc), selon les contextes, peuvent être suivis de l'une ou de l'autre structure.

Ex. : *He told me to stop to get some gas.* = Il m'a dit de m'arrêter pour faire le plein.

Observez et raisonnez

(texte p. 29)

• *A secondary school has instructed its pupils to stop using slang words.*

• *Pupils were told to replace hiya, cheers and ta with good morning and thank you.*

1 Dans ces énoncés, isolez les structures verbe + verbe.

2 Justifiez la structure employée.

3 Traduisez les énoncés.

Entraînez-vous

1 Cartoon fun

Que dit l'homme au chapeau à sa femme ? *"That reminds me, dear – did you remember bringing the sandwiches."* ou *"did you remember to bring the sandwiches?"* Justifiez votre réponse.

"That reminds me, dear– did you remember the sandwiches?"

2 Expression

V + *to* + BV *ou* **V + V-ing ?**

a. The Sheffield Springfield academy want ...... (make) sure their students speak proper English.

b. They also ask the students not ...... (use) slang words.

c. They think some students' language wants ...... (clean up).

d. But outside the school gates the students keep ...... (use) very colloquial language.

3 Dites-le en anglais.

a. Ils ne nous autorisent pas à utiliser des expressions familières ou argotiques.

b. Ils ne cessent de nous répéter les mêmes conseils.

c. Ils devraient essayer de nous comprendre davantage.

d. Moi, j'adore parler l'argot, je trouve cela très imagé.

e. Moi, je déteste entendre mes enfants s'exprimer grossièrement.

Improve your
VOCABULARY

1 British or American?

Make it British! MP3 8

Listen to the three conversations between Americans.
Use the following words to transform what they say into British English.
There are three words or expressions to change in each conversation.

bill • boot • car park • cupboard • dustbin • lift • petrol • toilet • trousers

2 Similes

Match the words

Some of the most common similes in English involve animals.
Match the adjectives to the nouns.

	Adjective		Noun
as	blind	as a	bat
	brave		bird
	free		dog
	gentle		lamb
	proud		lion
	quiet		mouse
	sick		ox
	strong		peacock

3 Formal or colloquial?

Find the pairs

a. Find the 12 pairs of sentences that mean the same thing.
Then decide which sentence of each pair is more colloquial, i.e. less formal. WBT n° 26

b. Work in pairs. Choose two of the more colloquial expressions and write a short dialogue that uses them. Read the dialogue to the class.

- Check it out. (US)
- *The movie was a terrible failure.*
- *You've got to be kidding.*
- That's nonsense.
- How annoying!
- I don't mind.
- That's a load of rubbish.
- Cool it. (US)
- Relax.
- It pays peanuts.
- You're joking.
- He won't budge an inch. *(UK)*
- The movie bombed. (US)
- What a drag!
- *The salary is extremely low.*
- He annoys me.
- *He spent all the money on a BMW.*
- He blew it all on a beemer.
- I'm easy. (UK)
- She's very attractive.
- He's a pain in the neck.
- He refuses to change his mind.
- *She's really fit. (UK)*
- *Have a look at it.*

FINAL TASK

Create a language game

Your school is holding a Foreign Languages Week. You have been asked to create a game that teaches English idioms. The game is based on a poster.

1 Before you start

- Make sure you know what an idiom is. Look at the definition.

> **What is an idiom?**
> An idiom is an expression that cannot be understood from the meaning of its separate words. For example, *"He has his head in the clouds"* means *"He is detached from reality"*. It has nothing to do with clouds!

- Look at the examples. Can you fit the explanations to the idioms?

> **Explanations**
> • A person who is very intelligent.
> • Blissfully happy.
> • Directing your efforts towards the wrong person or thing.
> • Not feeling well.
> • Someone who lies around and barely moves.
> • Someone who tries to be perfect.

2 Create your poster

- Work in groups of four or five. Choose five English idioms.
- Design a poster (either on paper or on a computer). For each idiom:
  – write the idiom,
  – illustrate its literal meaning,
  – leave a blank space for the explanation.
- Prepare the ten explanations separately.

3 Play the game

- Present your poster and the explanations to the class. They must match the explanations to the idioms.

PREPARE FOR THE BAC

Expression orale

FICHE MÉTHODE PAGE 41

Sujet Espaces et échanges

Modalités de l'épreuve

- Tirage au sort de l'une des quatre notions sur lesquelles porte le programme du cycle terminal.
- Préparation de l'exposé. (10 min.)
- Exposé oral en continu, en anglais : présentation de la notion. (5 min.)
- Expression orale en interaction : conversation entre l'examinateur et l'élève (5 min.)

Série L

- Le candidat apporte ses dossiers constitués dans l'année. L'examinateur choisit la notion.
- Préparation (10 min.). Exposé oral en continu (10 min.). Expression orale en interaction (10 min.).

Attention : les citations ci-dessous sont proposées dans le cadre d'un entraînement ; elles fournissent des pistes pour préparer votre épreuve pendant l'année. Le jour de l'épreuve, aucun document ne vous sera fourni.

Changing country

"Remember, remember always, that all of us, and you and I especially, are descended from immigrants and revolutionists."

Franklin D. Roosevelt (1882-1945), US President 1933-45.

"A simple way to take measure of a country is to look at how many want in. And how many want out."

Tony Blair (b. 1953), British Prime Minister 1997-2007.

Interconnections

The welfare of each is bound up in the welfare of all."

Helen Keller (1880-1968), American writer.

"Whatever affects one directly, affects all indirectly.

Martin Luther King, Jr. (1929-1968), baptist minister and Civil Rights leader.

Languages

"England and America are two countries separated by the same language."

George Bernard Shaw (1856-1950), Irish playwright.

"One language sets you in a corridor for life. Two languages open every door along the way."

Frank Smith, English educationalist.

Le monde se construit sur les échanges culturels, politiques, économiques et linguistiques. Les trois chapitres que vous avez étudiés montrent comment ces échanges modifient l'espace dans lequel les individus interagissent et vous permettent d'avoir une variété de points de vue sur la notion. Suivez les étapes ci-dessous pour construire votre présentation.

Fiche méthode	Application guidée
Étape 1 Constituer un dossier	
➔ Pour préparer votre présentation orale, créez un **dossier sur la notion**. Attention, seuls les élèves de la série L pourront apporter ce dossier le jour de l'épreuve !	➔ Le dossier doit regrouper les différents aspects de la notion traités dans l'année (*different kinds of English / why learn foreign languages / saving endangered languages*) et comporter différents supports (images, textes, enregistrements, etc.).
Étape 2 Trouver la problématique et construire le plan	
➔ La **problématique** est la question que l'on pose dans l'introduction et à laquelle on répond dans la conclusion. Vous devez toujours vous demander si vous pouvez répondre à votre question avec les arguments et les exemples que vous donnez. ➔ Le **plan** peut être **thématique** ou binaire (présenter deux points de vue différents). Deux parties suffisent.	➔ Exemples de problématiques : • *Why share what we have? (p. 12-13)* • *Why do people learn foreign languages? (p. 30-31)* • *Why do people change country? (p. 44-45)* ➔ Votre plan peut être thématique : *Reasons for learning languages (travel/leisure, career, personal life, personal development)* ; ➔ ou binaire : *Couchsurfing: just free accommodation or a chance to discover a new culture? (p. 12).*
Étape 3 Rédiger l'introduction	
➔ L'introduction doit contenir plusieurs éléments : - une définition générale de la notion ; - la présentation du sujet choisi ; - l'annonce de la problématique ; - l'annonce du plan.	➔ Pour la définition de la notion, appuyez-vous sur les mots clés des sujets étudiés ou sur une citation que vous aurez apprise dans l'année (ex. p. 40). **Exemple :** *Exchange: the act of giving or taking one thing in return for another thing / an occurrence in which people talk to each other / a conversation.*
Étape 4 Rédiger la conclusion	
➔ Elle doit être la synthèse de tout ce que vous avez dit, mais elle doit aussi permettre d'**élargir votre problématique** de départ. Vous devez proposer une ouverture, la plupart du temps sous forme de question. La conclusion est la dernière chose qu'entend votre auditoire. Elle doit donc être soignée !	➔ Pour élargir la problématique : • *Is bartering the key solution to avoid overconsumption? (ch. 1)* • *Is it always necessary to learn a foreign language? (ch. 2)*
Étape 5 Mettre au point le développement	
➔ C'est la **partie principale** de votre présentation. Entraînez-vous à préparer vos notes sous forme de mots-clés, de façon à ne pas lire votre présentation mot à mot.	➔ Pour chaque partie, notez sur votre plan les mots-clés (*opportunities / new culture / new way of thinking / new values*), les supports choisis (textes, photographie, etc.) et les connecteurs logiques utiles ! (voir p. 226)

Your turn!

Pour améliorer votre aisance à l'oral, entraînez-vous devant un miroir ou une webcam et chronométrez-vous. Essayez de ne pas trop lire vos notes. Faites un effort de prononciation car cette dernière est évaluée au même titre que le contenu de votre présentation.

Improve your **SKILLS**

Why emigrate?

1 In search of a new life

B1

Push factors	Pull factors
• Population pressure • Poor infrastructure • Inadequate job offer • Bad educational chances • Poor health care • Ecological problems • Natural disasters • Social compulsions	• Improvement in the standard of living • Better health care and availability of services • Varied employment opportunities • Higher wages • Quality of education • No social compulsions • Future prospects

Adapted from *https://omega7geo.wordpress.com/2013/07/13/push-and-pull-factors-by-chong-hui-jane/*

Analyse and explain

1. Use the diagram to deduce the meaning of *push* and *pull* factors.
2. Say what push factor(s) would drive you to move to another country.

2 Why emigrate to Britain?

B1 B2

The reason why people from developing countries want to live here is obvious[1]: life is better here than in the impoverished countries from which they came. But that is true of all the developed economies of Europe. All are much better places in which to live than the nations of Africa, for instance, or the Indian subcontinent.

So what explains why so many immigrants target[2] Britain, and why there are such queues at the Sangatte centre in France to get across the Channel to England?

Word has got out that Britain is more hospitable to immigrants than other European countries – which it is. The legacy of empire means we are more used to receiving them and are more willing to integrate them. One of the great virtues of the British people is their tolerance. Our society is much less closed to outsiders than most countries of continental Europe. It is easier to get a job here – less restrictive employment legislation means it is easier to fire people, so employers are more willing to hire migrants they can pay less in the first place. British employers are less suspicious of foreigners than their counterparts in countries such as Italy or France.

Add the fact that it is easier for immigrants who arrive here to claim benefits, get council housing[3] and access health and education services for themselves and their children and it becomes clear why Britain is a target for migrants.

Alasdair Palmer, *The Daily Telegraph*, March 21, 2009.

1. obvious (adj.) : *évident*. **2.** target (v.) : *cibler, viser*.
3. council housing (n.) : *habitation à loyer modéré (HLM)*.
More help WBT n° 27

Staff members of a London hotel. A very high percentage of London hotel staff come from overseas.

Comment and read

1. Comment on the photo and its caption.
2. Read the article and list the reasons why so many migrants want to come to Britain.
3. Say how the journalist explains this.
Go into detail. WBT n° 28

Activity

You have just arrived in London where you've decided to live. On your Facebook page, you post the reasons why you've made this choice and you compare your new life with life back in your home country.

3 Memories B2

The memory of my journey, or should I say my struggle to America, is buried deep inside of me. I was four years old when I was lifted into the arms of two strange men. They guided me down through the Rio Bravo[1] in the dead of night[2], from Mexico to Texas. The river is called the Rio Bravo, meaning the "angry river", because its huge waves are very strong. It has taken the lives of many people who have tried to cross it. [...]

After my brothers, sister, mother, and I made it across the river, we were taken to a man's house. He was a "coyote" and was supposed to help us get through our second obstacle – the border, without getting caught by Immigration. I guess you could say he knew what he was doing because I am here today.

Since I'm an illegal immigrant, the obstacles didn't stop once I got across the border. My freshman year[3], I thought I was going to be kicked out of school because of Proposition 187. Now I can't get a part-time job, or apply to college. On one occasion, I even blamed my mother for all of the troubles that I've had, because I don't have the necessary papers to be in this country. Blaming my mother was the biggest mistake I've ever made. She only wanted what was best for us. If she had known that in this country of "dreams" everybody talked about, things would be harder than they seemed, she wouldn't have brought us here. She would have raised us in our own country to the best of her ability. To this day I can't decide whether my journey here was taken in vain. I was brought here to have a golden opportunity, but unfortunately, it's not being given to me. I know it won't be easy, but I won't stop until I have gotten what I came here to get: my education. You know, come to think of it, my journey here was for that purpose. I must fulfill my dream of becoming an educator and helping young people like myself.

The Freedom Writers Diary, 1999.

1. Rio Bravo : *nom mexicain pour le Rio Grande.* 2. in the dead of night : *au plus profond de la nuit.* 3. freshman year (US) : *année de seconde.*

More help WBT n° 29

Read the extract

1. Relate the extract to the pictures.
2. Say as much as you can about the narrator: who he is, his family, his journey, his feelings, his ambition…
3. Find out what Proposition 187 was. Go into detail. WBT n° 30

Role play

Work in groups of at least five. Imagine the narrator has finally fulfilled his dream: he has become an American citizen and an educator. He is interviewed on television and is asked to tell his story in front of an audience. One of you is the immigrant, another is the interviewer. The others are in the audience and can ask the immigrant more questions.

Grammar

Phrases conditionnelles p. 52
- ***If she had known** [...] **she wouldn't have brought** us here.*

Natures, sens et prononciations du mot *used* p. 53
- *We **are** more **used to receiving***

Subordonnées de temps WBT n° 31
- *I won't stop **until I have gotten what I came here to get**.*

Your task

Do research to determine whether the situations described in the table and the texts above have changed and if so to what extent. Have they improved or got worse? Prepare and present your findings.

Immigrants:

1 Success stories B1

This week, [...] Asian cultural assimilation reached new heights with the appointment of Sajid Javid as Culture Secretary. Javid, son of a Pakistani bus conductor, is the first Asian male to lead a government department and is said to be one of the most promising members of government, whose talents took him to be vice-president of Chase Manhattan bank at 25. What makes him more remarkable is that he took a reported 98 per cent pay cut to fulfil his political ambition. [...]

[Personally] I have also had the luxury of growing up in a Britain with an unprecedented diversity of role models. Previously, popular understanding of the Asian immigrant experience was dominated by the twin stereotypes of curry houses and corner shops. Later Indian immigrants often – like my family – arrived with more education, skills and money than their Bangladeshi and Pakistani counterparts[1]. Those, like my parents, aware of the sacrifices made by their own parents in India, invested heavily in education for their children and typically favoured risk-averse career choices. Second- and third- generation Indians became associated with success in law and medicine.

Shashank Joshi, *The Daily Telegraph*, April 12, 2014.

1. counterpart (n.) : *homologue.*

More help WBT n° 32

Shappi Khorsandi (b. 1973) is an Iranian-born stand-up comedian who grew up in England after her parents immigrated during the Iranian revolution. She is regarded as one of the best comic talents in Britain.

Dev Biswal (b. 1977) is a chef who grew up in Calcutta. He moved to London in 2003. He now owns several restaurants and is acclaimed for his promotion of gourmet Indian food.

Read and compare

1. Sum up what each of the two paragraphs is about.
2. Say as much as you can about Sajid. Why, according to the writer, is he "remarkable"?
3. Compare Sajid's background with that of the two other people in the photos and that of the writer. Go into detail. WBT n° 33

Guess who it is

Think of one famous person in your own country who is a second-generation immigrant. Imagine you are him/her and write two or three sentences about yourself without mentioning your name. The rest of the class must guess who you are.

2 Don't send my Mom home! B1

Watch and explain DVD MP3 9

1. In what way does the photo illustrate the video?
2. Explain the intentions and aims of (a) President Obama, (b) the Democrats, (c) Latin American immigrants. Go into detail. WBT n° 35

Help

- staunchly (adv.) ['st :nt li] : *fermement, catégoriquement*
- get something through (v.) : *faire aboutir quelque chose*
- spouse [spa s] (n.) : *conjoint*

More help WBT n° 34

Grammar

Intention et chose déjà prévue WBT n° 36

- *Tomorrow night **I am going to** be announcing...*

settling in

3 Mexicans in the USA B1

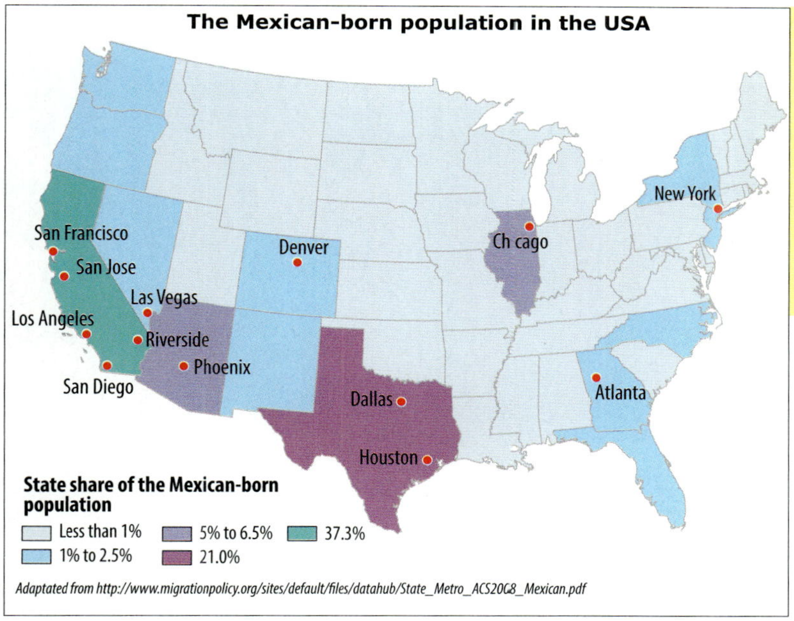

The **1980 census** recorded the foreign born from Mexico as the largest immigrant group in the United States, and this group remains the largest today. In 2006, more than 11.5 million Mexican immigrants resided in the United States, accounting for 30.7% of all US immigrants and one-tenth of the entire population born in Mexico. Over half of all Mexican immigrants reside in the United States illegally.

Comment on the map

1. Say in which states Mexican immigrants have settled and explain why.
2. Say if any of the statistics surprise you, and why.

4 Hispanics and English B1

There is no evidence whatsoever that Mexican and other Latin American immigrants are assimilating more slowly than did previous waves of immigrants. Take language acquisition: Contrary to popular belief, Latino immigrants acquire English as quickly as, or more quickly than, Asian and European immigrants. Although Mexican immigrants lagged behind on language acquisition in 1980, the gap was closed by 2000, the researchers found.

First-generation Mexican immigrants still lag behind on learning English, but second-generation Americans, including those who live with their first-generation parents, acquire English just as fast as do Asian or European immigrants. Non-Latino second-generation immigrants acquire English even faster. Filipino immigrants beat everyone, perhaps owing to the Philippines' half-century under US sovereignty.

Dylan Matthews, *The Washington Post*, January 1, 2013.

http://network.nshp.org/profiles/blog/list?month=11&year=2007

Analyse and comment

1. Explain what the graph shows about Hispanic immigrants' fluency in English.
2. Relate the graph to the newspaper article. Compare their findings.
3. Say what you learn about the different groups of immigrants in the USA. Go into detail. WBT n° 37

How important is language

Do you think language acquisition is the only way to assimilate well in a country? What other ways can you think of? Discuss.

Your task

Work in groups of four. You run a charity that organises classes to help immigrants settle in (in either the UK or the USA). Each immigrant has the right to language classes and 12 hours of other classes. Plan the curriculum of the 12 hours.
What aspects of the British or American way of life will they need to become familiar with?
Present your curriculum to the class and decide on the best one.

Treating immigrants

1 Hard-working foreigners B1

The research from the National Institute for Economic and Social Research found that recruiting skilled foreigners allows companies to become more efficient and expand their businesses.

The economists' findings follow a Government-backed study this week showing that foreigners are filling a fifth of jobs in key industries such as engineering because of a lack of skills in Britain.

The study may fuel[1] the debate about whether British workers have the skills and work ethic needed to compete with foreign counterparts in an increasingly international labour market.

The researchers studied official figures on employment and concluded that foreign workers employed in Britain are on average better-educated and work longer hours than British recruits.

Hiring foreign workers can make companies more productive, the study suggested. Recruiting from outside the UK has "allowed employers to fill skilled and specialist roles and enabled some organisations to expand", the researchers said.

James Kirkup & Peter Dominiczak,
The Daily Telegraph, November 5, 2013.

1. fuel (v.) : *alimenter*.

More help WBT n° 38

A group of workers in Wales. Some are Poles who can earn more doing manual work in Britain than doing jobs they are qualified for in their own countries.

Read and explain

1. Sum up in one sentence what the article is about.
2. Explain why foreign workers are hired in the UK.
3. From what is said in the article and in the picture caption, say what you can deduce about the Polish workmen in the photo.
4. Say what impact hiring foreign workers can have on British companies.
Go into detail. WBT n° 39

Grammar

Éviter d'employer une relative WBT n° 40

- *[...] a Government-backed study this week* ***showing*** *that...*

Role play

Work in pairs: **A** and **B**.

A: You have a British boyfriend/girlfriend. You don't want to emigrate because you won't be able to get a job in your own field.

B: You are A's British boyfriend/girlfriend. Try and persuade him/her to join you in Britain.

2 The problem of being undocumented B1

Read and explain

Using the cartoon (opposite) and the article (next page), explain why some employers hire undocumented workers.

fairly

Millions of workers [...] toil in industries like construction, casual day labour[1], agriculture or the food industry across America and [...] standing up[2] and complaining can result in an employer reporting them to the immigration authorities.

Experts point out that some employers are all too eager to take on undocumented workers and exploit them for their willingness to work long hours for low pay. If no one complains, questions about immigration papers are rarely asked. But if problems do arise – such as being injured on the job or workers demanding better pay or access to a union – a swift phone call to the police or ICE will result in the difficult employees being deported.

Paul Harris, *The Guardian*, March 28, 2013.

1. casual day labour (n.) : *travail temporaire (journalier).*
2. stand up (v.) : *(ici) se rebiffer, se faire entendre.*

What may happen?

Using information in the article, say what may happen to undocumented immigrant workers if they are injured or complain about their working conditions.

Discuss solutions

Work in groups of 3 or 4 and think about what measures could be taken to prevent undocumented workers from being exploited. Make a list of your proposals and compare your list with those of the other groups.

3 The way forward? B1

Use your imagination

Look at the photo and imagine who these people are and what they want. (If you have studied *"Don't send my Mom home"* [p. 46], use the information in that video to help you.)

Watch the video DVD MP3 10

1. Say what President Obama has decided to do.
2. Say who is opposed to the decision and why.
3. List the conditions under which undocumented workers will be able to stay in the USA.
Go into detail. WBT n° 42

State your point of view

Do you think it's fair that undocumented immigrants should be deported even if they have already been living and working in the USA for a long time? Why/Why not? Give your reasons.

Help

- vow [vaʊ] (v.) : *jurer de.*
- pledge (v.) : *s'engager à, promettre.*
- felon ['felən] (n.) : *criminel.*

More help WBT n° 41

Your task

You are applying for a job in England. You have to send an application form together with a cover letter. Write the cover letter, explaining why you want to work in England and why they should hire you. (180 words)

CROSS CULTURE

Famous immigrants

A new life in the USA

These people all moved to the USA – for various reasons. Some became American citizens. All of them had great ambitions.

Albert Einstein (1879-1955).

Charlie Chaplin (1889-1977).

Henry Kissinger (b. 1923).

Charlize Theron (b. 1975).

Cary Grant (1904-1986).

Arnold Schwarzenegger (b. 1947).

A new life in the UK

These people all moved to the UK – for various reasons. Some became British citizens. Some were famous before they emigrated, some achieved fame in Britain.

Anish Kapoor (b. 1954).

Karl Marx (1818-1883).

Henry James (1843-1916).

Sigmund Freud (1856-1939).

T. S. Eliot (1888-1965).

Activities

1. Divide into groups of four and choose two immigrants from the ones shown on these pages. Browse the internet and find:
– their countries of origin,
– the reasons why they decided to leave their countries and move to the USA or the UK,
– their achievements.
2. Compare their stories to the ones of the people on page 46. What are the similarities and differences?
3. Present the two people to the rest of the class.

Improve your

GRAMMAR

Phrases conditionnelles (PG p. 251)

MÉMO

Quel temps emploie-t-on en français pour exprimer une condition dans un contexte présent ?

• L'imparfait. Ex. : Si j'étais britannique...

Quel temps emploie-t-on en anglais dans la même situation ?

• Le prétérit modal. Ex. : *If I were British*...

Quels temps et mode emploie-t-on en français pour exprimer l'action soumise à condition dans un contexte présent ?

• Le présent du conditionnel. Ex. : ... je vivrais à Londres.

Quelle forme verbale emploie-t-on en anglais pour exprimer l'action soumise à condition dans un contexte présent ?

• Le modal *would* + base verbale. Ex. : ... *I would live in London*.

Que se passe-t-il quand les mêmes notions sont exprimées par rapport à un repère passé ?

• En français, comme en anglais, on emploie le plus-que-parfait pour exprimer la condition.

• L'action soumise à la condition est exprimée au conditionnel passé en français et avec *would* + *have* + participe passé en anglais (voir l'exemple ci-dessous).

Observez et raisonnez

(texte p. 45)

• *If she had known that in this country of "dreams" [...] things would be harder than they seemed, she wouldn't have brought us here.*

1 Combien de propositions cet énoncé contient-il ?

2 Isolez chacune d'elles.

3 Quelle est celle qui contient (a) la condition ? (b) l'action soumise à condition ?

4 À quoi voit-on que la condition porte sur une situation passée ?

5 Traduisez l'énoncé.

6 Quel sentiment cet énoncé exprime-t-il ?

Entraînez-vous

1 Cartoon fun

Faites une phrase pour expliquer comment l'accident aurait pu être évité.

2 Trouvez un exemple

Trouvez dans le texte p. 45 un autre exemple d'action soumise à une condition passée.

3 Expression et traduction

Reconstituez des phrases avec les éléments suivants. Puis, traduisez les phrases obtenues.

a. doing / guide / hadn't / have / he / if / known / never / reached / Texas / the / was / we / what / would

b. able / been / cross / had / hadn't / hard / have / if / Rio Grande / tires / the / to / we / we / wouldn't

c. authorities / deported / had / have / if / known / the / they / undocumented / us / we / were / would

d. ambitions / come / country / fulfilled / hadn't / have / I / I / if / my / this / to / wouldn't

4 Dites-le en anglais

a. Si mon rêve s'était réalisé, je serais devenu enseignant.

b. Si j'avais su, je n'aurais pas blâmé ma mère.

c. Si nous n'avions pas eu de guide, nous aurions été pris par la patrouille frontalière (*Border Patrol*).

Natures, sens et prononciations du mot *used* (PG p. 239)

MÉMO

Quelles sont les natures du mot used ?

• Selon les contextes et les emplois, c'est le passé du verbe lexical *use* (utiliser), ou l'expression figée *used* (*to* + BV) qui marque l'habitude passée ou une situation révolue, ou encore l'adjectif *used* (+ *to* + nom ou gérondif) qui marque l'habitude (habitué à).

1. *They used dogs to patrol the border.*
2. *They used to swim across the river.* (voir PG p. 239)
3. *They were not used to being treated so well.*

La prononciation de used varie-t-elle avec la nature du mot ?

• Oui. Dans l'ordre où les mots sont présentés dans les exemples ci-dessus, on obtient respectivement les prononciations suivantes :
[ju:zd + tu:] / [jʊst + tə] / [ju:st + tu:]. Entraînez-vous à prononcer les trois exemples donnés.

Comment traduire ces 3 phrases ?

1. Ils ont utilisé/utilisaient des chiens pour patrouiller la frontière.
2. Autrefois ils traversaient le fleuve à la nage.
3. Ils n'étaient pas habitués à être traités aussi gentiment.

Observez et raisonnez

(texte p. 44)

• *We are more **used to receiving** them and are more willing to integrate them.*

1 Analysez le groupe en gras et identifiez la nature (nom, verbe, adjectif, etc.) des mots qui le composent.

2 À laquelle des trois tournures décrites dans le mémo cet énoncé appartient-il ?

3 Traduisez l'énoncé.

4 Pouvez-vous justifier l'emploi de V-*ing* après *to* dans cet énoncé ? (Voir les structures verbales dans le PG p. 254)

Entraînez-vous

1 Dites quelle est la nature du mot *used* dans le dessin suivant.

2 Expression

Faites cinq phrases pour exprimer ce à quoi vous êtes habitué ou ce à quoi vous ne pouvez pas vous habituer.
Ex. *I can't get used to getting up early!*

3 Dites-le en anglais.

a. Nous sommes habitués à voir des gens de toutes origines dans les rues de Londres.

b. Beaucoup ont eu du mal à s'habituer à vivre à l'occidentale.

c. Moi, je ne peux pas m'habituer à manger des plats si relevés (*hot/spicy*).

d. Elle n'a pas l'habitude de conduire à gauche.

4 Choisissez

Choisissez entre *used to* + *V-ing* et *used to* + BV.

a. When we lived in India we used to ...... (help) with the running of the local orphanages.

b. But we never got used to ...... (see) all the poverty around us.

c. I still hesitate a lot before saying something because I'm not yet used to ...... (live) in this country.

d. She used to ......(be) much more tolerant of other cultures.

Improve your

VOCABULARY

1 Immigration

Match the descriptions MP3 11

Check that you know the meaning of these nouns. Then listen and say which one is being described.

an alien • citizenship • a Green Card • health benefits • a menial job • moonlighting

Complete

Use these words to complete the paragraph.

border • illegal • living • provide • unskilled • wetback

The origin of the American word "......", the slang name for ...... Latin American immigrants (usually Mexican), comes from the fact that they avoided ...... controls by swimming the Rio Grande and therefore got wet. In their own countries, they were unable to ...... for their families and believed that they could earn a good ...... in the USA, even as ...... workers.

Imagine an interview

The woman in the picture came to Britain from Romania a year ago. She is being interviewed by a journalist who is writing a series of articles about immigrants in Britain. Imagine the interview and use these expressions (check their meaning if necessary).

make ends meet • put money aside • support my/your family back home • a better standard of living

2 Getting a job

People and paper...

a. Say which of the nouns below are people and which are written documents.

b. Find two pairs of synonyms in the list.

c. Translate the words into French.

an applicant • a candidate • a CV • a jobseeker • a reference • a referee • a résumé

Find the right verb

Choose the right verb from the list to complete each blank in this email sent by a headhunter to a Human Resources Director. Put the verbs in the correct form.

apply • attach • interview • make • shortlist • suggest • take

From	jonathanredding@hotmail.com
To	gillianmcpherson@RBY.uk
Subject	Recruitment of production supervisor (ref. 05685B)
Attached	

Hello Gillian,

Fifteen people have ...... for the post. After ...... them all, I have ...... three (CVs and cover letters ......). I ...... that, when you have ...... your final choice, you ...... the person on for a trial period of 6 months.

Best regards,

Jonathan Redding

FINAL TASK

A TV show about immigration

**A TV channel is making a programme about immigration.
The aim is to look at the question from the immigrants' point of view – to tell their stories.
The two hosts interview several families who have immigrated.**

1 Choose your roles

- Choose the English-speaking country where the programme is being made (the UK, Canada, the USA, Australia, New Zealand, etc.).
- Designate the two chat show hosts and the families (3 or 4 people in each family).

2 Prepare for the programme

Families

- Give yourselves new identities (names, ages, nationality, etc.).
- Think about why you emigrated (economic, political, personal, etc.) and how you got here.
- Imagine what has happened since (jobs, schools, integration, friends, etc.).
- Think about your feelings (when you left your home country, when you arrived, how you feel now, etc.).

Hosts

- Choose a name for the programme.
- Prepare a short introduction to present the show.
- Listen to the "families" as they prepare their stories and use this information to prepare an introduction to each family.
- Think about the questions you will ask them.

3 Make the programme

- The hosts introduce the programme and their guests.
- They interview each family in turn.

PREPARE FOR THE BAC

Compréhension de l'écrit (10 points)

FICHE MÉTHODE PAGE 57

Sujet Immigrants from India

Dad and Anwar lived next door to each other in Bombay and were best friends from the age of five. Dad's father, the doctor, had built a lovely low wooden house on Juhu beach for himself, his wife and his twelve children. Dad and Anwar would sleep on the veranda and at dawn run down to the sea and swim. They went to school in a horse-drawn rickshaw. At weekends they played cricket, and after school there was tennis on the family court. The servants would be ball-boys. The cricket matches were often against the British, and you had to let them win. There were also constant riots and demonstrations and Hindu-Muslim fighting.

Dad had had an idyllic childhood, and as he told me of his adventures with Anwar I often wondered why he'd condemned his own son to a dreary suburb of London . [...]

It was only later, when he came to England, that Dad realized how complicated practical life could be. He'd never cooked before, never washed up, never cleaned his own shoes or made a bed. Servants did that. Dad told us that when he tried to remember the house in Bombay he could never visualize the kitchen: he'd never been in it. He remembered, though, that his favourite servant had been sacked for kitchen misdemeanours; once for making toast by lying on his back and suspending bread from between his toes over a flame, and on a second occasion for cleaning celery with a toothbrush – his own brush, as it happened, not the Master's, but that was no excuse.

London, the Old Kent Road, was a freezing shock. It was wet and foggy; people called you 'Sunny Jim'; there was never enough to eat, and Dad never took to dripping[1] on toast. "Nose drippings more like," he'd say, pushing away the staple diet[2] of the working class. "I thought it would be roast beef and Yorkshire pudding all the way." But rationing was still on, and the area was derelict after being bombed to rubble during the war. Dad was amazed and heartened by the sight of the British in England, though. He'd never seen the English in poverty, as roadsweepers, dustmen, shopkeepers and barmen. He'd never seen an Englishman stuffing bread into his mouth with his fingers, and no one had told him the English didn't wash regularly because the water was so cold – if they had water at all.

Hanif Kureishi, *The Buddha of Suburbia*, 1990.

1. dripping *(n.) : graisse de cuisine récupérée après cuisson d'un rôti.* 2. staple diet *(n.) : régime de base.*

Questions

- ***Tous les élèves traiteront les questions suivantes.***

1. Where did the narrator and his father each spend their childhood?
2. Find three details which indicate that the father was from a wealthy background.
3. Say whether the following are true or false. Quote from the text to justify your choice.
a. Life was not always idyllic for Dad in Bombay.
b. Dad was well-prepared for his new life in Britain.
c. His first impressions of Britain were very positive.
4. Explain what "You had to let them win" (l. 5) suggests about the difference between the father's relationship with the British during his childhood and when he moved to London.

- ***Seuls les élèves de l'option LVA traiteront les questions 5 et 6.***

5. Describe the tone of the narrator. Quote from the text to justify your answer.
6. What do you learn about India from this text?

Expression écrite (10 points)

- ***Tous les élèves traiteront les questions suivantes.***

1. Write the letter the father sends to his family a few weeks after his arrival in London. (150/200 words)
2. Would you ever change country? Why/Why not? (150 words)

- ***Seuls les élèves de l'option LVA traiteront la question suivante.***

3. If you have visited a country very different from your own, write about your first impressions of it. If not, choose such a country and imagine your first impressions. (250 words)

Compréhension écrite

Fiche méthode	Application guidée

Étape 1 Lire le texte et les premières informations

Fiche méthode	Application guidée
➜ Lisez attentivement le texte deux fois, sans regarder les consignes, pour identifier les **éléments essentiels** (thème, personnages, époque…) et la notion à laquelle se rapporte le texte. Le paratexte, peut fournir des informations précieuses. ➜ Si vous ne connaissez pas un mot, utilisez le **contexte** pour en comprendre le sens.	➜ Repérez les éléments qui permettent d'identifier le narrateur (qui est-il ?), de situer l'action dans le temps (quels détails montrent quand l'action principale se déroule ? ; citez une date), de situer le ou les lieux mentionnés (quels pays ?), d'identifier les personnes (sont-ils nombreux ? présents ?) ➜ Exemple : *rubble (derelict, bombed…)* = décombres.

Étape 2 Lire et comprendre les consignes

Fiche méthode	Application guidée
➜ Les consignes éclairent le contenu du texte. **Lisez-les toutes** une première fois, puis relisez le texte en surlignant les informations importantes. Soyez attentif à ce qui est demandé dans les consignes pour répondre avec précision. Apprenez le **lexique** des consignes ! ➜ Les questions vont du plus simple au plus complexe. du global au plus détaillé.	➜ La **question 1** attire votre attention sur les lieux (*Where*) et les personnages. Les **1/2/3** vous amènent, notamment, à vous concentrer sur un personnage (*father*). La **4** permet de faire le lien avec la notion (Espaces et échanges). Dans plusieurs questions, on demande d'être précis *(Find details, quotes, justify)*. ➜ Pour les questions **5** et **6**, il faut comprendre l'implicite, donc s'appuyer sur le contexte. Relisez le texte en entier.

Étape 3 Répondre aux questions

Fiche méthode	Application guidée
➜ Répondez aux questions **dans l'ordre**, en indiquant les numéros ou les lettres. **Relisez** chaque réponse immédiatement après l'avoir écrite. À la fin, relisez l'ensemble. Attention aux **fautes d'étourderie**.	➜ Vous devez citer le texte à plusieurs reprises : soyez précis, sélectionnez les passages les plus pertinents. Référez-vous au texte pour vérifier l'orthographe des mots que vous utilisez (ex. : *court, matches, shock*).

Expression écrite

Fiche méthode	Application guidée

Étape 1 Lire les sujets

Fiche méthode	Application guidée
Sujet 1 ➜ Lisez attentivement les consignes et soulignez les **termes clés**. ➜ Déterminez le **type de production** écrite que l'on vous demande : lettre, discours, essai, récit, dialogue…	**Sujet 1** ➜ *letter / father / family / after his arrival in London / impressions / feels / native country.* ➜ Une lettre à un membre de la famille (Writing a letter, p. 225). Attention au ton de la lettre (contexte familial).

Étape 2 Préparer la rédaction

Fiche méthode	Application guidée
➜ Sur votre **brouillon** : – notez les formules d'introduction et de conclusion ; – les mots et expressions que vous allez utiliser dans votre lettre.	➜ **Sujet 1** – *Dear …, / First of all, let me say… / That's all for now / Your loving husband/father*, etc. – *I felt / I had the impression / I couldn't help feeling / I didn't know what to think / it really shocked me…*, etc.

Étape 3 Rédiger au propre

Fiche méthode	Application guidée
➜ Variez les **structures de phrases** et le **vocabulaire**. N'oubliez pas les mots de liaison. ➜ Pensez à vous **relire** !	➜ *However much I thought I knew about Britain, … / I couldn't have been more surprised / Nevertheless, you have to admire them for…*, etc. ➜ Attention à l'orthographe (*thought, heartened*, etc.).

The Orphanage

Konstantia Kombuis, the restaurant where Piet and I have arranged to meet for lunch, is set off the beaten cuisine path of downtown Paarl with its jazzy eateries, art stores, and gift shops. Rather, Drosty Street has a row of Cape Dutch homes, most of them converted to small businesses. One of them is this slightly decrepit cafe - its thatched roof worn, the shutters shedding their bottle-green paint, and its austere dining room empty. Instead of boasting the region's finest KWV wines like its more frequented counterparts on Main Street, it offers a special on Windhoek lager. I order a shandy and take in the decor, which is a mishmash of French colonial and tribal hut. Before long Piet breezes in wearing coveralls, a backpack slung over his shoulder, and a lit cigarette perched on his lower lip in defiance of the anti-smoking ban. The restaurant manager claps his back and says, 'Piet! *Jou blerrie skilpad!* At your age you can't afford to keep such a beautiful woman waiting!'

"Luister, ou pal, instead of reminding me of my age, why don't you make yourself useful and pour me a cup of coffee – or has it been so long since you've had a customer that you've forgotten how to serve one?" he volleys back, winking at me.

When he approaches our table he is scowling as the smoke hits his eyes. "Abbe! What a pleasure to see you," he says, removing the cigarette from his mouth so he can kiss the back of my hand. "So long; too long." [...]

We order the specialty of the day – kudu kebobs – and he pulls from his backpack a folder with the offer from the firm, five percent more than asking price, which Piet says he set deliberately high. They hope to finish construction of the resort[1] before the winter rains next year, he tells me. A win-win, Piet concludes his report.

"I heard the local council members aren't too happy about the idea of another big resort," I say.

"Ja nee," he confirms. "It's going to be competition for all the local establishments, but progress is progress. And none of those people who are so unhappy about this deal are offering to buy the place, so there you are." He drains his second cup of coffee. "Rhiaan still on board?"

I nod. "He has wanted to sell the farm for years. I was the one who wanted to hang on to it – you know, in case." In case what? In case I ever stopped running away and returned? In case my mother was right – that it would all still be here waiting for me when I came back?

Piet leans over and holds my hand. "It was your home, I understand." After the waiter has set down our entrees, he says, "Perhaps we should take a drive out to the farm first, before you sign the papers, and clear the air, so to speak. After all, we're talking about your home."

"It was never my home," I protest.

"Ag, skat, but it is where you left your heart, *ne?"*

Whether or not this is true, it is still not a good idea to visit the farm. There is a deal to make, papers to sign. Maybe afterward, when the land with its withered fruit trees is the site of the Kabbeljou Resort, I can visit. When all the ghosts have been evicted. "I need the money, Piet, and I mean in the food-on-the-table sense. I don't want any nostalgia trips cluttering this decision. Let's just do it; the sooner the better."

"Yes, of course." Piet goes over the contract, the estimated settlement statement, the government transfer charges and the tax implications. The final number, after all the required adjustments, is staggering even when you divide by two.

1. resort (n.) : *complexe touristique.*

Paarl, a town in the Western Cape province of South Africa.

He finishes his food in a dozen mouthfuls and lights a cigarette. "There is just one small matter to clear up, which, hopefully, can be accomplished by the buyer's deadline."

"What's that?"

"The school." Although initially supposed to educate twenty elementary-aged black children, the farm is now schooling forty, half of whom are staying on the property. Nobody quite has the answer for the number of children orphaned from AIDS, or the matter that nobody wants to go to school with kids who are infected. These little start-up schools pop up on farms and church properties everywhere, modest projects of the well-intentioned. But before you know it, there is twice, thrice the number of kids expected. "Quite frankly," Piet continues, "I am pleased we are going to be out from under the burden of liability." Piet goes on to explain that there is a state-sponsored orphanage closer to Cape Town that can take a few of the children, and he is hoping the Catholics might be able to do something about the rest. Suddenly the euphoria of inheriting a small fortune is sanded down by the realization that for some, for many, there is no relief, neither from poverty nor an early grave. What is to become of children without mothers, without teachers?

"What if I talk to Rhiaan and see about taking some of the money from the sale and establishing a trust? Something that can provide scholarships for a few of these children."

"That would be very generous indeed, Abbe. But you are not responsible for these kids, you know. You and your brother have already been more than generous, letting them use the farm."

"I wouldn't call it generous – we both know that no one else wanted anything to do with the place. But a scholarship fund – that's something my grandmother would have approved of."

"Indeed," he agrees.

"So when do I sign the papers?"

Isla Morley, *Come Sunday*, 2009.

Read and understand

1. Where does the conversation take place?
2. Identify the narrator, the characters present and those who are only referred to.
3. What do we learn about the narrator?
4. Show that she is coming back after a long absence.
5. What has she come back for? Make sure you understand what "the farm" and "the resort" refer to.
6. What shows that a large amount of money is at stake?
7. What may stand in the way of the transaction that is planned?
8. How does the narrator solve the problem?
9. How important is it to know that the narrator is in urgent need of money to appreciate what she finally decides to do?

Go further LVA/LELE

1. Study how the author manages to paint a realistic picture of the place where the conversation takes place. Would you say she has succeeded in creating what is called "local colour"?
2. How is the reader made to understand the reasons why the narrator left "the farm"?
3. How does the author manage to make the reader feel empathy towards the narrator?

Going to America in 1901

Ours was a terrible twenty-four-day journey to *la 'Merica,* made unbearable by spoiled food, tainted[1] water, and rolling seas. A broken propeller delayed us off the coast of Portugal for three extra days and nights of hell. Worst of all was the darkness and stink of life below, inside the belly of the big ship. Where there is sun and fresh air, there is hope, but here the sun did not shine and the air we breathed was stale and fetid. Aboveboard, bands played and the filthy rich dined off china and drank from fancy glasses. We in steerage[2] lived like rats. Women and children sobbed, men fought each other over trifles, and everyone suffered the stench of vomit and excrement. There was a stabbing[3] en route, and the birth of a baby, and the death of the child's mother two days later. That crying *bambino* was passed from breast to breast after that, and we prayed for its fate. All our fates. That baby cried for us all!

There were rats, too, plenty of them; nighttime was when those goddamned creatures prowled[4]. One night I woke to find one sitting on my neck, sniffing at my mustache. I screamed out, waking even my brother Pasquale, who always slept like a dead man. After that night, I took no chances, napping[5] as best I could while sitting or leaning against beams and walls. Day and night fell together on that hellish journey across the sea, and my mind existed in a place between sleep and vigilance.

During the voyage, my brother Vincenzo was as shamefully behaved as always – pinching women's behinds, boasting about his mischief, cheating at cards against men with bad and worsening tempers. Vincenzo was forever wandering away from Pasquale and me and getting himself in trouble, then calling for me to settle some dispute he had provoked. It is the firstborn's burden to unravel the knots that younger brothers make.

Throughout that endless and terrible journey across the ocean, I was afflicted with lice and worry – scratching and haunting myself with the cold fear of what would come

1. tainted (adj.) : *contaminé.*
2. steerage (n.) : *entrepont.*
3. stabbing (n.) : *agression à l'arme blanche.*
4. prowl (v.) : *rôder.*
5. nap (v., n.) : *(faire) un somme.*
6. taut (adj.) : *tendu.*
7. omen (n.) : *augure, présage.*
8. squint (v.) : *plisser les yeux.*
9. Poveri si, sporchi no = Being poor is no excuse for being filthy.
10. hold (n.) : *cale.*
11. Il mondo e fatto a scale, chi le scende e chi le sale = The world is made of stairs: there are those who go up and those who go down.

to pass once we landed in this place I had risked everything to reach. For a Sicilian, home is everything. How could I have done this? Had I been bewitched into thinking that the unknown would be preferable to putting up with the petty nuisances of a stonemason who would die off in time anyway? The rumbling every few years of a distant *vulcano?* As much as I hated Etna for the damage it had visited upon my *famiglia*, the lives it had claimed, at least it was an enemy I could watch. What enemies awaited me in this *Mundo Novu* toward which we sailed? My heart was sick from thinking and worrying and pinching those goddamned lice between my fingernails!

The little rest I stole came to me in short, interrupted naps made terrible with nightmares. In my dreams, I saw flowing lava, cracking earth, screaming women stuck in fiery trees. Somewhere in the middle of one of those desperate nights, I promised myself that I would never again put myself through such a hellish journey – that I would never return home. That night I said farewell to Sicily forever. Whatever *la 'Merica* held in store for me, it was where I would stay for the rest of my days. The vow was small comfort, but comfort nonetheless.

Sometimes as the other steerage travelers slept, I crept amongst them and over them and did what was forbidden: climbed the narrow stairs to the ship's deck where the wealthier travelers strolled and where I might take into my lungs the clean salt air or watch the moon's rippling reflection against that endless sea. In the school run by the good Sisters of Humility, I had envied the rich boys their supplies of India ink. Now, here in the moonlight, was an ocean full of it through which we traveled – enough *inchiostro di china* in which to drown the whole world, let alone Domenico Tempesta. But I would not give those haughty boys at the convent school the satisfaction of dying! I was not weak. I had been the best of them – the student most loved by the good sisters – and I would prevail!

On one such night of watching the endless ocean, the moon shone brighter than usual, illuminating a small school of dolphins that jumped and swam alongside the SS *Napolitano*. I have always been a modern man who leaves superstition to ignorant old women, but the sight of those *delfini* that night – their bodies arcing toward the sky, their taut[6] skin glistening in the moonlight – it seemed to me a powerful omen[7]. That night, I stood smiling through my tears and was comforted. I knelt on the ship's deck to pray and, in that position, fell into the only sweet, deep sleep I enjoyed during that long and horrible journey.

I awakened next morning to the blinding sun, a mocking voice, and a kick in the ribs! When I squinted[8] and looked up, I was peering into the arrogant face of a ship's waiter. Nearby, a well-dressed couple stood staring at me with looks of disdain. "Get back down where you belong," the haughty waiter ordered – commanding me, the son of a hero! The grandson of landowners! A man who had once been singled out by the Blessed Virgin herself!

The rich woman shook her head and chattered like a squirrel. *"Poveri si, sporchi no*[9]*,"* she told the rich man.

Still half-asleep, I rose and stumbled toward the ship's hold[10], and the waiter and the well-dressed couple moved on. My dignity returned along with my consciousness. Boldly, I turned back, shouting to the three of them, *"Il mondo e fatto a scale, chi le scende e chi le sale!*[11]*"*

One day, I vowed, I would have power and money enough to spit in the faces of those who had humiliated me! In America, my destiny would be realized and I would be avenged!

Wally Lamb, *I Know This Much Is True*, 1998.

Read and understand

1. Say where and when the action takes place.
2. Name the three main characters and say how they are related to each other.
3. Say where they come from. Quote from the text and give your reasons.
4. Say what social background they come from. Quote from the text and give your reasons
5. Say where they are going to and why they left their country. Quote from the text to justify your answer.
6. Find elements in the text which show that the travelling conditions for the narrator and the people from the same social background were appalling.
7. What childhood memory comes back to the narrator's mind and why?
8. Quote passages from the text showing that the wealthy people and the staff have no respect for people like the narrator.
9. Say what kind of life the narrator dreams of when he gets to this new country.

Go further LVA/LELE

1. Explain why some sentences are written in Italian and in italics.
2. Quote passages from the text showing that, despite the situation, the narrator remains proud and determined.
3. How does the narrator feel about having to leave "home"?
4. Explain the role of the passage about the dolphins and the omen. What does it tell us about the narrator's vision of the future?
5. To what extent is the text linked to the notion you have studied in this chapter.

Improve your SKILLS

What makes a hero?

1 Are these your heroes? B1

Writers, activists, political leaders, soldiers, volunteers... We all have our own heroes. Yet, although some criteria for heroism are universally accepted, people often disagree when it comes to deciding who can really be called a hero.

Talk about tne photos

1. Say who you recognise and what you know about them.
2. Would you say that any of these people are heroes? Why/Why not?

2 Definitions B1 B2

"I think of a hero as someone who understands the degree of responsibility that comes with his freedom."

Bob Dylan (b. 1941), musician.

"If I were the blushing[2] kind, I would blush to be called a hero."

Aung San Suu Kyi (b. 1945), Burmese politician.

"A hero is someone who has given his or her life to something bigger than oneself."

Joseph Campbell (1904-1987), American writer.

"I am of certain convinced that the greatest heroes are those who do their duty in the daily grind of domestic affairs whilst the world whirls as a maddening dreidel."

Florence Nightingale (1820-1910), English nurse.

"I don't see myself as a hero because what I'm doing is self-interested: I don't want to live in a world where there's no privacy and therefore no room for intellectual exploration and creativity."

Edward Snowden (b. 1983), "whistleblower"[1].

"Imagine young people would grow up with the feeling that you have to be a hero to do your human duty. I am afraid nobody would ever help other people, because who is a hero? I was not. I was just an ordinary housewife and secretary."

Miep Gies (1909-2010), Dutch woman who hid Anne Frank's family during World War II.

1. whistleblower (n.) : *personne qui alerte l'opinion.*
2. blush (v.) : *rougir.*

What do you think?

1. Read the quotes, then say who these people are or were. If necessary, use the Internet to find more information about them.
2. Say what you need to be a hero, according to these quotes.
3. Do you agree with them? Can you think of other criteria? Share them with your classmates.

Your task

Use the ideas from the quotes and those shared with your classmates to write your own definition of what makes a hero.

Recognition for

1 A schoolgirl's fight for education B1

"One child, one teacher, one book, one pen can change the world."

Malala, a 16-year-old Pakistani education activist, has written her memoirs in "I Am Malala".
Now living in England, she explains that, although the regime in her part of Pakistan officially prevented her from attending school, this didn't stop her from studying. "It was school that kept me going," she says.

How much do you know?

Say what you know about Malala. The title, the picture and the text will help you.

Discuss

Why do you think Malala said "It was school that kept me going"? Exchange your views.

2 Nobel prizewinners call for action B1

Watch the video DVD MP3 12

1. In what way do the two NobelPeace Prize winners fulfil the criteria specified by Nobel (see the picture caption).
2. Say what Satyarthi wants. Guess what he means by "the dreams of our children".
3. Identify the three things that children want, according to Malala. Go into detail. WBT n° 43

Research and discuss

Find out who the winners of the Nobel Peace Prize were over the last ten years (http://nobelpeaceprize.org/en_GB/laureates/).
Do you agree with all the choices? Choose one winner and argue why the person (or the organisation) should or should not have received the award. Exchange your views.

Grammar

Les mots se terminant en *-ing* p. 72

- *the regime [...] prevented her from going to school.*
- *this didn't stop her from studying.*
- *it was school that kept me going.*

Help

- plea (n.) : *plaidoyer*
- prayer [preə] (n.) : *prière*
- expenditure (n.) : *dépenses*
- heed (v.) : *tenir compte de*

The Nobel Peace Prize medallion. Alfred Nobel (1833-1896) – the inventor of dynamite – willed most of his fortune to a series of prizes. The Peace Prize was to be awarded to "the person who shall have done the most or the best work for fraternity between nations, for the abolition or reduction of standing armies and for the holding and promotion of peace congresses."

our heroes

3 Britain honours its teen heroes

B1

Next Sunday in London the first BBC Radio 1 Teen Awards will be held, to celebrate the achievements of British teenagers who make a difference to their communities, have overcome difficulties in an inspirational way, or display entrepreneurial talent. The winners will be presented with glass statues on stage at the Hammersmith Apollo, alongside music stars including Katy Perry and JLS, who are also up for awards.

Lauren Gander, 12, Sussex

Teen Community Hero Award nominee

Proving wrong the doctors who said she would never walk, spina bifida[1] sufferer Lauren is a tireless fundraiser, completing runs, walks and night treks for charity.

"Now that I can walk, I thought, 'I'm not going to sit on my bottom and not do anything!' My ambition is to be a dancer, but if not I'd like to be a physiotherapist or an occupational therapist in the future. I like to help people."

Josh Worley, 14, Norfolk

Teen Community Hero Award nominee

The schoolboy founded his own radio station after raising nearly £50,000. The station is run by young people and helps teens – particularly the unemployed and those in care – to gain experience working in radio. "If teenagers aren't seen as hoodies attacking people, they are perfect teens in magazines. Young people who want to make a difference in their communities are forgotten because it is seen as boring."

Rachel Shields, *The Independent*, November 7, 2010.

1. spina bifida (n.) : *malformation de la colonne vertébrale.*

More help WBT n° 44

The award ceremony for BBC Radio 1's Teen Awards (2014).

Brainstorm

Use the title and the photo to work out what the BBC Radio 1 Teen Awards are. Guess what sort of radio station BBC Radio 1 is.

Read and explain

1. Explain briefly what these awards are. Compare what you now know with your guesses in the previous activity.
2. Say what Lauren has been doing despite her handicap.
3. Say what Josh founded and what his main aim is.
4. Explain what makes them both young heroes.

Go into detail. WBT n° 45

Present a hero

Use the links to learn more about young British heroes. Choose one of them and present him or her to the class. Then, as a class, decide which of them is the most heroic teenager.

http://www.dailymail.co.uk/health/article-2550057/All-lifesavers-YOUR-young-hero-From-10-year-old-saved-choking-mother-Army-Cadet-rescued-stranger-having-fit-street-The-five-finalists-Young-Hero-Year.html

http://www.independent.co.uk/news/uk/home-news/britain-honours-its-teen-heroes-2127503.html

Your task

Work in pairs. Imagine a project that will qualify you to run for the BBC Radio 1 Teen Awards. It should be a project that fulfils the criteria of the Awards (see the text on the left). Present the project to the class and be prepared to answer questions on it. The rest of the class then decides if you are worthy or not of being nominated.

Female heroes

1 Deanie Parrish B1

Deanie Parrish served in the Women Airforce Service Pilots (WASP) during World War II. […] Parrish joined WASP because "my country needed me and I felt that was the best thing that I could do." Though the WASP logged hundreds of hours of flight time in numerous aircraft, they were not part of an official military team[1]. When they tried to get Congress to militarize them, they voted it down. Parrish believes this was because "Women primarily were thought to be housewives and mothers, they weren't considered professionals like the men."

Convincing Congress to award the long-neglected WASP the Congressional Gold Medal became Parrish's mission. She wanted the award to be "a way of educating America about the history of this group of women that most of America had never heard of." In 2009, her mission was completed when President Obama awarded the WASP the Congressional Gold Medal. The medal was never for the publicity, rather, Parrish felt it important because "it's inspirational and it's motivational, especially for young girls to know that they too can do whatever they want to do if they put their mind to it and keep persevering."

US Army Educational Package, June 8, 2014.

1. not part of an official military team = i.e. women pilots were not allowed to take part in military operations; they were civil pilots.

Four members of WASP (Women Airforce Service Pilots) leaving their plane on an airfield in Ohio.

Comment on the photo

1. Describe the photo, read the caption and say when you think the photo was taken. How do you know?

Read and explain

1. Say what Deanie Parrish did during World War II and why.
2. Explain what her aim has been since the war ended.

Go into detail. WBT n° 46

Discuss a quote

Parrish said, *"Women primarily were thought to be housewives and mothers, they weren't considered professionals like the men."* What does this tell us about the role of women in 1940s society? Exchange your views.

2 Harriet Tubman B1

Brainstorm

1. Have you ever heard of Harriet Tubman and the Underground Railroad?
2. Imagine why there is a statue of her in this particular district of New York City.

Listen and find out MP3 13

Listen and say what you now know about (a) Harriet Tubman, (b) the Underground Railroad, (c) the statue.

Go into detail. WBT n° 48

What do you think?

Give your opinion of Harriet Tubman. She is a hero/heroine in the eyes of many people, especially African-Americans. Do you think she deserves her place in this chapter? Give your reasons.

The Harriet Tubman Memorial, Harlem, NYC

Help

- **unveil** [ʌn'veɪl] **(v.)** : *(ici) inaugurer*
- **bondwoman (n.)** : *servante, femme esclave*

More help WBT n° 47

3 Victoria Soto B1

Victoria Soto died a hero as she protected her students from Adam Lanza, shielding[1] the children by putting herself between them and the gunman.

Ms Soto was one of four adults at Sandy Hook Elementary School who sacrificed themselves for the youngsters in their care. Three were teachers, the other was the school psychologist.

One teacher, Natalie Hammond, 40, was shot in the arm and leg and is the only wounded survivor of the massacre. Her injuries[2] are not thought to be life-threatening.

When Lanza began his murderous rampage[3], some staff members dived under tables. But Ms Soto, 27, rushed towards the killer, blocking the bullets with her body.

Her cousin, Jim Wiltsie, said police had told him that she was trying to usher[4] her pupils into a storage room when she came face-to-face with Lanza.

"She put herself between the gunman and the children and that's when she was tragically shot and killed," Mr Wiltsie said. "I'm proud that Vicki had the instincts to protect her kids from harm. In our eyes she's a hero."

Ms Soto died alongside colleagues Dawn Hochsprung, 47, the school principal, and Mary Sherlach, 56, school psychologist. Mrs Sherlach had worked at Sandy Hook for 18 years and was a year from retirement.

Martin Delgado, *The Daily Mail (The Mail on Sunday)*, December 16, 2012.

1. shield [ʃiəld] (v.) : *faire écran.* 2. injuries (n.) : *blessures.*
3. rampage ['ræmpeɪdʒ] (n.) : *fureur, folie.*
4. usher (v.) : *conduire.*

More help WB T n° 49

75¢ - NYDailyNews.com

SPORTS FINAL

Mostly cloudy, 46/41. Thursday, December 20, 2012

DAILY NEWS

NEW YORK'S HOMETOWN NEWSPAPER

BELOVED NEWTOWN TEACHER LAID TO REST

'She gave her life to save her kids, and if that's not true strength and heroism, I don't know what is.'

SUPER HERO

PAGES 2-8

Grammar

Ce qui/que/dont : *what, which*
- ***what's*** *astonishing is...* p. 73
- *It is the first ever statue of an African-American woman in New York,* ***which*** *is remarkable enough.*

Work it out

Look at the magazine cover and work out who Victoria Soto was and what she did.

Read and comment

Read the article and find out:
- who was injured or killed in the incident;
- the order of events.

Go into detail. WB T n° 50

Heroism or not?

Think about the magazine's analysis of Victoria's actions.
Did she show "true strength and heroism" or was it something else? Exchange your views.

Your task

Choose one woman you consider to be a heroine and write at least two sentences about her. Read the paragraph to the class and see if they can guess your heroine's name. Don't make it too easy for them! Here is an example. Do you know who the heroine is?

In 1955, this woman stood up for her rights by remaining seated on a bus. What she did sparked off a movement that led to equal rights for African Americans.

CROSS CULTURE

Inspirational people in the movies

People who have led exceptional lives have always inspired movie directors. Numerous films have been made about them. Here are a few examples.

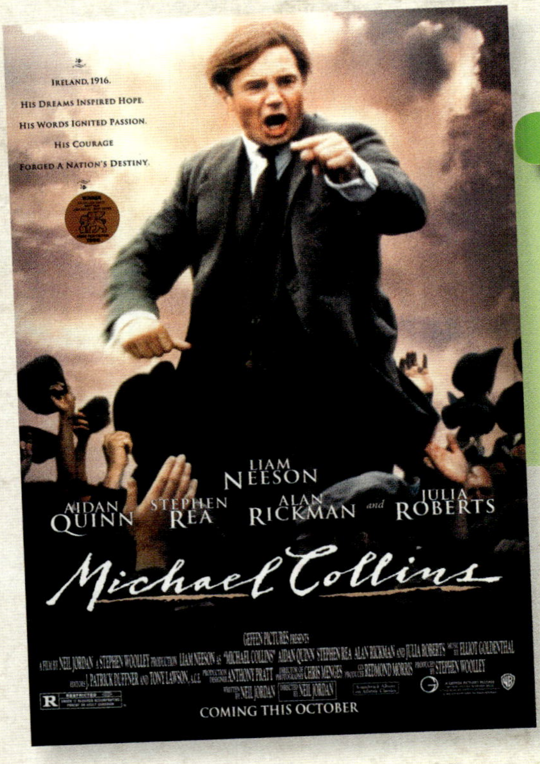

Michael Collins

The depiction of the controversial life and death of Michael Collins, the "Lion of ireland", who led the IRA against British rule and founded the Irish Free State (Eire) in 1921 (http://www.imdb.com/title/tt0117039plotsummary).

Pride

UK gay activists work to help miners during their lengthy strike of the National Union of Mineworkers in the summer of 1984. Their leader: Mike Jackson.

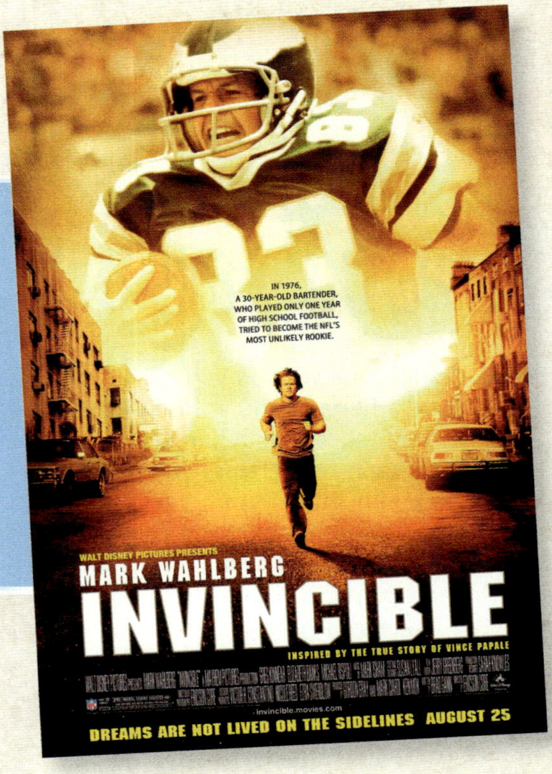

Invincible

A Philadelphia Eagles fan who has just lost his wife and his teaching job decides one day to show up for an open tryout for his favorite NFL team, only to see his wildest dreams come true (http://www.imdb.com/title/tt0445990/plotsummary). His name: **Ernie Davis.**

The Butler

As **Cecil Gaines** serves eight presidents during his tenure as a butler at the White House, the civil rights movement, Vietnam, and other major events affect this man's life, family, and American society (http://www.imdb.com/title/tt1327773/plotsummary). Based on the life of Eugene Allen.

12 years a slave

An incredible true story of one man's fight for survival and freedom. In the pre-Civil War United States, **Solomon Northup**, a free black man from upstate New York, is abducted and sold into slavery (http://www.imdb.com/title/tt2024544/plotsummary).

A Beautiful Mind

At Princeton University, **John Nash** struggles to make a worthwhile contribution to serve as his legacy to the world of mathematics. He finally makes a revolutionary breakthrough that will eventually earn him the Nobel Prize (http://www.imdb.com/title/tt0268978/plotsummary).

The Wolf of Wall Street

A movie based on the true story of **Jordan Belfort**, from his rise to a wealthy stockbroker living the high life to his fall involving crime, corruption and the federal government (http://www.imdb.com/title/tt0993846/plotsummary).

Activities

1. Work in groups, choose one of the movies from this double page, then browse the net to find information on the person the movie was based on.
2. Take notes and work out why it was decided to make the movie (a vehicle for a particular actor? audience appeal? other reasons?).
3. From what you have found out, decide if the movie sticks to the truth or not.
4. Report back to the class with your findings.

Improve your **GRAMMAR**

Les mots se terminant en *-ing* (PG p. 247)

MÉMO

Les mots anglais se terminant en -ing sont-ils tous de même nature ?

• Absolument pas ! Les natures des mots en *-ing* sont nombreuses.

À quoi sert le suffixe -ing ?

• À dériver des mots à partir d'un verbe. Les linguistes disent que *-ing* a un effet « nominalisant ».

Quels sont les mots concernés ?

• Des participes présents dérivés de l'infinitif du verbe : *cry* → *crying* (pleurer / pleurant).

• Des gérondifs ou noms verbaux indénombrables indiquant le fait de faire quelque chose (*firing* : le fait de licencier quelqu'un).

• Des noms courants dénombrables dérivés de verbes : *begin* → *the beginning* (commencer → commencement).

• Des adjectifs verbaux dérivés de verbes : *frighten* → *frightening* (effrayer → effrayant).

Comment différencier les adjectifs verbaux des participes présents et des gérondifs ou noms verbaux ?

• Les premiers sont épithètes ou attributs d'un nom ou d'un pronom ; les seconds ont un sujet placé avant ou après selon les contextes et les constructions de phrases.

Observez et raisonnez

(texte p. 66)

• *the regime [...] prevented her from going to school.*
• *this didn't stop her from studying.*
• *it was school that kept me going.*

1 Relevez les mots en *-ing* présents dans les énoncés ci-dessus et dites quelle est leur nature.

2 Quels types de mots cités dans le Mémo sont absents de ces exemples ?

Entraînez-vous

1 Cartoon fun

Étudiez la légende de ce dessin et indiquez la nature des mots en *-ing*.

"I'm trying to be more active. Which one burns more calories, Twittering, Blogging or Googling?"

2 Complétez

Complétez les phrases par l'un des mots suivants, puis traduisez les phrases.

crowdfunding • including • life-threatening • raising • receiving • shopping • working

a. In some countries girls, are barred from ...... an education.

b. In some other countries men forbid their wives to go ....

c. None of the injuries the girl suffered from was ....

d. Many people attended Malala's lecture, ... some heads of states.

e. The boy founded his own company after ...... a lot of money through ....

f. I got a lot of experience ...... as a volunteer on an organic farm.

3 Dites-le en anglais

a. Au lieu de se plier aux exigences des hommes, la jeune fille se dressa pour défendre ses droits à l'éducation.

b. Les propos menaçants qu'elle entendait ne l'empêchèrent pas d'étudier en secret.

c. À l'hôpital, pendant sa convalescence, elle passait ses journées à lire et réviser ses cours.

d. Apprendre est pour elle une façon de trouver la liberté.

Ce qui/que/dont : *what, which* (PG p. 251)

MÉMO

De quoi les formes « ce qui », « ce que », « ce dont » dépendent-elles en français ?

• Uniquement de la fonction du relatif dans la subordonnée, respectivement ici : sujet, COD, COI (ou, plus rarement, complément circonstanciel, d'adjectif, etc.).

Il s'agit en français de ce qu'on appelle une déclinaison : changement de la forme d'un mot due à sa fonction grammaticale.

Comment le relatif double français est-il traduit en anglais ?

• Le choix de *what* ou *which* en anglais ne dépend pas de la fonction grammaticale du relatif mais du rôle qu'il joue dans la phrase : *what* annonce ce qui va suivre, *which* rappelle ce qui précède. (Voir exemples ci-dessous.)

Observez et raisonnez

(enregistrement p. 68)

• *but what's astonishing is that she went back again and again.*

• *it is the first ever statue of an African-American woman in New York, which is remarkable enough.*

1 Dans ces phrases, lequel de *what* ou *which* :
– annonce l'information à venir ?
– rappelle l'information déjà donnée ?

2 Précisez quelle est cette information dans chacune des phrases.

3 Traduisez les deux phrases.

4 Justifiez la forme du relatif double français.

Entraînez-vous

1 Cartoon fun

a. Dans la légende, dites à quoi *which* fait référence.

b. Traduisez la légende et justifiez la forme du relatif double français.

The cat taught her to live life to the fullest. Which, for an indoor cat, means eat, sleep and stare out the window.

2 Complétez

Complétez par *what* ou *which*, puis traduisez les phrases.

a. To me …… is real heroism is the fact that Victoria Soto shielded her pupils by putting herself between them and the gunman.

b. Other adults dived under the tables, ……, although understandable, might look like an act of cowardice.

c. …… we still do not know is what motivated the man to carry out the attack.

d. I really can't say …… I would do under similar circumstances.

e. One of the victims was only a few months away from retirement, …… I would call a terrible case of bad luck.

3 Dites-le en anglais

a. Nous montrons aux visiteurs ce qu'il y a d'important dans le fait d'avoir érigé la statue de Harriet Tubman à Harlem.

b. On ne sait pas exactement quand Harriet est née entre 1820 et 1825, ce qui illustre la façon dont les esclaves étaient considérés.

c. Ce dont je ne me souviens jamais, c'est du nom de la célèbre romancière qui a écrit *La Case de l'Oncle Tom.*

d. Ce que je trouve incroyable, c'est qu'Harriet n'ait jamais été capturée pendant ses raids dans les États du Sud.

Improve your
VOCABULARY

1 Heroic qualities

Adjectives MP3 14

a. Read the list below and find the six pairs of adjectives with very similar meanings.

b. Listen to the six sentences and say which pair of adjectives is concerned in each case.

brave • charismatic • fearless • foolhardy • forthright • indefatigable • inspirational • modest • outspoken • reckless • self-effacing • untiring

Complete

Complete the passage with the following words and expressions. Put the verbs in the correct form.

a blind eye • abolish • campaign *(v.)* • cause *(n.)* • champion *(v.)* • dedication • driving force • pass *(v.)* • precedence • social

William Wilberforce (1759-1833) was the ...... behind the abolition of slavery in Britain. As an MP, he ...... many causes, but his ...... to abolitionism took ...... over everything else: he ...... indefatigably for abolition. It became his obsession and, because of this, many accused him of turning ...... to other examples of social .... He lived just long enough to see slavery ...... in 1833, dying just three days after the law was ....

2 Awards and recognition

Match WB n° 51

Match each award or honour to its explanation.

a. the Purple Heart	**a.** the UK's highest award for bravery
b. a knighthood	**b.** the USA's highest award for bravery
c. a life peerage	**c.** The highest award for bravery in the US (for military personnel only)
d. the Medal of Honor	**d.** a British title of nobility that is not hereditary; life peers have the right to sit in the House of Lords
e. the George Cross	**e.** the US award given to any military personnel wounded in action
f. the Congressional Gold Medal	**f.** a British (or Australian) honour bestowed on a man; as a knight, he is addressed as "Sir" + his first name

A purple heart

The George Cross

The Medal of Honor

A congressional Gold Medal

Accepting an award MP3 15 WB n° 51

Listen to the acceptance speech. Which one of these pairs of expressions do you hear? They are in chronological order.

a.	❑ on behalf of	❑ for half of	**e.** ❑ I would like to express	❑ I would like to address
b.	❑ it is with great pleasure	❑ it is a great pleasure	**f.** ❑ my hearty thanks	❑ my heartfelt thanks
c.	❑ gain the recognition	❑ earn the recognition	**g.** ❑ all those who have given	❑ others who have given
d.	❑ it serves	❑ it deserves	**h.** ❑ put a stop to	❑ put us up for

FINAL TASK

A project for "Action Radio"

1 Choose your role

- Read the information about SNYA and Josh Worley.
- Work in groups of four. Three of you are young people who have come up with a project that corresponds to the **aims of SNYA Radio** (see the Eastern Daily Press article). Give yourselves new names. The other person is Josh Worley, who is interviewing the other three people on his radio station.

South Norfolk South Action Radio was the brainchild of [...] Josh Worley and is run by and for young people in South Norfolk.

"I wanted to start a radio station to give other young people the chance to have the same fun and buzz as I did when I was broadcasting silly little shows from my bedroom. I also wanted to stop young people being treated like criminals, just because they wear hoodies or skateboard." (Josh Worley)

bbc.co.uk, March 3, 2010.

2 Choose your project

- You can use the ideas below, suggested by the **newspaper headlines** or invent your own.

YOUTH CLUB TO BE RENOVATED

YOUNG PEOPLE TO CONVERT HOMES FOR THE DISABLED

YOUNG VOLUNTEERS TO HELP THE ELDERLY

- Prepare **a 3-minute radio interview**. The aim is to present the project, explaining why it deserves to be mentioned on the programme.

SNYA Radio was praised for having done the most to inspire children and young people in cultural activities, especially among disadvantaged groups, and developing innovative collaborations between children's services and the cultural sector.

Eastern Daily Press, December 28, 2010.

3 Do the radio interview

- The guests introduce themselves.
- Josh gets as much information as possible about the project.
- After the interview, the whole class decides if the project deserved to be mentioned on the programme.

PREPARE FOR THE BAC

Compréhension de l'écrit (10 points)

FICHE MÉTHODE PAGE 77

Sujet The rescue

The narrator has just got caught in a gigantic mudslide that has buried the road and the houses of the small city he was driving by.

Again, as I said, I'm no hero – I'm barely capable of taking care of myself, if you want to know the truth – but I fell in beside her without a word. She was sobbing now, her face slack with shock and the futility of it all – we needed a shovel, a pick, a backhoe[1] for Christ's sake – but the tools were buried, everything was buried. "I was at the store," she kept saying, chanting it as her fingers raked and bled and her nails tore and the blouse clung wet to the hard frenetic muscles of her digging, "at the store, at the store," and my mind flew right out of my body. I snatched up a length of two-by-four[2] and began to tear at the earth as if I'd been born to it. The dirt flew. I knew nothing. I was in a trench up to my knees, up to my waist, the mud sliding back in almost as fast as I could fling it out, and she was right there beside me with her martyred hands.

At some point a neighbor appeared with a shovel, and I couldn't tell you whether this guy was thirty or eighty, ten feet tall or a hunchbacked dwarf, because in one unbroken motion I flung down the two-by-four, snatched the shovel from him, and started stabbing at the earth all on my own, feeling the kind of ecstasy only the saints must know. I don't know how long it was after that – five minutes maybe, no more – until I broke through. I was stabbing at the bottom of the hole like a fencer parrying with an invisible opponent, thrusting away, when all at once the shovel plunged in all the way to my fist and everything went still. This was the miracle: he was in there, the husband, and the little girl with him, preserved in a pocket where the refrigerator and stove had gone down under a section of the wall and held it in place.

As soon as I jerked the blade of the shovel back his arm came thrusting out of the hole. I could hear him now – he was shouting his wife's name, *Julie! Julie!* – and the arm vanished to show a sliver of his face, one eye so intensely green it was as if all the vegetation of the hillside had been distilled and concentrated there underground, and then his hand thrust out again and she was there, the wife, clinging to it.

T. C. Boyle, "La Conchita", in *Wild Child*, 2010.

1. backhoe: *pelleteuse*. 2. two-by-four: *planche de bois*.

Questions

- ***Tous les élèves traiteront les questions suivantes.***

A. Give as many details as possible about each of the characters mentioned in the extract.

B. Where was the woman when the mudslide buried her house?

C. What was the narrator's state of mind while digging? Quote from the text to back up your answer.

D. Say if the following sentences are true or false. Quote from the text to justify your answers:

1. The narrator is used to dealing with such catastrophic situations.
2. The husband and the daughter are safe and sound.

- ***Seuls les élèves de l'option LVA (Langue vivante approfondie) traiteront les questions E et F.***

E. Explain the expression "the futility of it all". Give your reasons, quoting from the text.

F. What is the narrator's digging compared to (lines 8-10)? Explain the simile.

Expression écrite (10 points)

- ***Tous les élèves traiteront les questions suivantes.***

1. Explain what is meant by "feeling the kind of ecstasy only the saints must know". Relate this to the notion of heroism. (150 words)
2. Imagine the conversation between the woman and the narrator after the rescue. (150 words)

- ***Seuls les élèves de l'option LVA traiteront au choix l'une des deux questions suivantes.***

1. Explain the narrator's behaviour. Would you behave in the same way in these circumstances? Why/Why not? (200 words)
2. You are a journalist who has witnessed the rescue. Write an article for your newspaper.

Compréhension écrite

Fiche méthode	Application guidée
Étape 1 Lire le texte et les premières informations	
→ Lisez attentivement le texte deux fois, sans regarder les consignes, pour identifier les **éléments essentiels** (thème, personnages, époque, etc.) et la **notion** à laquelle se rapporte le texte. Le paratexte peut fournir des informations précieuses. → Si vous ne connaissez pas un mot, utilisez le **contexte** pour en déduire le sens.	→ Repérez les éléments qui permettent d'identifier les personnages (combien ? lesquels sont présents et lesquels sont juste mentionnés ? quelle est leur relation ?), de repérer la saison et la durée de l'action, de visualiser la scène, les actions et leurs conséquences. → Aidez-vous des mots transparents et décomposez les mots composés (*underground* = *under* + *ground* = *sous terre*).
Étape 2 Lire et comprendre les consignes	
→ Les consignes éclairent le contenu du texte. **Lisez-les toutes** une première fois, puis relisez le texte en surlignant les **informations importantes**. Soyez attentif à ce qui est demandé dans les consignes pour répondre avec précision. Apprenez le lexique des consignes ! → Les questions vont du plus simple au plus complexe.	→ La question **A** attire votre attention sur les personnages (*characters*) ; soyez exhaustif *(as many details as possible)* : nom, âge, relations, etc. La **D** vous pousse à une lecture plus détaillée : repérez les mots clés (*barely capable, knew nothing, ecstasy, miracle*, etc.). → Pour **E / F**, il faut se concentrer sur deux passages précis afin de les expliquer (*explain*). Utilisez le contexte pour vous aider.
Étape 3 Répondre aux questions	
→ Répondez aux questions dans l'ordre, en indiquant les numéros ou les lettres. **Relisez** chaque réponse immédiatement après l'avoir écrite. À la fin, relisez l'ensemble. Attention aux fautes d'inattention (s à la 3e pers. sing, etc.).	→ Lorsque vous citez le texte (**C / D / E** : *quote from the text*), sélectionnez les passages les plus pertinents, recopiez-les sans faire de fautes et ne coupez pas d'éléments essentiels. Vérifiez l'orthographe de certains mots : *snatch, stabbing, opponent*, etc.

Expression écrite

Fiche méthode	Application guidée
Étape 1 Lire les sujets	
→ Lisez les consignes et soulignez les **termes clés**. → Déterminez le **type de production écrite** que l'on vous demande : lettre, discours, essai, récit, dialogue, etc.	**Sujet 1** → *Explain / feeling ecstasy / saints / notion of heroism* → Vous devez commenter une citation du texte et de la relier à une des notions du programme.
Étape 2 Préparer la rédaction	
→ Rédigez **au brouillon** : – un plan détaillé ; – une introduction ; – un développement ; – une conclusion.	→ **Exemple de plan pour le sujet 1** **1.** The meaning of "feeling the kind of ecstasy only the saints must know" (being in an abnormal state). **2.** Relation to the notion of heroism (no concern for oneself, helping others, not giving up...) (N'oubliez pas de définir les mots *ectasy, saints, heroism*.)
Étape 3 Rédiger au propre	
→ Variez les structures de phrases et le vocabulaire, utilisez la **rhétorique du discours**. N'oubliez pas les mots de liaison ! → Aérez votre copie et pensez à vous relire. Attention aux fautes d'inattention !	→ *It means that... / In saying he was... / This can be taken to be heroic because... / Thanks to his selflessness, ... / By persevering in his task,... / Despite his inexperience,...* → Commencez chaque paragraphe par un alinéa et allez à la ligne à chaque changement d'idée.

Chapter 5 Everyday heroes

1 Saying thank you a few days after 9/11.

3 The Red Cross in action.

2 Miep Gies with a photo of Anne Frank, whose family hid in her house.

React!

1. Relate the badge to the photo of the man with the flag. Who is being thanked and why?
2. Do any of the photos make you think of the word "heroic"? Give your reasons.

Unsung heroes

1 A pardon for a pioneer B1

Alan Turing (1912-1954).

Although never confirmed by Apple staff, the logo of the famous computer brand could be a tribute to Turing who committed suicide by biting into an apple he had laced with cyanide.

The World War II codebreaker and computer pioneer Alan Turing has been granted a royal pardon, more than 60 years after being convicted[1] in 1952 of homosexuality, an offence[2] in Britain at the time. His punishment was chemical castration.

He died two years later; the verdict of suicide was disputed. His wartime research breaking Nazi codes was said to have greatly shortened the conflict and saved thousands of lives.

Euronews, December 12, 2013.

1. convict [kən'vɪkt] (v.) : *reconnaître coupable*. 2. offence [ə'fens] (n.) : *délit*.

Read and comment

1. Say what you find out from the article about:
(a) Turing's role in World War II,
(b) what happened to him in 1952,
(c) how he died.
2. In what way does the picture caption for the Apple logo conflict with what you learn from the text?

2 Giving a hero his due B1 B2

Brainstorm

Why does the film poster use the phrase "The true enigma was the man who cracked the code"? Try and guess.

Watch and compare DVD MP3 16

1. Say what new information you now have about Turing (compared to the information in the article above).
2. Identify the three key periods of Turing's life which are portrayed in the film.
Go into detail. WBT n° 53

Write a letter

In order to obtain a royal pardon for Turing, the Justice Minister had to make an official request to the Queen in writing. Imagine what the Minister put in the letter. (150 words)

Poster for the movie about the life of Alan Turing.

"The true enigma was the man who cracked the code."

3 The secret friend B2

I walked downstairs and slipped outside, using my tactical military training to follow Franz for several minutes to a house I did not recognize. I didn't know the residents, but it looked as if nobody was home. The shutters were drawn, the house in a state of disrepair. Yet when Franz knocked, the door opened to admit him.

I waited for about fifteen minutes, hiding behind a hedge, until my brother reappeared, his book bag slack and empty against his hip.

I stepped out from behind the shrubbery. "What are you up to, Franz?"

He pushed past me. "I'm bringing books to a friend. As far as I know that's not a crime." [...]

"Who lives here that you don't want me to know you are visiting?" I raised my brows, grinning, suddenly wondering if my little brother had become a ladies' man in my absence. "Is it a girl? Has something other than poetic meter finally got you twitching[1]?" Playfully, I cuffed[2] him on the shoulder, and he ducked away[3] from me.

"Stop it," he muttered.

"Ah, poor Franz. If you'd asked me I would have told you to bring her chocolates, not books –"

"It's not a girl," Franz blurted out. "It's Artur Goldman. That's who lives here."

It took me a moment to place the name. The Jew from Franz's class at *Gymnasium*.

Most of the Jews in our town had left. I didn't know where they'd gone – to the big cities, maybe Berlin. I had not given any thought to it, really. But obviously, my brother had. "Jesus. Is this why you won't join the SS? Because you're a Jew-lover?"

"Don't be an idiot –"

"I'm not the idiot here, Franz," I said. "I'm not the one fraternizing with enemies of the Reich."

"He's my friend. He misses school. So I bring him books. That's it."

"You have a brother who is an SS officer candidate," I said quietly. "You will stop fraternizing with a Jew."

"No," my brother replied.

No.

No.

I could not remember the last time someone had told me that.

I grabbed him by the throat. "How do you imagine it will look when the Gestapo finds out?"

Jodi Picoult, *The Storyteller*, 2013.

1. twitch (v.) : *(ici) frétiller*. 2. cuff (v.) : *donner une tape*. 3. duck away (v.) : *esquiver*.

More help WBT n° 54

Grammar

When et les contextes futurs p. 88
- *How do you imagine it will look* ***when*** *the Gestapo* ***finds*** *out?*

Selfportrait by Felix Nussbaum, 1943.

Read and explain

1. Read the extract and find out when and where the story is set. Give details to back up your answers.
2. Say who the two characters are and who is telling the story.
3. Say why you think the Nussbaum self portrait was chosen to illustrate this extract. Go into detail. WBT n° 55

What do you think?

Would you say Franz's behaviour is heroic? Give your reasons.

Your task

Work in pairs and choose one of the following role plays.
1. Act out the scene from the novel. Think about the way each character talks and moves...
2. A little later when he's sure his brother can't follow him, Franz goes back to the house to warn the Goldman family that his brother has discovered where they are living. Imagine his conversation with one member of the family.

First on the scene

1 9/11: First responders B1

Comment

Using the title and the picture, identify the event and say what you know about it.

Watch the video DVD MP3 17

1. Relate Ken George's experience to the title above and the picture. Explain what Ken did.
2. Say what you know about Ken's present situation, his health problems and their causes.
3. Say how 9/11 has affected most first responders. Go into detail. WBT n° 57

Role play

Work in pairs. A journalist is interviewing a firefighter who was one of the first on the scene on September 11, 2001. The journalist wants to know what the firefighter did and why. Does he/she consider him/herself a hero? Prepare a 4-minute interview and act it out in front of the class.

Help

- **first responder (n.)** : *premier intervenant*
- **makeshift** ['meɪkʃɪft] **(adj.)** : *de fortune*

More help WBT n° 56

2 The intrepid journalist B1

Cao Junwu is known for intrepid coverage[1] of breaking news events such as the Sichuan earthquake and Shandong flood and for enterprise pieces on China's computer game industry. [He] was one of the first on the scene of the 2008 Sichuan earthquake. He traveled by helicopter and hiked along cliffs to reach the devastated area, which was cut off from the world. His moving blog and newspaper coverage conveyed the despair, courage and resilience of the survivors.

In 2007, when a flood in Jinan, Shandong Province's capital city, killed 34 and injured 171, Cao exposed the cause: flaws[2] in the city's sewer system.

In another story he described how children in a remote village could get to school only by sliding along steel cables above the rushing Nu River. The public outpouring[3] of support brought in more than $200,000, enough to build two bridges for the village.

Amanda Ernst, adweek.com, June 24, 2009.

1. coverage (n.) : *reportage*. 2. flaw (n.) : *défaut*.
3. outpouring (n.) : *déferlement, effusion*.

Cao Junwu of China, co-winner of the 2009 Knight International Journalism Award

Read and explain

1. Say what aspect of journalism the article highlights.
2. Say why you think Cao won the Knight Award (as mentioned in the picture caption).
3. Summarise the three subjects that Cao wrote about and which are mentioned in the text.

Go into detail. WBT n° 58

What do you think?

In what way did Cao show "heroic" qualities? Do you think he is representative of journalists in general?

3 The invincible photographer B1 B2

Bosch had spent most of 1969 and 1970 in Vietnam. He had encountered many journalists and photographers in the base camps and out in fire zones as well. In all of them, he had seen a unique form of fearlessness. Not a warrior's fearlessness but almost a naive belief in one's ultimate survival. It was as though they believed that their cameras and press passes were shields that would save them, no matter the circumstance.

He had known one photographer particularly well. His name was Hank Zinn and he worked for the Associated Press. He had once followed Bosch into a tunnel in Cu Chi. Zinn was the kind of guy who never turned down an opportunity to go out into Indian country and get what he called "the real thing." He died in early 1970 when a Huey[1] he had jumped on for transport to the front was shot down.

One of his cameras was recovered intact in the debris field and somebody at base developed the film. It turned out Zinn was shooting frames the whole time the chopper[2] was taking fire and then going down. Whether he was valiantly documenting his own death or thinking he was going to have great shots[3] to file when he got back to base camp could never be known. But knowing Zinn, Bosch believed he thought he was invincible and the chopper crash would not be the end of the line.

Michael Connelly, *The Black Box*, 2012.

1. Huey [hjuːɪ] : *type d'hélicoptère américain*.
2. chopper (n. fam.) : *hélicoptère*. 3. shots (n.) : *(ici) clichés*.

More help WBT n° 59

David Hume Kennerly, photographer and Pulitzer Prize winner.

Read and explain

1. Say what you know about Zinn (job, character...) and how he died.
2. Draw a parallel between Zinn and David Hume Kennerly (in the photograph).
3. According to Bosch, Zinn thought he was invincible. What makes Bosch think this? Go into detail. WBT n° 60

Write an email

You are a photographer working in a war zone for a TV station. Your boss has emailed you to return home as the situation is worsening. Email your boss, saying that you intend to stay. Give your reasons. (150 words)

Grammar

Les structures causatives WBT n° 61
- *His health situation* **caused him to retire** *in 2006.*

Les verbes de perception WBT n° 62
- *I've* **seen** *the buildings* **burning**.

Your task

1. Organise a TV debate. The title is "Should overseas correspondents and photographers risk their lives in war zones?" There are two teams who take opposing views, a host who chairs the debate and a studio audience.
2. Each team prepares its arguments and then tries to persuade the audience that they are right.
3. The audience decides who has won the debate.

Improve your SKILLS

Just ordinary people?

1 Giving something back

B1

Jorge Muñoz arrived in America from Columbia as an illegal immigrant in the early '80s. He became a citizen in 1987. One evening as he left a bar he noticed all the destitute and illegal day laborers and the flame in his heart was lit. He found out that most of the men slept under a bridge or in the Elmhurst Hospital's emergency room and skimped[1] on meals in order to send money to their loved ones at home.

Since then, he has been cooking enough food to feed dozens of day laborers in Queens[2] which he delivers at the corner of Roosevelt Avenue and 73rd Street in Jackson Heights every evening at 21:30. Munoz delivers the warm, cooked meals in rain, snow, thunder and lightning. He estimates that he has served food to more than 70,000 people since 2004.

The whole operation is financed from the $600 he receives weekly for driving a school bus and donations. On August 4, 2010, Munoz was awarded the Presidential Citizens Medal by President Barack Obama.

Hestie Barnard Gerber, listverse.com, May 31, 2013.

1. skimp (v.) on : *lésiner sur.*
2. Queens: the largest borough of New York City.

What do you think?

1. Describe the photo and work out what "giving back" means in the context of volunteering.
2. Do you think volunteering is an act of heroism? Exchange your views.

Read and explain

1. Say who Jorge Muñoz is (origin, nationality, occupation...).
2. Explain (a) whom he helps, (b) what he does to help them, (c) why he decided to help them.
Go into detail. WBT n° 63

Give your opinion

1. Do you consider Jorge Muñoz a hero? Why/Why not?
2. Do you know other examples of "ordinary people" who have devoted their life to helping people in need?
3. Would you consider being a volunteer? If so, in what field?
Give your reasons.

2 Red Cross volunteers

B1 B2

Brainstorm

Look at the title and say what you know about this organisation.

Watch and find out DVD MP3 18

1. Say what event the video deals with. (What happened? Where?)
2. Explain what the volunteers are doing and why.
Go into detail. WBT n° 65

Help

- scramble (v.) : *(ici) se démener*
- gale force wind [wɪnd] (n.) : *vent soufflant en tempête*
- cramped [kræmpt] (adj.) : *(être) à l'étroit*

More help WBT n° 64

3 Miscellaneous[1] Heroes

B1

"How long have you been here?" Mitchell asked the beekeeper[2].

"Couple of weeks. Brought the whole family. This is our Christmas vacation. And New Year's. My wife and kids are working in one of the orphanages[3]. I figured this place might be a little tough on the kids. But taking care of cute little babies? Yeah, sure." With his suntanned skin and blond curls, the beekeeper looked like a surfing legend or an aging quarterback. His gaze was level and serene. "Two things brought me here," he said, before leaving Mitchell on his own. "Mother Teresa and Albert Schweitzer. Couple years ago I went on a real Schweitzer kick. Read everything he wrote. Next thing I know I'm taking pre-med classes. At night. Bio-logy. Organic chemistry. I was twenty years older than anybody else in the class. But I kept going. Finished my pre-med requirements last year, applied to sixteen medical schools, and got into one. I start next fall."

"What are you going to do with your bees?"

"I'm selling the farm. Turning over a new leaf. Starting a new chapter. Pick your cliché."

Mitchell took it easy that day, settling in. He helped serve lunch, ladling daal[4] into bowls. He brought the patients glasses of water. On the whole, the men were cleaner and healthier than he'd anticipated. A dozen or so were superannuated[5], with skeletal faces, lying immobile in their beds, but quite a few were middle-aged, and a few even young. It was often hard to tell what they were suffering from. No charts hung from their beds. What was plain was that the men had nowhere else to go. [...]

The other volunteers were a miscellaneous bunch. There was a group of Irish women who believed in papal infallibility. There was an Anglican minister who spoke of the resurrection as "a nice idea". There was a sixty-year-old (gay) New Orleanian who, before coming to Calcutta, had walked the pilgrimage route in Spain, stopping off to run with the bulls in Pamplona. [...] There were married couples who came to volunteer for a week and college students who stayed a half year or a year. No matter who they were or where they came from, they all tried their best to follow the guiding philosophy.

Jeffrey Eugenides, *The Marriage Plot*, 2011.

1. miscellaneous [misəˈleɪnɪəs] (adj.) : *divers et varié.*
2. beekeeper (n.) : *apiculteur.*
3. orphanage [ɔːfənɪdʒ] (n.) : *orphelinat.*
4. daal: Indian lentils.
5. superannuated [suːpəˈrænjueɪtɪd] (adj.) : *très âgé.*

More help WBT n° 66

Comment and read

1. Relate the photo to the text. Say exactly where you think the scene takes place. Give your reasons.

2. Say as much as you can about the beekeeper, Mitchell and the other volunteers mentioned.
Go into detail. WBT n° 67

Write a flyer

The NGO (non-governmental organisation) in charge of the field hospital described in the text wants you to write a flyer for their volunteers that explains its "guiding philosophy" in ten "dos and don'ts". Add a logo, a slogan or a motto and the contact details of the NGO.

Grammar

La notion d'intention p. 89

- *What **are you going to** do with your bees?*
- *I'**m selling** the farm.*

Your task

Work in groups of four. You are representatives of an NGO. One of you is the head of the organisation, the others are volunteers who have been involved in the NGO for a few years. In order to recruit new volunteers, prepare and make a 5-minute slideshow presentation of the NGO for a class of college students.

CROSS CULTURE

Memorials to fortitude

Some of the most touching memorials – monuments that honour the memory of someone – are collective ones. They have been erected in recognition of the devotion, fortitude and sacrifice of different groups of people.

The pilots of the Battle of Britain

This bronze memorial showing pilots running to their planes (by Paul Day, 2002) is in **London**, on the banks of the Thames. It commemorates the heroism of these young men in the summer of 1940 when England's fate lay in their hands.

The marines of Iwo Jima

Based on a famous 1945 photograph by Joe Rosenthal, The bronze Iwo Jima Memorial in **Washington D.C.** (by Felix de Weldon, 1954) depicts the end of a decisive World War II battle. It is dedicated to all marines who have given their lives in battle.

The firefighters of New York

This **bronze monument in Albany NY** (by Robert J. Eccleston, 1998) is dedicated to the many firefighters who have lost their lives in the line of duty in New York State.

The veterans of Vietnam

The Vietnam Veterans Memorial **in Washington D.C.** (by Maya Lin, 1982) is a black granite wall inscribed with the names of the 58,195 men and women who died or went missing during the Vietnam War – the longest in US history.

The Women in World War II

This bronze memorial **in London** (by John W. Mills, 2005) has 17 sculpted sets of clothing and uniforms around its sides, symbolising the hundreds of different jobs **women** undertook during WWII. Until 2005, Britain had never erected a monument to women's achievements in wartime.

The starving people of Ireland

The Famine Memorial **in Dublin** (by Rowan Gillespie, 1997) pays tribute to the millions of victims of the Great Famine (1845-1849). The memorial consists of bronze sculptures of weary, emaciated figures walking towards the docks in the hope of a better life in North America.

Activities

1. Choose one of the memorials from this double page. The city where the memorial is located has commissioned you to produce a new and original audio guide for the memorial as one of a series of guides called "The memorial heroes talk to you".
2. Search the Net to find more information about the memorial (the artist, the location, the event/people it commemorates, the historical context...) and take notes.
3. Using your notes, write the script of your audio guide. Write in the first person as if you were one of the heroes from the memorial.
4. Record the audio file.

When et les contextes futurs (PG p. 250)

MÉMO

Quelles formes verbales faut-il employer après when ?

• Tout dépend de la nature du mot *when*.

Quelles sont les natures du mot when ?

• *When* **adverbe interrogatif** est suivi de toutes les formes verbales marquant le passé, le présent ou l'avenir.

Ex. : *When does he arrive? / When did she say that? / When shall we tell him? When will they leave?*

• *When* **pronom relatif** est, lui aussi, suivi de toutes les formes verbales marquant le passé, le présent ou l'avenir.

Ex. : *I'm looking forward to the day when this country will rise again.*

• *When* **conjonction de subordination**, comme toutes les conjonctions de subordination indiquant le temps (*once, till, before, as soon as*, etc.), ne peut être suivi que du passé ou du présent, ce qui exclut les modaux *shall, will, would*.

On peut donc trouver après ces conjonctions de temps : le présent, le prétérit, le *present perfect*, le *pluperfect*.

NB : Attention à l'emploi des temps quand *when* introduit une subordonnée interrogative indirecte (dans ce cas, il reste adverbe interrogatif).

Observez et raisonnez

(texte p. 81)

• *How do you imagine it will look when the Gestapo finds out?*

1 Décomposez la phrase, isolez les trois propositions qu'elle contient et indiquez leur nature (principale, subordonnée…).

2 Quelle est la nature du mot *when* (adverbe, conjonction, relatif) ? Justifiez votre réponse.

3 Analysez l'emploi des formes verbales dans cette phrase et vérifiez que ce qui est expliqué dans le mémo fonctionne bien ici.

4 Traduisez la phrase et comparez l'emploi des temps dans les deux langues.

5 Mettez la phrase ci-dessus au passé : *How did you imagine…* Que remarquez-vous ?

Entraînez-vous

1 Cartoon fun

Répondez à la question.

When do you think the fish will come back and play here ?

I used to play here as a kid, but of course, that was before Humans built that sewer pipe…

2 Complétez les phrases suivantes avec les verbes donnés.

a. What …… (happen) as soon as he …… (crack) the Enigma code?

b. They couldn't do anything with the messages until someone …… (crack) the code.

c. We …… (not know) what their plans are until we …… (understand) the code.

d. My brother advised me to stop visiting my friend before the secret police …… (find out) I was hiding a Jew.

e. I …… (feel) safe as long as they …… (not discover) my secret.

3 Dites-le en anglais

a. Quand ils trouveront le mot de passe, ils pourront faire fonctionner la machine.

b. Et quand vont-ils y parvenir ?

c. Dès qu'ils auront recruté un petit génie de l'informatique. *(computer nerd)*

d. Le jour où ils l'auront trouvé, je veux être là.

La notion d'intention : *be going to* et *be* + V-*ing* (PG p. 234)

MÉMO

Quelles sont les notions véhiculées dans l'expression be going to ?

• Il en existe deux, selon le contexte et l'énonciateur.

– La certitude (ou son contraire) de l'énonciateur concernant des événements à venir :

He's going to help them. = Il va les aider.

Is he going to help them? = Va-t-il les aider ?

– L'intention de l'énonciateur :

I'm going to help them as much as I can. = Je vais les aider du mieux que je peux.

• Notez que le changement d'énonciateur et de sujet grammatical peut faire changer le sens du message :

Is he going to help them? marque le manque de certitude du locuteur, pas l'intention du sujet grammatical *he*.

En revanche, *he says he's going to help them* marque bien l'intention du sujet *he* ; l'énonciateur, lui, n'exprime alors ni l'intention ni la certitude.

La forme be + V-ing exprime-t-elle également l'intention ?

• C'est l'une des nombreuses notions exprimées par cette forme verbale : elle marque une décision prise après réflexion.

Ex. : *I'm not marrying him. That's out of the question.* = Je ne l'épouserai pas ; c'est hors de question.

Observez et raisonnez

(texte p. 85)

• *What are you going to do with your bees?*
• *I'm selling the farm. Turning over a new leaf.*

1 Reportez-vous au contexte p. 85 et identifiez les auteurs des deux énoncés ci-dessus.

2 Quelle notion le premier véhicule-t-il : intention ou certitude/incertitude ? Les deux ?

3 Qu'en est-il du second énoncé ?

4 Justifiez votre opinion.

Entraînez-vous

1 Cartoon fun

Qu'indiquent les textes de ce dessin : intention ou certitude ? Justifiez votre réponse en décrivant le contexte.

2 Exprimez le sens

Qu'exprime chacun des énoncés suivants (texte p. 85) ?

a. My wife and kids are working in one of the orphanages.

b. Next thing I know I'm taking pre-med classes.

c. I'm starting a new chapter.

3 Dites-le en anglais

a. Qu'allez-vous faire maintenant ?

b. Je vais travailler avec les religieuses de l'hôpital de Bombay.

c. Et votre maison aux États-Unis ? – Je la loue. Mais je vais sans doute la vendre.

d. J'ai pris ma décision. Je quitte les États-Unis.

e. Je tourne une page. Je change de vie. Je vais aider les autres.

4 Comment le dire ?

Be going to ou *be* + V-*ing* ? Utilisez les verbes donnés entre parenthèses.

a. Vous ne voulez pas que vos enfants vous suivent en Inde. Que leur dites-vous ? (*stay*)

b. Votre conjoint veut vous accompagner. Que dit-il ? (*come*)

c. Il vous demande où vous allez vous loger là-bas. Que dit-il ? (*live*)

d. Vous lui répondez de ne pas s'inquiéter, que vous n'avez pas l'intention de dormir à la belle étoile. (*sleep*)

Improve your

VOCABULARY

1 Saving lives

Listen and choose MP3 19

Check the meanings of the words and expressions in the list below. Then listen to the five interviews and choose two words from the list that fit each interview: (a) the person being interviewed, (b) the situation.

a bomb attack on an embassy • a casualty • a coastguard • an earthquake • a lifeguard • a multiple pile-up on the motorway • a paramedic • a rescue worker • a shark attack near a beach • a shipwreck

Explain

Explain these words and expressions from the interviews above. Listen again if necessary.

1. it went off
2. rubble
3. I hope she pulls through
4. a check-up
5. the lifeboat

Complete

Complete the passage with the following verbs. Put the verbs in the correct form.

cause • engulf • overcome • revive • spread • trap

The fire had …… rapidly from the kitchen to the living-room. Smoke had …… the stairs and had …… the family on the first floor. By the time the fire brigade arrived, they had all been …… by smoke. Luckily, the paramedics managed to …… them. It was discovered that the fire had been …… by faulty wiring.

2 Secrets

Choose the expression

a. Which of the following sentences refer to people who (a) keep secrets or are secretive, (b) don't keep secrets?

b. Which expression is illustrated in the picture?

- My lips are sealed.
- She's always telling tales.
- He plays his cards close to his chest.
- She keeps herself to herself.
- I let the cat out of the bag.
- They won't let on.
- Someone tipped off the police.

Complete the conversation MP3 20

Listen to the short conversation. The last line is missing. Choose one of the sentences above to complete it.

Which sentence?

Work in pairs and imagine your own conversation, ending it with another of the sentences above. Act out the conversation, leaving out the last line. The rest of the class must guess what it is.

Write about Enigma

Alan Turing (see page 80) was instrumental in breaking the Enigma code. You can find out more about Enigma on http://archive.iwm.org.uk/upload/package/10/enigma/. Use what you know to write about 100 words about it. Try and include these words and expressions.

encode message • type keyboard • crack the code • cleverest mathematicians • strict security • prevent leaks

FINAL TASK

The "Unsung Hero Award"

As members of the Unsung Hero Award jury, you must choose the nominee that you think best deserves the award.

The criteria

The Unsung Hero is a special person who has done extraordinary things for his/her fellow men – for the needy, for those unable to do things for themselves… He/she may have saved lives or contributed to the advancement of medical or social care. He/she has shown that an ordinary person can make a real difference.

The nominees

Robert Kuba

In February 2014, high school science teacher Robert Kuba saw one of his students pull out a .22 caliber rifle from beneath a blanket. Instantaneously, Kuba approached the student and tore the weapon away from him.

http://www.nysut.org/news/2014/february/a-modest-science-teacher-performs-a-heroic-act

Rick Rescorla was the security director for Morgan Stanley during 9/11. Thanks to his preparedness, he helped all but 13 of Morgan Stanley's 2700 employees escape.

http://www.buzzfeed.com/ailbhemalone/unsung-heroes-who-will-inspire-you-to-be-a-better-person#.weKAAYQ6K9

Hideaki Akaiwa

When the 2011 Tohoku earthquake shook his world apart, a Japanese surfer, Hideaki Akaiwa, scuba-dived to rescue tsunami victims.

http://www.cracked.com/article_20516_6-awesome-stories-bystanders-becoming-heroes.html

Pushpa Basnet

Bashnet's non-profit organisations in Nepal provide a children's day-care program and are a residential home for the older children to live in throughout the year.

http://www.waitingformamu.com/pushpa.html

1 Make your choice

- Work in teams of four.
- Read the criteria and the information about the nominees.
- Choose the nominee that you think should win the award.
- Prepare to talk about him/her (achievements, reasons for your choice…).
- Present your nominee to the other groups.

2 Choose the winner

- As a class, vote for the winner.

PREPARE FOR THE BAC

Compréhension de l'oral (10 points)

FICHE MÉTHODE PAGES 92-93

Modalités de l'épreuve

- Un **enregistrement** audio ou vidéo en lien avec une notion du programme. **(1 min. 30)**
- Le **titre** vous est communiqué avant la première écoute.
- **Trois écoutes/visionnages** espacés chacun(e) d'une minute, durant lesquels vous pouvez prendre des **notes**.
- Un **compte-rendu** en français, par écrit. **(10 min)**

Attention *! Il ne vous est pas demandé d'écrire le script de l'enregistrement, ni de commenter ce qui est dit, ni de prendre parti mais uniquement de* ***rendre compte de ce que vous avez compris****.*

Sujet d'entraînement

US couple rescued Austrian children in WWII

DVD

Lisez attentivement la fiche méthode en cachant la partie « Application guidée », puis reportez-vous à l'aide, au fur et à mesure des difficultés rencontrées.

Fiche méthode	Application guidée
Étape 1 Anticiper à partir du titre donné	
➔ **Analysez le titre** pour préparer votre écoute. Cela vous guidera dans la compréhension du texte. ➔ Mobilisez le **vocabulaire** utile à ce support spécifique. Vous serez ainsi plus apte à comprendre certains termes utilisés.	➔ Repérez le **thème abordé** et la notion à laquelle il se rattache (Mythes et héros). ➔ **Listez** tous les mots, phrases et expressions que vous connaissez et que vous êtes susceptible d'entendre dans cette vidéo (*war / rescue / danger / courage / persecution / Nazi, etc.*).
Étape 2 Écouter et noter au brouillon	
➔ **Première écoute** Valorisez une compréhension **globale** : – **repérez** le type de support, la nature du document, le nombre d'intervenants, les indices sonores ; – **relevez** quelques mots ou expressions sans noter de phrases entières. Les images peuvent vous aider à comprendre le texte, mais elles peuvent aussi n'avoir qu'un rôle illustratif.	➔ **Première écoute** – type de support : vidéo / nature du document : reportage / voix : homme, femmes (s'agit-il du metteur en scène ? du journaliste ? d'une personne interviewée ?) – mots et expressions : *children / rescue / heroic stories / Holocaust / war / evacuate / infants / persecution / America / Vienna, etc.*
➔ **Deuxième écoute** • Notez un maximum de mots et expressions accentués et répétés.	➔ **Deuxième écoute** *rescue mission / war / courage / children / safety / unknown / extraordinary / inspire / guilt(y) / leave*
➔ **Troisième écoute** • Concentrez-vous sur les informations manquantes. Relevez des informations plus précises (noms, dates, lieux, données chiffrées, etc.).	➔ **Troisième écoute** *message remains relevant / American couple who travelled to Vienna / ordinary people / at risk of persecution / healthiest / survivor guilt*

Étape 3 Rédiger le compte-rendu

➔ Détachez-vous de l'anglais et pensez maintenant uniquement **en français**.
➔ Réutilisez toutes vos **notes** pour rédiger votre compte-rendu et n'oubliez pas de faire une **introduction**. Si le support est une vidéo, ne décrivez pas les images, mais concentrez-vous sur ce que vous avez entendu.
➔ Écrivez des phrases courtes et simples.
Utilisez des verbes **introducteurs** et variez le vocabulaire.
➔ Aérez votre copie et pensez à vous relire !

➔ Pensez en français pour faire un compte-rendu cohérent.
Utilisez vos notes (étapes 1 et 2) pour la rédaction.
Dans l'introduction, présentez le type de support, la nature du document et le contexte : qui ? où ? quand ? quoi ? *(vidéo / documentaire / couple d'Américains / Vienne / Seconde Guerre mondiale / sauver des enfants.*
➔Pensez aux verbes introducteurs (*le journaliste présente / explique, ajoute / la survivante raconte, précise, etc.)*
➔Commencez chaque paragraphe par un alinéa et allez à la ligne à chaque changement d'idée.

À votre tour !

Heroism of rescuers in eruption disaster

À présent, appliquez la méthodologie à cet enregistrement.

Voici une grille de notation sur 10 correspondant aux attentes du baccalauréat pour essayer de vous situer selon que vous êtes en LV1 ou LV2.

CONTENT	LEVEL	LV1	LV2
COMPRÉHENSION TRÈS INSUFFISANTE **Vous n'avez repéré que des mots isolés (peut-être uniquement basés sur les images ou le titre), mais sans établir de liens entre eux.**		1	2
COMPRÉHENSION SUPERFICIELLE **Vous avez relevé des mots isolés, des expressions courantes et des phrases simples. Votre compréhension reste superficielle.**	A1	3	4
COMPRÉHENSION PARTIELLE **Vous avez su identifier le thème majeur de la discussion et identifier chaque locuteur sans comprendre toutes les informations.**	A2	5	7
COMPRÉHENSION SATISFAISANTE **Vous avez su relever les points principaux (contexte, objet, sentiments des interlocuteurs, conclusion de l'échange) et les mettre en relation.**	B1	8	10
COMPRÉHENSION FINE **Vous avez su relever les points principaux et un nombre suffisant de détails significatifs vous permettant de rendre compte du point de vue.**	B2	10	

Two icons of

1 King Arthur B1

John Garrick, *The Death of King Arthur*, 1862.

"Yet some men say in many parts of England that King Arthur is not dead, but carried by the will of our Lord Jesus into another place; and men say that he shall come again."

Thomas Malory, *Le Morte d'Arthur*, 1485.

The young Arthur in the TV series Merlin (2008).

Brainstorm

What do you know about King Arthur? Piece together as many elements as you can (events, places, people…).

Listen and explain MP3 21

1. Say what you now know about Arthur. Was he a real person or not? When was he supposed to have lived?
2. List the legendary elements that appeared in the Middle Ages.
3. Say why Arthur is so special. In what way do the two literary extracts (with the pictures) highlight his uniqueness? Go into detail. WBT n° 69

What do you think?

Choose one of the following elements from the legend of King Arthur, find out more about it if necessary, and present it in your own words. Write about 150 words.

Camelot • the Round Table • the quest for the Holy Grail • Excalibur • Sir Lancelot

"The best thing for being sad," replied Merlyn, beginning to puff and blow, "is to learn something. [...] That is the only thing which the mind can never exhaust, never alienate, never be tortured by, never fear or distrust, and never dream of regretting. Learning is the only thing for you. Look what a lot of things there are to learn."

T. H. White, *The Sword in the Stone*, 1938.

Help

- quest [kwest] (n.) : *quête*
- Holy Grail (n.) : *Saint Graal*
- ingrained (adj.) : *ancré, enraciné*

More help WBT n° 68

English legend

2 Robin Hood B1

Robin has just become an outlaw[1] and has gone to live in Sherwood Forest.

Fivescore or more good stout yeomen[2] gathered about Robin Hood, and chose him to be their leader and chief. Then they vowed that even as they themselves had been despoiled they would despoil their oppressors, whether baron, abbot, knight, or squire, and that from each they would take that which had been wrung[3] from the poor by unjust taxes, or land rents, or in wrongful fines; but to the poor folk they would give a helping hand in need and trouble, and would return to them that which had been unjustly taken from them.

Beside this, they swore never to harm a child nor to wrong a woman, be she maid, wife, or widow; so that, after a while, when the people began to find that no harm was meant to them, but that money or food came in time of want to many a poor family, they came to praise Robin and his merry men, and to tell many tales of him and of his doings in Sherwood Forest, for they felt him to be one of themselves.

Howard Pyle, *The Merry Adventures of Robin Hood of Great Renown in Nottinghamshire*, 1883.

1. outlaw (n.) : *hors-la-loi.*
2. yeomen (pl. yeomen) [ˈjəʊmən] (n.) : *paysan propriétaire de terres.*
3. wring [rɪŋ] (wrung, wrung) (v.) : *(ici) extorquer.*

More help WBT n° 70

http://www.boldoutlaw.com/robbeg/robbeg5.html
1938 film: https://www.youtube.com/watch?v=Ist_bZLP9u4
2010 film: https://www.youtube.com/watch?v=NVx3GxiaAxc

Brainstorm

What do you know about the legend of Robin Hood?
Why is he called *Robin des Bois* in French? Exchange your views.

Read and comment

1. Say why so many men joined Robin in the forest.
2. List the principles that Robin and his men would live by.
3. What did local people think of Robin Hood?

Go into detail. WBT n° 71

Your task

Work in pairs. First, find out more about Robin Hood. Then watch the trailers of the 1938 and 2010 film versions of Robin Hood (see the links). Compare the two different treatments of the legend and list the good and bad points of both. Present your findings to the class.

Would you believe it?

1 A monster hoax B1

The "Surgeon's Photograph" of the Loch Ness Monster (1934), now known to be a hoax.

Explain

Explain what a hoax is, then guess why the word is used in the caption to this picture.

Listen to the recording DVD MP3 22

1. Explain what has been found out about the photograph.
2. Say how the Loch Ness Monster Centre has reacted to revelations about the photo.
3. How have local people reacted?

What do you believe?

Do you believe in anything that may be considered extraordinary (e.g. UFOs, ghosts, witches...)? Say if you believe in anything like that and explain why. React to what your classmates say.

Help

- fake (n.) : *faux*
- clockwork toy (n.) : *jouet mécanique*
- conning tower (n.) : *kiosque de sous-marin*
- hump (n.) : *bosse*

More help WBT n° 72

2 Hoax or not? B1 B2

In your experience...

1. Have you, or has anyone you know, ever been the victim of a hoax (by phone, by email...)? If so, say what it was and whether it was successful or not.
2. Do you think the internet favours hoaxes? Why/ Why not?

The "rumors game"

Work in pairs. Go to http://www.snopes.com/info/whatsnew.asp. and choose two "rumors" – one of which must be true and the other a hoax (you can find out on the site). Then read them out to the rest of the class. They must guess which one is true.

3 An urban legend B2

Sewers[1] are dark, dangerous, and scary places. There's lots of nasty stuff down there, from rats to garbage and, well, sewage. But what about the infamous colonies of alligators?

That claim has been around for decades, and you've probably heard some version of the tale that started it, in which a young boy gets a baby alligator for his birthday and flushes it down the toilet, not knowing what else to do about it. Years later, as the story goes, that same boy reaches into a sewer grate for a lost baseball, and his arm is ripped off by his former pet, now monstrous and ravenous[2] for blood.

According to folklorist Jan Harold Brunvand in his *Encyclopedia of Urban Legends* (2001, ABC-CLIO) the story is widely known and has appeared in many forms, including TV shows and horror films. Indeed, "queries about the sewergator rumors regularly arrive at the offices of the New York City Bureau of Sewers and are routinely denied... [One source for the story is] Robert Daley's 1959 book *The World Beneath the City* which included an interview with a man claiming to have been sewer commissioner in the 1930s when a campaign was mounted to clean all the gators out of the sewer system."

This seemed like solid evidence that, even if alligators no longer lurk in the city's sewers, they did at one time and were enough of a menace that the city initiated a program to eradicate them. However, Brunvand notes, further investigation revealed that the man "had never been commissioner, and, in fact, had delighted in spinning outrageous yarns[3]."

Trumping[4] all myths, however, is the fact that alligators wouldn't survive long in sewers. [...]

Still, New York City is a big place, and known for its strangeness. Some people have exotic pets, and it's possible that there are one or more doomed, miserable baby alligators somewhere. But finding (or putting) an alligator in a New York City sewer does not mean that decades of stories about giant alligators in sewers are true.

Benjamin Radford, *Live Science*, June 3, 2011.

1. sewers ['su:əz] (n.) : *égoûts*. 2. ravenous ['rævənəs] (adj.) : *affamé*. 3. yarn (n.) : *récit, conte*. 4. trump (v.) : *prendre le dessus sur*.

More help WBT n° 73

Brainstorm

Say everything you know about the subject of urban legends. Do you know any?

Read and explain

1. Say how this urban legend began. Relate it to the picture.
2. Could the legend be a true story? Summarise the arguments for and against.

Go into detail. WBT n° 74

Grammar

Dater et mesurer le temps p. 104

- *Sixty years **ago**, a surgeon said he took this photo.*
- *many **have since claimed** the existence of Nessie.*

Your task

What story, myth or legend did you believe in when you were younger? Do you think children need to believe in such things or should they always be told the truth? (150 words)

Irish myths

1 Finn MacCool and the Giant's Causeway B1

The story goes that Finn invited the Scottish giant, Benandonner, to visit Ireland for a contest of strength. Finn, deciding as an act of hospitality to build a walkway between Scotland and Ireland so that Benandonner would not get his feet wet while he crossed the Irish Sea, started to lay down the hexagonal stones.

After a few weeks of intensive work, the pathway was nearing completion and Benandonner's home, Fingal's Cave, was only a stride away.

Finn, exhausted, lay down to sleep. At dawn break the next morning, Finn's wife, Oonagh, woke to the thundering footsteps of Benandonner striding towards their home. Quickly realising the still resting Finn would be no match for Benandonner, she woke Finn and dressed him in one of her nightgowns and, placing a bonnet on his head, she urged him to pretend to sleep.

Walking into the cave, Benandonner roared, "Right, where is he hiding?"

Pointing to the sleeping form of Finn, Oonagh replied, "Be quiet or you'll wake our baby!"

Thinking Finn was indeed their child, Benandonner beat a hasty retreat as he did not want to wait around to meet the father. He was last seen running back across the causeway tearing it up in his wake[1] leaving visitor after visitor to marvel at the spectacular coastline that is Finn's legacy[2] to Ireland.

www.yourirish.com/fionn-maccumhal.

1. in his wake (n.) : *après son passage*.
2. legacy (n.) : *héritage*.

More help WBT n° 75

The Giant's Causeway. "Causeway" comes from the French *chaussée* and means a path across water.

Read and explain

1. Say where the story takes place and who the characters are.
2. Find out what Finn builds and why. Relate this to the picture.
3. Describe the trick that Oonagh plays on Benandonner and explain her reasons. Does it work? Go into detail. WBT n° 76

http://www.theemeraldisle.org/irish-myths-legends/
http://www.toptenz.net/top-10-irish-myths-and-legends.php
http://irelandnow.com/myths.html

Present a myth

1. Work in pairs. Choose another Irish myth (see the links), take notes and prepare a slideshow.
2. Make a 2-minute presentation, telling the story and saying why you have chosen this particular myth.

2 The Children Of Lir B1

Brainstorm

The painting depicts an episode from the myth of the Children of Lir. Imagine the story that is told in the myth.

Listen and explain MP3 23

1. Say what you find out in the beginning about Lir and his family.
2. Explain what Aoife (pronounced [iːfə]) did to the children and why. Relate this to the picture.
3. Say what happened after Lir died.

How does it end? MP3 24

1. Imagine how the story ends. Say what you think will happen.
2. Listen to the real ending and compare it with your version. Which ending do you prefer?
Go into detail. WBT n° 78

Help

- cast a spell (v.) : *jeter un sort*
- turn someone into something (v.) : *transformer quelqu'un en quelque chose*

More help WBT n° 77

"Instead of the four children what did she behold", from *The Children Of Lir*, 1930's.

3 The wailing Banshee B1 B2

A banshee, a supernatural creature from Irish mythology whose name has become synonymous with unbearable wailing.

Listen to the story MP3 25

1. From what the story tells us, say what it means when a banshee appears.
2. Which elements of the story are shown in the picture?

Help

- wail (v.) : *gémir*
- hideous ['hɪdɪəs] (adj.) : *hideux*
- bear (v.) : *supporter*

More help WBT n° 80

Grammar

L'emploi des auxiliaires p. 105

- *She would like to have killed them, but knew that, if she* ***did*** *[...].*

Le conditionnel dans les subordonnées de temps WBT n° 79

- *The spell would only be broken after 900 years when the children heard the ringing of a bell.*

Your task

Using the Banshee story and picture as a model, find a picture that portrays a supernatural character or illustrates an episode from a myth and write your own short story to be included in a book of stories for young children.

Improve your

VOCABULARY

1 Playing tricks

Match the pairs

Find the seven pairs of words or expressions that mean the same thing.

believable • claim • convincing • deceive • easily led • fool • gullible • invent • maintain • make out • make up • pretend • take in • trick

Use the words WBT n° 81

Replace the words in bold type with their synonyms from the list above.

Candid Camera is a very popular TV programme. The object is to **trick** people into doing things that makes them look silly. It's surprisingly easy to **deceive** someone – people are more **gullible** than you think. All you have to do is **invent** a story that is **convincing**. In one famous case, the presenter **pretended** he was an alien from Venus who was looking for a place to park his spaceship. The first person he talked to offered him his back yard. Afterwards, the victim **claimed** he knew it was a Candid Camera trick from the word go, but no one believed him.

Criminal tricks MP3 26

a. Check that you know the meaning of these words. Then listen to the conversations. Which word is concerned in each case?

embezzle • counterfeit • fake • scam

b. Use the words to make sentences that sum up the situations.

2 The supernatural

Match the words WBT n° 81

Match each word to its explanation.

a spell •	• a sort of ghost
a curse •	• an imaginary being in human form
a spirit •	• a person (usually a woman) claiming to have magical powers
a fairy •	• a punishment inflicted by a supernatural force
a witch •	• wicked, malevolent
evil •	• a word or formula with magic powers

Use the words WBT n° 81

Complete the sentences with words from the previous exercise.

a. A ...... was placed on the house: everyone who came to live there would die a horrible death.

b. What he thought was a butterfly was in fact a ...... : a tiny creature that looked like a little girl with wings.

c. He was turned into a frog when the witch cast a ...... on him.

d. In Dickens' novel *A Christmas Carol*, Scrooge meets three ...... who show him the past, the present and the future.

Making predictions

a. Imagine you are a fortune-teller, palmist and astrologer (check the meanings of these words).

b. Work in pairs. Find out your partner's astrological sign (see the list below). Then use the following expressions to interview your partner and predict his/her future.

beware of... • have (no) money problems • travel widely • marry young • find love late in life • have a long and happy life • achieve your ambitions • be fabulously rich • find true happiness

Signs of the Zodiac

Aries ['eəri:z]	*Bélier*
Taurus ['tɔ:rəs]	*Taureau*
Gemini ['dʒemɪnaɪ]	*Gémaux*
Cancer ['kænsə]	*Cancer*
Leo [li:əʊ]	*Lion*
Virgo [vɜ: gəə]	*Vierge*
Libra ['lɪ:brə]	*Balance*
Scorpio [skɔ:pɪəu]	*Scorpion*
Sagittarius [sædʒɪ'teəriəs]	*Sagittaire*
Capricorn ['kæprɪkɔ:n]	*Capricorne*
Aquarius [a'kweərɪəs]	*Verseau*
Pisces ['paisi:z]	*Poissons*

FINAL TASK

The hoax contest

If you have ever wanted to play a trick on someone – or on everyone in the world – now is your chance! But your hoax must be well-thought-out. If someone can prove it's not true, then you won't win the contest!

Did aliens invade Earth in 1938?

http://www.transparencynow.com/welles.htm

Did they find the missing link in 1912?

http://en.wikipedia.org/wiki/Piltdown_Man

Was an autopsy performed on an alien in 1995?

http://hoaxes.org/archive/permalink/alien_autopsy

1 Find out about hoaxes

- Look at the three hoaxes illustrated on this page. Find out more about them and discuss how the perpetrators managed to convince people they were true.

2 Create your own hoax

- Work in groups of four.

a. Imagine the incredible story you want to tell.

b. Put together the so-called evidence of your story (photographs, interviews…).

c. Create a slideshow or a short film and write the commentary.

3 Present your hoax

- Present your hoax to the class and try to convince them that your story is real.

It is the job of your classmates to try and debunk your hoax!

- As a class, decide who created the best hoax and explain your choice!

PREPARE FOR THE BAC

Expression orale

FICHE MÉTHODE PAGE 109

Sujet **Mythes et héros**

Modalités de l'épreuve

- Tirage au sort de l'une des quatre notions sur lesquelles porte le programme du cycle terminal.
- Préparation de l'exposé. (10 min.)
- Exposé oral en continu, en anglais : présentation de la notion. (5 min.)
- Expression orale en interaction : conversation entre l›examinateur et l'élève (5 min.)

Série L

- Le candidat apporte ses dossiers constitués dans l'année. L'examinateur choisit la notion.
- Préparation (10 min.). Exposé oral en continu ; (10 min.) Expression orale en interaction. (10 min.)

Attention : *les citations ci-dessous sont proposées dans le cadre d'un entraînement ; elles fournissent des pistes pour préparer votre épreuve pendant l'année.*
Le jour de l'épreuve, aucun document ne vous sera fourni.

Heroes

"A hero is someone who has given his or her life to something bigger than oneself."

Joseph Campbell (1904-1987), American writer.

"What is a hero without love for mankind."

Doris Lessing (1919-2013), British writer.

"I think a hero is any person really intent on making this a better place for all people ."

Maya Angelou (1928-2014), American writer.

Myths

"I believe in everything until it's disproved."

John Lennon (1940-1980), British musician.

"Myths which are believed in tend to become true."

George Orwell (1903-1950), British writer.

"I believe that legends and myths are largely made of truth."

J. R. R. Tolkien (1892-1973), British writer.

Les héros et les mythes font partie des piliers fondateurs d'une société ; ils incarnent les valeurs et préoccupations d'une époque. Les trois chapitres que vous avez étudiés vous permettent d'avoir différents points de vue sur la notion. Suivez les étapes ci-dessous pour construire votre présentation.

Fiche méthode	Application guidée
Étape 1 Constituer un dossier	
→ Pour préparer votre présentation orale, créez un **dossier sur la notion**. Attention, seuls les élèves de la série L pourront apporter ce dossier le jour de l'épreuve !	→ Le dossier doit regrouper les différents aspects de la notion traités dans l'année (*Irish myths, urban legends, today's heroes,* etc.) et comporter différents supports (images, textes, enregistrements, etc.).
Étape 2 Trouver la problématique et construire le plan	
→ La **problématique** est la question que l'on pose dans l'introduction et à laquelle on répond dans la conclusion. Vous devez toujours vous demander si vous pouvez répondre à votre question avec les arguments et les exemples que vous donnez. → Le **plan** peut être thématique ou binaire (présenter deux points de vue différents). Deux parties suffisent.	→ **Exemples de problématiques** • *Are heroes always recognised as they should be?* (p. 80-81) • *What makes a hero?* (p. 64-65) • *To what extent do myths explain our history/an era?* (ch. 6) → Votre plan peut être thématique (*Who are today's young heroes?* ch. 4) ou binaire (*Are myths true or always legends?* ch. 6).
Étape 3 Rédiger l'introduction	
→ L'introduction doit contenir **plusieurs éléments** : – une définition générale de la notion ; – la présentation du sujet choisi ; – l'annonce de la problématique ; – l'annonce du plan.	→ Pour la définition de la notion, appuyez-vous sur les mots clés des chapitres étudiés ou sur une citation que vous aurez apprise dans l'année (ex. ci-contre). ***Exemples :*** *Hero: a person admired for his/her courage, outstanding achievements or noble qualities. Myth: a traditional story, often about the distant past and usually involving the supernatural.*
Étape 4 Rédiger la conclusion	
→ Elle doit être la synthèse de tout ce que vous avez dit, mais elle doit aussi permettre **d'élargir votre problématique** de départ. Vous devez proposer une ouverture, la plupart du temps sous forme de question. La conclusion est la dernière chose qu'entend votre auditoire. Elle doit donc être soignée	→ Pour élargir la problématique. Exemples : • *Why do we need examples to follow?* • *Why are some people ready to sacrifice their lives to save others?*
Étape 5 Mettre au point le développement	
→ C'est la **partie principale** de votre présentation. Entraînez-vous à préparer vos notes sous forme de mots-clés, de façon à ne pas lire votre présentation mot à mot.	→ Pour chaque partie, notez sur votre plan : les mots-clés (*myth / superstition / insecurity / power / pride / tradition*, etc.), les documents choisis (textes, photographie, etc.) et les connecteurs logiques utiles ! (voir p. 226)

Your turn!

Pour améliorer votre aisance à l'oral, entraînez-vous devant un miroir ou une webcam et chronométrez-vous. Essayez de ne pas trop lire vos notes. Faites un effort de prononciation car cette dernière est évaluée, au même titre que le contenu de votre présentation.

Hiding a Jew

1939. Nazi Germanwy. The country is holding its breath. Death has never been busier. Liesel, a nine-year-old girl, is living with a foster[1] family on Himmel street. Her parents have been taken away to a concentration camp. One day, her foster parents decide to hide a young man and they let him sleep in Liesel's bedroom.

Max Vandenburg slept for three days. [...]

Sometimes, towards the end of the marathon of sleep, he spoke.

There was a recital of murmured names. A checklist.

Isaac. Aunt Ruth. Sarah. Mama. Walter. Hitler.

Family, friend, enemy.

They were all under the covers with him, and at one point, he appeared to be struggling with himself. "*Nein*," he whispered. It was repeated seven times. "No."

Liesel, in the act of watching, was already noticing the similarities between this stranger and herself. They both arrived in a state of agitation on Himmel street. They both nightmared.

When the time came, he awoke with the nasty thrill[2] of disorientation. His mouth opened a moment after his eyes and he sat up, right angled.

"Ay!"

A patch of voice escaped his mouth.

When he saw the upside-down face of a girl above him, there was the fretful[3] moment of unfamiliarity and the grasp of recollection – to decode exactly where and when he was currently sitting. After a few seconds, he managed to scratch his head (the rustle of kindling[4]) and he looked at her. His movements were fragmented, and now that they were open, his eyes were swampy[5] and brown. Thick and heavy.

As a reflex action, Liesel backed away.

She was too slow.

The stranger reached out, his bed-warmed hand taking her by the forearm.

"Please."

His voice also held on, as if possessing fingernails. He pressed it into her flesh.

"Papa!" Loud.

"Please!" Soft.

It was late afternoon, grey and gleaming, but it was only dirty-coloured light that was permitted entrance into the room. It was all the fabric of the curtains allowed. If you're optimistic, think of it as bronze.

When Papa came in, he first stood in the doorway and witnessed Max Vandenburg's gripping fingers and his desperate face. Both held on to Liesel's arm. "I see you two have met," he said.

Max's fingers started cooling.

Max Vandenberg promised that he would never sleep in Liesel's room again. What was he thinking that first night? The very idea of it mortified him.

He rationalized that he was so bewildered[6] upon his arrival that he allowed such a thing. The basement was the only place for him as far as he was concerned. Forget the cold and the loneliness. He was a Jew and if there was one place he was destined to exist, it was a basement or any other such hidden venue of survival.

"I'm sorry," he confessed to Hans and Rosa on the basement steps. "From now on I will stay down here. You will not hear from me. I will not make a sound."

1. foster (adj.) : *adoptif, adoptive.*
2. thrill (n.) : *sensation forte.*
3. fretful (adj.) : *agité.*
4. the rustle of kindling : *le bruissement du petit bois.*
5. swampy (adj.) : *marécageux.*
6. bewildered (adj.) : *confus.*
7. steep in (v.) : *s'imprégner de.*
8. predicament (n.) : *situation délicate.*
9. sloppily (adv.) : *de façon désordonnée.*
10. spurred on by (adj.) : *poussé par.*
11. twinge (n.) : *élancement.*

Still from *The Book Thief,* directed by Brian Percival, 2013.

Hans and Rosa, both steeped in[7] the despair of the predicament[8], made no argument, not even in regard to the cold, they heaved blankets down and topped up the kerosene lamp. Rosa admitted that there could not be much food, to which Max fervently asked her to bring only scraps, and only when they were not wanted by anyone else.

"*Na na,*" Rosa assured him. "You will be fed, as best I can."

They also took the mattress down, from the spare bed in Liesel's room, replacing it with dust sheets – an excellent trade.

Downstairs, Hans and Max placed the mattress beneath the steps and built a wall of dust sheets at the side. The sheets were high enough to cover the whole triangular entrance, and if nothing else, they were easily moved if Max was in dire need of extra air.

Papa apologized. "It's quite pathetic, I realise that."

"Better than nothing," Max assured him. "Better than I deserve – thank you."

With some well-positioned paint tins, Hans actually conceded that it did simply look like a collection of junk gathered sloppily[9] in the corner, out-of-the-way. The only problem was that a person needed only to shift a few tins and remove a dust sheet or two to smell out the Jew.

"Let's just hope it's good enough," he said.

"It has to be." Max crawled in. Again, he said it. "Thank you."

Thank you.

For Max Vandengurg, those were the two most pitiful words he could possibly say, rivalled only by I'm sorry. There was a constant urge to speak both expressions, spurred on by[10] the affliction of guilt.

How many times in those first few hours of awakeness did he feel like walking out of that basement and leaving the house altogether? It must have been hundreds.

Each time, though, it was only a twinge[11].

Which made it even worse.

He wanted to walk out – Lord, how he wanted to (or at least he *wanted* to want to) – but he knew he wouldn't. It was much the same as the way he left his family in Stuttgart, under a veil of fabricated loyalty.

To live.

Living was living.

The price was guilt, and shame.

Markus Zusak, *The Book Thief*, 2011.

Read and understand

1. Who is Max Vandenburg? Give as many details as possible.
2. What is Max Vandenburg's nationality? Give your reasons and quote from the text.
3. Read the first paragraph carefully and say if Isaac, Sarah and Walter are Max's family, or friends.
4. Find one word in the text that best sums up Max Vandenburg's main objective.
5. Who are Hans and Rosa?
6. Explain in your own words what Hans and Rosa do to make Max Vandenburg as comfortable as possible.
7. Read again the paragraph starting with "Downstairs, Hans and Max placed the mattress..." and guess what Hans's job is.

Go further LVA/LELE

1. Knowing Liesel's situation, explain why she calls her foster father "Papa". (50 words)
2. Explain the last sentence of the text: "The price was guilt, and shame." (50 words)
4. In the second paragraph, from "When the time came" to "Max's fingers started cooling", the author uses the word "fragmented" to portray Max Vandenburg. Analyse the passage and say how the author manages to convey this idea. What image of Max does it give?

Of Dwarfs and Their Sometimes Irascible Nature

Grumpy, one of the seven dwarfs.

David is a 12 year-old boy lost in a world of myths and legends.

He got to his feet, put his pack on his shoulder, and almost fell over a dwarf who had just climbed up on the road from the low ditch on the left.

"Mind where you're going," said the dwarf. He was about three feet tall and wore a blue tunic, black trousers, and black boots that came up to his knees. There was a long blue hat on his head, at the end of which was a little bell that no longer made any sound. His face and hands were grubby[1] with dirt and he carried a pickaxe over one shoulder. His nose was quite red, and he had a short white beard. The beard appeared to have pieces of food trapped in it.

"Sorry," said David.

"So you should be."

"I didn't see you."

"Oh, and what's that supposed to mean?" said the dwarf. He waved his pick threateningly. "Are you sizeist? Are you saying I'm small?"

"Well, you are small," said David. "Not that there's anything wrong with that," he added hurriedly. "I'm small too, compared to some people."

But the dwarf was no longer listening and had instead commenced shouting at a column of squat[2] figures heading for the road.

"Oy, Comrades!" said the dwarf. "Bloke[3] over here says I'm small."

"Bloody cheek![4]" said a voice.

"Hold him till we get there, Comrade," said another, who then appeared to reconsider. "Hang on, how big is he?"

1. grubby (adj.) : *pas très propre.*
2. squat [skwɒt] (adj.) : *ramassé, trapu.*
3. bloke (n. fam., UK) : *type, mec.*
4. bloody cheek! : *quel culot !*
5. mutter (v.) : *marmonner.*
6. filthy (adj.) : *très sale.*
7. shin (n.) : *tibia.*
8. ditch (n.) : *fossé.*
9. idly ['aɪdlɪ] (adv.) : *négligemment.*
10. shackled (adj.) : *enchaîné.*

The dwarf examined David. "Not very big," he said. "Dwarf and a half. Dwarf and two-thirds at most."

"Right, we'll 'ave him," came the reply.

Suddenly, it seemed as if David was surrounded by short, unhappy men muttering[5] about 'rights' and 'liberties' and having enough of 'this sort of thing'. They were all filthy[6] and they all wore hats with broken bells. One of them kicked David in the shin[7].

"Ow!" said David. "That hurt."

"Now you know how our feelings, er, feel," said the first dwarf.

A small, grubby hand tugged at David's pack. Another tried to steal his sword. A third appeared to be poking him in his soft places just for the fun of it.

"That's enough!" shouted David. "Stop it!"

He swung his pack wildly and was rather pleased to feel it connect with a pair of dwarfs, who immediately fell into the ditch[8] and rolled around theatrically for some time.

"What did you do that for?" asked the first dwarf. He looked quite shocked.

"You were kicking me."

"Was not."

"Were so too. And someone tried to steal my bag."

"Did not."

"Oh, this is just ridiculous," said David. "You did and you know it."

The dwarf lowered his head and kicked idly[9] at the road, sending a little puff of white dust into the air.

"Oh, all right then," it said. "Maybe I did. Sorry."

"That's all right," said David.

He reached down and helped the dwarfs raise their two fellows from the ditch. Nobody was badly hurt. In fact, now that it was all over, the dwarfs seemed rather to have enjoyed the whole encounter.

"Reminder of the Great Struggle, that was," said one."Right, Comrade?"

"Absolutely, Comrade," replied another. "The workers must resist oppression at every turn."

"Um, but I wasn't really oppressing you," David said.

"But you could have, if you'd wanted to," said the first dwarf. "Right?"

He looked up at David quite pathetically. David could tell that he really, really would have liked someone to try unsuccessfully to oppress him.

"Well, if you say so," said David, just to make the dwarf happy.

"Hurrah!" shouted the dwarf. "We have resisted the threat of oppression. The workers will not be shackled![10]"

"Hurrah!" shouted the other dwarfs in unison. "We have nothing to lose but our chains."

"But you don't have any chains," said David.

"They're metaphorical chains," explained the first dwarf.

He nodded once, as if he had just said something very profound.

"Riiight," said David. He wasn't certain what a metaphorical chain was, exactly. In fact, David wasn't entirely sure what the dwarfs were talking about at all. Still, there were seven of them altogether, which seemed about right.

"Do you have names?" asked David.

John Connolly, *The Book of Lost Things*, 2006.

Read and understand

1. Give information about the physical appearance of David and those he meets.
2. What does David say to apparently upset the first dwarf?
3. Say how the dwarf interprets what David said and why this attracts the attention of the other dwarfs.
4. What do some dwarfs do to David and what happens to them?
5. Find an element showing that the dwarfs wanted to appear hurt and two elements to show that they were not, in fact, hurt.
6. Explain the last line of the extract.

Go further LVA/LELE

1. Do you think the author is sympathising or making fun of the dwarfs? If not, what could be his other aim? Give your reasons by quoting from the text.
2. What point do you think Connolly is trying to make about the use of language in political struggles?
3. What do you think Connolly's own political leanings are? Give your reasons.
4. Study how the author makes his tale humorous.

Improve your SKILLS

A question

1 Waiting to exhale

B1

Observe, describe and comment

1. Describe the cartoon and the characters.
2. Check the definition of "exhale", "belch" and "harmful".
3. Explain what the cow is doing here.
4. Find out what the EPA is and explain its decision. (See the link.)
5. Comment on the cartoonist's message.

http://www.epa.gov

2 How do we fight global warming?

B1 B2

Interpret the map

Describe what the map shows and link it to the title.

Watch and take notes DVD MP3 27

Note down everything you understand about:

a. the event mentioned;
b. the part played by a Hollywood superstar in the event;
c. something else that happened while the event was taking place;
d. the demands made by the two speakers.

Go into detail. WBT n° 83

Write a letter

Write a letter to the UN environment committee on climate change. Say whether you approve or not of UN policy. Say what other things, other than those proposed by the speakers, should be done to tackle the problem and why. (200 words)

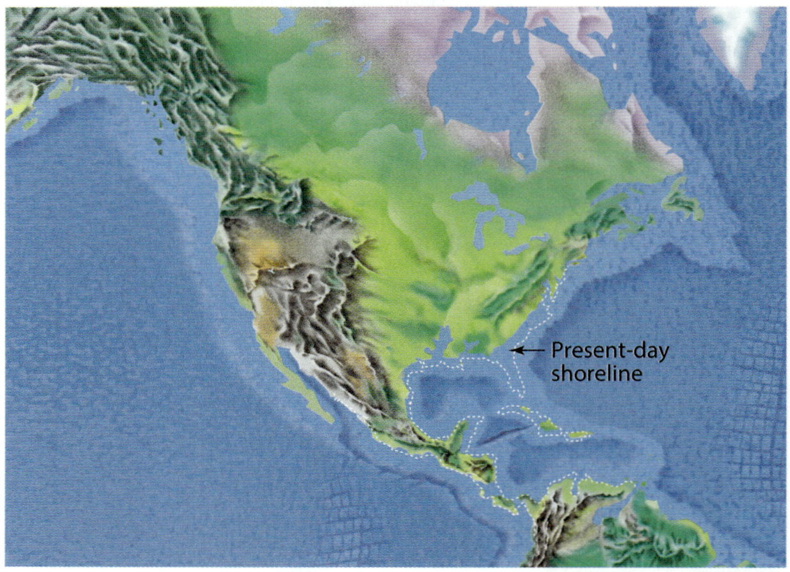

If all the ice melts...

Help

* pledge (n., v.) : *promesse formelle ; promettre*
* price tag (n.) : *(ici) coût*
* subsidies (n.) : *subventions*
* corporate (adj.) : *relatif à l'entreprise*

More help WBT n° 82

Grammar

Prétérit ou *present perfect* ? p. 124

- *All the oil wells, carbon, again! We **have evaporated** that into the air.*
- *He **called** for 100 billion dollars a year from governments for a global fund.*

# of temperature

3 Is global warming a myth? B2

According to a new study, something as small as a light icebreaker could go in the Arctic Ocean by the middle of the century, including straight over the North Pole, thanks to the ongoing effects of climate change.

Ovid's eyebrows lifted in a familiar way, almost amused. "I'm afraid you have missed the boat, Tina. Even the most recalcitrant climate scientists agree now, the place is heating up. Pretty much every one of the lot. Unless some other outcome is written on the subject line of his paycheck."

She raised her jaw slightly, an edgier[1] look, and started over once again. Her stamina for replays was unbelievable. "Dr. Byron, let's talk about global warming. Many environmentalists contend[2] that burning fuel puts greenhouse gases into the atmosphere."

He pulled back his chin in such skeptical dismay he looked like a startled turtle. "They *contend* this? That burning carbon puts carbon in the air, this is a *contention*?" His voice notched up so severely it squeaked a little. "Tina, Tina. Think about what you are saying. All the coal that has ever been mined, that's carbon. All the oil wells, carbon, again! We have evaporated that into the air. What's in the world stays in the world, it does not go *poof* and disappear. It's called the conservation of matter. The question was settled well before the time of Sir Isaac Newton."

Tina blinked once, twice. "Scientists tell us they can't predict the exact effects of global warming."

"Correct. We tell you that, because we are more honest than other people. We know evidence will keep coming in. It does not mean we ignore the subject until further notice. We brush our teeth, for instance, even though we do not know exactly how many cavities we may be avoiding."

"Well, a lot of people are just not convinced. We're here to get information."

He rolled his eyes to the ceiling and showed his teeth in a grimace, the tip of his tongue just visible between his front teeth. When he finally looked at her again, this seemed to cause him actual pain. "If you were here to get information, Tina, you would not be standing in my laboratory telling me what scientists think."

She opened her mouth, but he cut her off. "What scientists disagree on now, Tina, is how to express our shock. The glaciers that keep Asia's watersheds[3] in business are going right away. Maybe one of your interns could Google that for you. The Arctic is genuinely collapsing.

Barbara Kingsolver, *Flight Behavior*, 2012.

1. edgy (adj.) : *crispé, énervé.*
2. contend (v.) : *remettre en cause.*
3. watershed (n.) : *ligne de partage des eaux.*

More help WBT n° 84

Read and explain

1. Look at the picture caption and explain what the picture shows.
2. Read the passage and identify the two characters. What are their jobs?
3. Briefly explain the point of view of each character. How does the narrator feel? Go into detail. WBT n° 85

Activity

Work in groups.

1. Find as many sources of CO_2 and other greenhouse gases as you can and explain what happens to them when they are emitted into the atmosphere. Imagine solutions to the problem.
2. Report back to the class on your findings.

Your task

Draw your own cartoon on the subject of global warming, using the facts presented on these pages. The cartoon must have a caption or include characters speaking. Show your cartoon to the class and ask them to describe and interpret it.

Water: too little

1 An unstoppable flow of water B1

Explain and practise

1. Describe the picture and explain what it shows.
2. Practise pronouncing the words in the help box. This will help your understanding of the video.

Watch and find out DVD MP3 28

1. Say what problem the video focuses on.
2. How does the video relate to the picture?
3. Find out:
– what the consequences will be in the near future;
– how the data was collected;
– how Eric Rignot feels.

WBT n° 87

Help

* **glacier** ['gleɪsɪə] **(n.)** : *glacier*
* **glaciologist** [gleɪsɪ'ɔlədʒɪst] **(n.)** : *glaciologue*
* **data** ['deɪtə] **(n.)** : *données (details, information)*
* **radar** ['reɪdaː] **(n.)** : *radar*

More help WBT n° 86

2 Water statistics B1

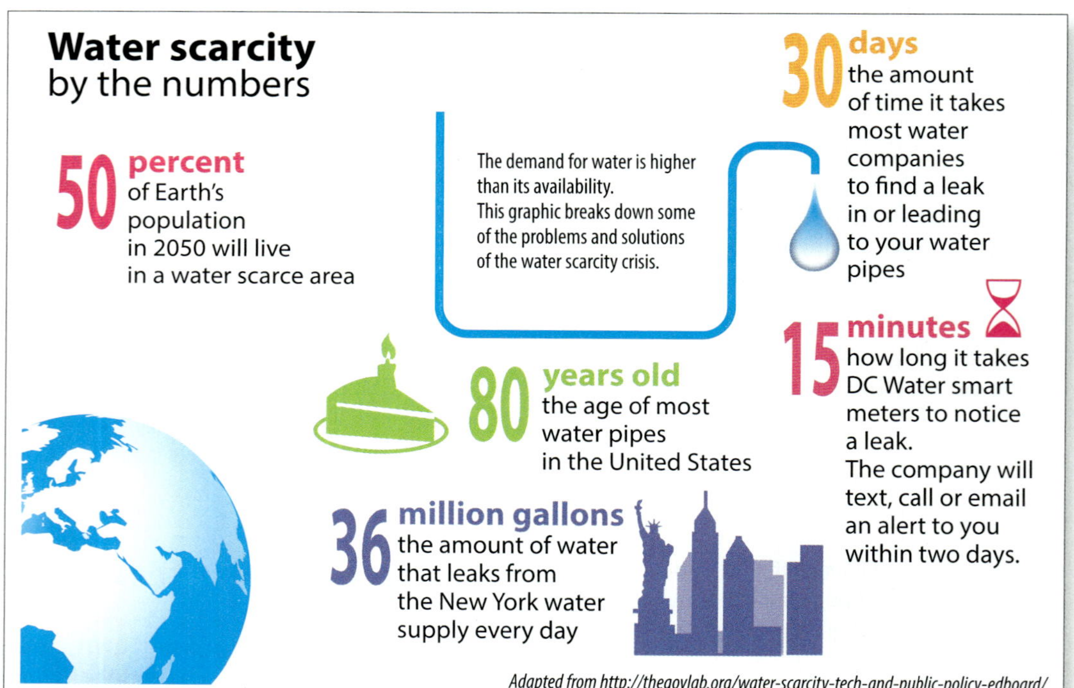

Comment on the statistics

1. Check the meaning of "scarcity". Say what the statistics tell us about the causes of water scarcity.
2. What solutions can you think of to stop us from wasting water?

or too much?

3 On the verge of disaster? B2

On 17 January, scientists downloaded fresh data from a pair of Nasa satellites and distributed the findings among the small group of researchers who track the world's water reserves. At the University of California, Irvine, hydrologist James Famiglietti looked over the data from the gravity-sensing Grace satellites with a rising sense of dread[1].

The data, released last week, showed California on the verge of an epic drought[2], with its backup systems of groundwater reserves so run down that the losses could be picked up by satellites orbiting 400 km above the Earth's surface.

"It was definitely an 'oh my gosh moment'," Famiglietti said. "The groundwater is our strategic reserve. It's our backup, and so where do you go when the backup is gone?"

That same day, the state governor, Jerry Brown, declared a drought emergency and appealed to Californians to cut their water use by 20%. "Every day this drought goes on we are going to have to tighten the screws on what people are doing," he said. [...]

There are other shock moments ahead – and not just for California – in a world where water is increasingly in short supply because of growing demands from agriculture, an expanding population, energy production and climate change.

Already a billion people, or one in seven people on the planet, lack access to safe drinking water. Britain, of course, is currently at the other extreme. Great swaths of the country are drowning in misery, after a series of Atlantic storms off the south-western coast. But that too is part of the picture that has been coming into sharper focus over 12 years of the Grace satellite record. Countries at northern latitudes and in the tropics are getting wetter. But those countries at mid-latitude are running increasingly low on water. [...]

The Middle East, north Africa and south Asia are all projected to experience water shortages over the coming years because of decades of bad management and overuse.

Watering crops[3], slaking thirst[4] in expanding cities, cooling power plants[5], fracking[6] oil and gas wells – all take water from the same diminishing supply. Add to that climate change – which is projected to intensify dry spells in the coming years – and the world is going to be forced to think a lot more about water than it ever did before.

Suzanne Goldenberg, *The Guardian*, February 9, 2014.

1. dread (n.) : *crainte*. 2. drought [draʊt] (n.) : *sécheresse*. 3. crop (n.) : *récolte*. 4. slake thirst : *étancher la soif*. 5. power plant (n.) : *centrale électrique*. 6. fracking (n.) [utilisé ici comme verbe] : *fracturation (pour créer un puits)*.

More help WBT n° 88

Read and explain

1. In what way is the article related to the picture (look carefully at the caption)?
2. Explain what alarming fact Grace has brought to light.
3. Find out about the causes of the problem and the regions concerned.

Go into detail. WBT n° 89

Activity

Work in groups.

1. Discuss what you can do on a personal level to combat water shortage.
2. Prepare a list of actions and report back to the class.

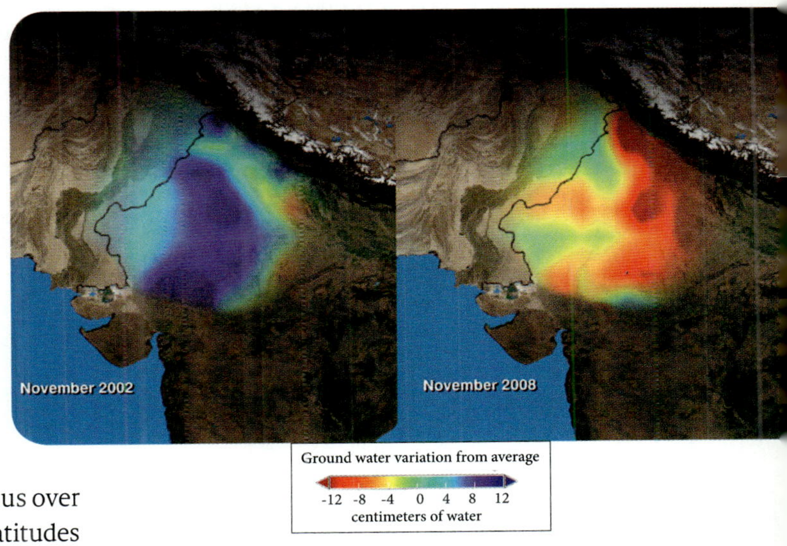

A photomontage from NASA's Grace satellites showing the depletion of groundwater in northwestern India between 2002 and 2008.

Your task

You are a blogger and environmentalist. Write a blog that defends the following point of view – from the same Guardian article as the extract above :"The world is going to be forced to think a lot more about water than it ever did before." Say what measures were not taken by governments in the past and must now be taken. (150 words)

Can our cities

1 Too much energy? B1

Watch the video DVD MP3 29

1. Sum up briefly what the video is about and how the word "energy" is defined.
2. Say what a "sustainable city" should be like.
3. Find out why energy consumption in cities is still a problem today. Go into detail. WBT n° 91

Activity

What should we do to limit our energy consumption? How far can we go along that road? Prepare your answers individually (in note form), then exchange your views in pairs or in groups.

Help

* sustainable (adj.) : *durable*
* decade ['dekeɪd] (n.) : *décennie*
* embodied (adj.) : *(ici) contenu*

More help WBT n° 90

Grammar

L'article Ø WBT n° 92

• *Ø Skylines and Ø skyscrapers that are built to impress.*

2 The city of tomorrow? B1

A group of designers has put together a proposal for a new floating city on the banks of the Mississippi to help prevent a tragedy similar to the one that happened in New Orleans in 2005.

It looks like something from a sci-fi film, but this bizarre floating metropolis may be the solution for cities devastated by extreme weather.

The incredible structure measures a staggering[1] 1,200ft high, covers 30 million square feet and is designed to house up to 40,000 residents. It comes with everything you would expect to find in a normal city – from hotels to shops, casinos and schools. The Space Age design is even equipped with gardens, special express elevators for 'vertical commuting[2]' and moving walkways for pedestrians.

The bizarre plans were inspired by the devastation caused when the American city of New Orleans was ravaged by Hurricane Katrina in 2005.

The damage was so extensive, the community is still in the process of rebuilding.

Now a group of designers, based in Boston, has put together a proposal for a new floating city. Called the New Orleans Arcology Habitat, or NOAH, the sturdy[3] triangular creation dissipates strong weather by allowing it to blow through. Fitted with hurricane panels, the structure can take the blast of a storm with little impact on the community inside. [...]

Although based on New Orleans, the design team believes their structure could be used in any coastal urban area.

Adapted from *MailOnline*, Mach 3, 2011.

1. staggering (adj.) : *époustouflant*. 2. commuting (n.) : *déplacement, trajet*. 3. sturdy (adj.) : *solide, robuste*.

More help WBT n° 93

Explain and read

1. Say what happened in New Orleans in 2005.
2. Read the article and say how this floating city can help prevent a similar tragedy.
Go into detail. WBT n° 94

Improvise

Choose a card from the ones offered you by your teacher. Improvise a one-minute dialogue with a friend on the topic you have just studied.
WBT n° 95

survive?

3 An underwater city B1 B2

Artists' impressions of the Ocean Spiral project off the coast of Japan.

Real or not?

1. Use the pictures to guess what the Ocean Spiral project is. Does it look like science fiction or reality?
2. Say what you know about the legend of the lost city of Atlantis and about the movie *Waterworld*. Use the links.

Listen to the recording MP3 30

1. Explain what Ocean Spiral is.
2. Sum up the project in your own words.
3. Would you want to live there? Why/Why not? Go into detail. WBT n° 96

http://www.livescience.com/23217-lost-city-of-atlantis.html
http://www.kidzworld.com/article/960-history-the-lost-city-of-atlantis
https://www.youtube.com/watch?v=oEp382HIisE

Grammar

La futurité dans les subordonnées de temps WBT n° 31

- *Until such times* ***arrive**..*

Action soumise à condition p. 125

- *What* ***would happen*** *if...*

Your task

It is the year 2023. You and your family decide to spend a weekend at the newly-built Ocean Spiral. When you get back home, the website you used to book your holiday asks you to write a review: accommodation, activities, etc. (150-200 words)

Improve your

VOCABULARY

1 Climate change

Match the descriptions MP3 31

Check that you know the meaning of these nouns. Then listen and say which one is being described.

a. a carbon footprint
b. a drought
c. an earthquake
d. exhaust fumes
e. a flood
f. the greenhouse effect
g. a monsoon
h. a tidal wave

Up or down?

Replace the words in bold type with the correct form of one of the verbs from the list below and add the adverb "up" or "down" in each case. Use the verbs only once.

break • cool • dry • put • warm

1. In a few years time, many of our rivers **will no longer flow.**
2. The Earth**'s temperature is** gradually **increasing.**
3. The polar ice caps **are disintegrating**.
4. More and more people will buy air-conditioning units in an effort to **reduce their body temperature.**
5. People who **raised** objections in the past to global warming theories are now changing their minds.

2 Energy

Fossil fuels: translations and definitions WBT n° 97

a. Match the English words and expressions with their French equivalents.

b. Identify the two important *faux-amis*.

c. Choose three items and write a sentence for each one, explaining what it is.

• diesel oil	*plate-forme pétrolière*
• fuel	*centrale*
• heating oil	*combustible*
• oil	*pétrole, huile*
• oil rig	*puits de forage*
• oil well	*gaz de schiste*
• petrol (UK), gasoline (US)	*fuel*
• power station	*essence*
• shale gas	*charbon*
• coal	*gazole*

Alternative energy sources: a two-minute exercise!

Use the words and expressions below to complete this Internet article as quickly as you can. Use each item only once.

central heating • convert • costly • farms • funding • heat • noise • plant • renewable • residential • tiles • turbines • unused • windmills

Wind energy

This was one of the first forms of alternative energy used – there are still thousands of ...... in use today. Many countries have developed wind ...... – both offshore and on the mainland – where groups of wind ...... produce a viable and ...... energy source. The problem with wind energy is that turbines can't be located near ...... areas because of the ...... they make.

Solar Energy

In many countries grants are now available to help pay for photovoltaic ...... which collect the ...... from the sun's rays and ...... it into an exceptionally safe form of alternative energy. Whether used to create electricity or to simply heat water or a ...... system, solar energy is easily obtained and not too ....

Biomass

Biomass is the creation of energy using ...... materials. It is still a relatively ...... form of energy in many parts of the world, but more and more money is being put into ...... it.

Adapted from http://EzineArticles.com/68287.

survive?

3 An underwater city B1 B2

Artists' impressions of the Ocean Spiral project off the coast of Japan.

Real or not?

1. Use the pictures to guess what the Ocean Spiral project is. Does it look like science fiction or reality?
2. Say what you know about the legend of the lost city of Atlantis and about the movie *Waterworld*. Use the links.

Listen to the recording MP3 30

1. Explain what Ocean Spiral is.
2. Sum up the project in your own words.
3. Would you want to live there? Why/Why not? Go into detail. WBT n° 96

http://www.livescience.com/23217-lost-city-of-atlantis.html
http://www.kidzworld.com/article/960-history-the-lost-city-of-atlantis
https://www.youtube.com/watch?v=oEp382HIisE

Grammar

La futurité dans les subordonnées de temps WBT n° 31
- *Until such times **arrive**...*

Action soumise à condition p. 125
- *What **would happen** if...*

Your task

It is the year 2023. You and your family decide to spend a weekend at the newly-built Ocean Spiral. When you get back home, the website you used to book your holiday asks you to write a review: accommodation, activities, etc. (150-200 words)

CROSS CULTURE

The new Atlantis?

Shaky foundations and encroaching seas are posing significant threats to some of the world's cities. Will one of them be the next Atlantis?

Atlantis

Whether real or legendary, the disappearance of **Atlantis** has fascinated us for centuries. Some scientists believe it did exist – maybe in the Bahamas – and was swept into the sea as a result of earthquakes and floods.

Venice

Preserving Venice has been a priority of the Italian government for about 30 years. Several billion euros have been spent on flood defence, but some say that the only way to save the city is to move it altogether.

New Orleans

It was not until after Hurricane Katrina that experts really took note of New Orleans downhill situation. In 2006, *National Geographic* reported that the city was sinking about a quarter of an inch every year.

Houston

America's fourth-largest city was built on sand and has been sinking for years. The sinking has been slowed down significantly by stopping the extraction of groundwater, but a permanent solution has yet to be found.

New York City

America's most densely populated city is doomed to suffer the effects of global warming. It is predicted that it will not just be flooded but will eventually disappear into the sea.

Activities

1. Find out more about seven cities that are disappearing (including the four mentioned here).
2. Working in groups, choose one of the cities and prepare a report on:
a. the dangers it is facing because of its foundations or climate change;
b. the possible solutions, if any,
3. Compare your reports and discuss the similarities and differences between the cities' problems.

http://travel usnews.com/features/7_Cities_About_to_Sink/

Traduction du passé composé : prétérit ou *present perfect* ? (PG p. 234)

MÉMO

A quoi sert le passé composé français ?

• Il a deux valeurs principales : il sert à évoquer des événements passés et à exprimer un bilan.
Ex. : Je me suis levé, ai pris ma douche et suis parti au lycée.
Ex. : Je n'ai jamais eu un aussi bon livre d'anglais.

Comment est-il traduit en anglais ?

• Dans le premier cas ci-dessus, on emploie le prétérit simple (*simple past*) : *I got up, took a shower and went to school.*

• Dans le second cas, on utilise le *present perfect* : *I've never had such a good English book.*

Y a-t-il une différence de structure entre le passé composé français et le present perfect ?

• L'auxiliaire utilisé dans les deux langues est suivi du participe passé du verbe conjugué.

• Mais en anglais on n'utilise que l'auxiliaire *have* :
Ex. : Je ne suis jamais monté au sommet de la tour.
I've never been to the top of the tower.
N.B. : le prétérit n'est pas toujours traduit par le passé composé !
Ex. : *She raised her jaw slightly [...] and started over once again. Her stamina for replays was unbelievable.*
Elle releva légèrement la tête [...] et reprit [son argumentation] à nouveau. Quand il s'agissait de se répéter, elle faisait preuve d'une endurance incroyable.

Observez et raisonnez

(texte p. 117 et video p. 116)

• *He called for 100 billion dollars a year from governments for a global fund.*

• *All the oil wells, carbon, again! We have evaporated that into the air.*

1 Repérez les temps utilisés dans les deux énoncés.

2 Reportez-vous aux contextes (texte et vidéo) et identifiez qui parle.

3 Expliquez et justifiez l'emploi des deux temps dans les énoncés.

4 Traduisez les énoncés.

Entraînez-vous

1 Cartoon fun

• Quel temps allez-vous utiliser pour expliquer l'état dans lequel se trouve cette mère de famille à la fin de la semaine ?

• Quel temps allez-vous utiliser pour dire ce qu'elle a fait vendredi, samedi et dimanche ?

2 Relisez, justifiez, traduisez

a. Relisez le texte p. 117.
b. Relevez les occurences du prétérit et du present perfect et justifiez leur emploi.
c. Traduisez-les.

3 Mettez les verbes indiqués au prétérit ou au *present perfect*.

We don't know what causes ice ages to begin or end. In 1875, a janitor turned geologist, James Croll, ... (propose) that small variations in Earth's orbit around the Sun ...... (be) responsible for climate change. This idea ...... (enjoy) its greatest heyday during the 1970s, when ocean sediment cores ...... (appear) to confirm the theory. But in 1992, Ike Winograd and his colleagues at the US Geological Survey ...... (falsify) the theory by demonstrating that its predictions ...... (be) inconsistent with new, high-quality data.
The climate of the ice ages is documented in the ice layers of Greenland and Antarctica. We ...... (core) these layers, ... (extract) them, and ...... (study) them in the laboratory. Not only ...... (be) ice ages colder than today, but the climates ...... (be) considerably more variable. Compared to the norm of the last million years, our climate is remarkably warm, stable and benign ....

Action soumise à condition : prédiction ou intention ? (PG p. 235)

MÉMO

Quels sont les mots qui introduisent la notion de condition ?

- En français : si, à condition que, sauf si.
- En anglais, les plus courants sont : *if, provided, unless*.

Quelles formes verbales (mode et temps) sont utilisées en français pour exprimer la condition ?

- Selon les contextes, le présent et l'imparfait.

Quelles formes verbales sont utilisées en français dans la partie de la phrase qui suit l'expression de la condition ?

- Selon les contextes, le futur de l'indicatif et le présent du conditionnel.

Qu'en est-il en anglais ?

- Le présent et l'imparfait de l'indicatif sont respectivement traduits par le présent et le prétérit. (ex. ci-dessous.)
- Dans la partie de la phrase qui suit l'expression de la condition, le futur français est traduit par le modal ***will + BV***, et le conditionnel par le modal ***would + BV***.

Qu'indique la partie de la phrase qui suit ou précède la condition ?

Un degré de certitude ou une intention (dans les deux langues).

Observez et raisonnez

(vidéo p. 116 et enregistrement p. 121)

- *The economy itself will die if our ecosystems collapse.*
- *What would happen if the legend of the Lost City of Atlantis was crossed with the screenplay of Kevin Costner's 1995 hit movie "Waterworld"?*

1 Dans ces deux énoncés, isolez la condition et l'action soumise à condition.

2 Qu'indiquent les parties d'énoncés suivantes : un degré de certitude ou une intention ?
The economy itself will die / What would happen

3 Dans lequel des deux cas le degré de certitude est-il le plus fort ?

Entraînez-vous

1 Cartoon fun

Faites trois phrases en anglais pour expliquer comment on pourrait éviter ce que le dessin montre.

2 Le changement climatique au cinéma...

Que feriez-vous si semblable événement se produisait ? Faites trois phrases.

3 Complétez (librement)

a. If temperatures go on rising, ...
b. Unless temperatures ....
c. If all the ice in the world melted, ...
d. If the USA, China and India ....
e. Unless the USA, China and India ....

4 Complétez

a. If sea levels go on rising, what ......?
b. If sea water came up to your door, what ......?
c. If Vesuvius erupts again, what ......?
d. If we keep raising more and more cattle, ...?
e. If we can't stop the ice cap melting, ...

Improve your

VOCABULARY

1 Climate change

Match the descriptions MP3 31

Check that you know the meaning of these nouns. Then listen and say which one is being described.

a. a carbon footprint
b. a drought
c. an earthquake
d. exhaust fumes
e. a flood
f. the greenhouse effect
g. a monsoon
h. a tidal wave

Up or down?

Replace the words in bold type with the correct form of one of the verbs from the list below and add the adverb "up" or "down" in each case. Use the verbs only once.

break • cool • dry • put • warm

1. In a few years time, many of our rivers **will no longer flow.**
2. The Earth**'s temperature is** gradually **increasing.**
3. The polar ice caps **are disintegrating**.
4. More and more people will buy air-conditioning units in an effort to **reduce their body temperature.**
5. People who **raised** objections in the past to global warming theories are now changing their minds.

2 Energy

Fossil fuels: translations and definitions WBT n° 97

a. Match the English words and expressions with their French equivalents.

b. Identify the two important *faux-amis*.

c. Choose three items and write a sentence for each one, explaining what it is.

• diesel oil	*plate-forme pétrolière*
• fuel	*centrale*
• heating oil	*combustible*
• oil	*pétrole, huile*
• oil rig	*puits de forage*
• oil well	*gaz de schiste*
• petrol (UK), gasoline (US)	*fuel*
• power station	*essence*
• shale gas	*charbon*
• coal	*gazole*

Alternative energy sources: a two-minute exercise!

Use the words and expressions below to complete this Internet article as quickly as you can. Use each item only once.

central heating • convert • costly • farms • funding • heat • noise • plant • renewable • residential • tiles • turbines • unused • windmills

Wind energy

This was one of the first forms of alternative energy used – there are still thousands of ...... in use today. Many countries have developed wind ...... – both offshore and on the mainland – where groups of wind ...... produce a viable and ...... energy source. The problem with wind energy is that turbines can't be located near ...... areas because of the ...... they make.

Solar Energy

In many countries grants are now available to help pay for photovoltaic ...... which collect the ...... from the sun's rays and ...... it into an exceptionally safe form of alternative energy. Whether used to create electricity or to simply heat water or a ...... system, solar energy is easily obtained and not too ....

Biomass

Biomass is the creation of energy using ...... materials. It is still a relatively ...... form of energy in many parts of the world, but more and more money is being put into ...... it.

Adapted from http://EzineArticles.com/68287.

FINAL TASK

Designing a "green" city

Imagine how you could turn your own city into a sustainable one.

1 Report on a video

- Divide into five groups. Each group chooses a video about Songdo, a new city in South Korea. (See the links.)
- Watch your video and, as a group, report back to the class. Explain what issue is dealt with and give your view on the sustainablility of the solutions.
- Take notes on the other reports and complete a table (which your teacher will give you). Identify all the issues, key words and key ideas.

2 Redesign your city

- In groups, and using the information from the videos, imagine if and how you could turn your own city into a really sustainable one. Say what you would need doing and why. Report back to the class.
- As a class, build a model of your ideal "green" city. Attribute the various issues to different groups so that everyone contributes.

http://newsroom.cisco.com/feature-content?type=webcontent&articleId=776681
http://newsroom.cisco.com/feature-content?type=webcontent&articleId=677558
http://newsroom.cisco.com/feature-content?4type=webcontent&articleId=677543
http://newsroom.cisco.com/feature-content?type=webcontent&articleId=677530
http://newsroom.cisco.com/feature-content?type=webcontent&articleId=668731

PREPARE FOR THE BAC

Compréhension de l'écrit (10 points)

FICHES MÉTHODE PAGE 129

Sujet A warning falls on deaf ears

The Grand Ballroom of the Mark Hopkins Hotel was darkened for the after-dinner speeches. The audience was elegant, the men in tuxedos[1], the women in ball gowns[2]. Beneath the ornate chandeliers, the voice of Nicholas Drake boomed from the podium. "Ladies and gentlemen, it is no exaggeration to say that we face an environmental crisis of unprecedented proportions. Our forests are disappearing. Our lakes and rivers are polluted.

The plants and animals that make up our biosphere are vanishing at unprecedented rates. Forty thousand species become extinct every year. That's fifty species every single day. At present rates, we will lose half of all species on our planet in the next few decades. It is the greatest extinction in the history of earth.

"And what is the texture of our own lives? Our food is contaminated with lethal pesticides. Our crops are failing from global warming. Our weather is growing worse, and more severe. Flooding, droughts, hurricanes, tornadoes. All around the globe. Our sea levels are rising – twenty-five feet in the next century, and possibly more. And most fearsome of all, new scientific evidence points to the specter of abrupt climate change, as a result of our destructive behavior. In short, ladies and gentlemen, we are confronted by a genuine global catastrophe for our planet."

Sitting at the center table, Peter Evans looked around at the audience. They were staring down at their plates, yawning, leaning over and talking to one another. Drake wasn't getting a lot of attention.

"They've heard it before," Morton growled. [...] Nicholas Drake appeared tall and ungainly, his tuxedo ill-fitting. The collar of his shirt was bunched up around his scrawny neck. [...] Evans thought no one would ever guess that Drake was paid a third of a million dollars a year to head the Fund, plus another hundred thousand in expenses. Or that he had no science background at all. Nick Drake was a trial attorney, one of five who had started NERF many years before. And like all trial attorneys, he knew the importance of not dressing too well.

"...the erosion of bio-reservoirs, the rise of ever more exotic and lethal diseases..."

"I wish he'd hurry up," Morton said. He drummed his fingers on the table.

Michael Crichton, *State of Fear*, 2004.

1. tuxedo [tʌk'siːdəʊ] (n.) : *smoking*. 2. ball gown (n.) : *robe longue*.

Questions

● ***Tous les élèves traiteront les questions suivantes.***

A. Where does the scene take place? What sort of people are in the audience?

B. Who is Nicholas Drake? What's his job?

C. What is the speech about?

D. Does the speaker sound optimistic about the future? Give your reasons and quote from the text.

E. What point is the speaker trying to get over to his audience?

F. How does the audience react? Quote from the text.

G. What do we learn about Drake? Does that make his speech more or less convincing?

● ***Seuls les élèves de l'option LVA (Langue vivante approfondie) traiteront la question H.***

H. Think carefully about how the author feels towards Drake. Is he trying to make him likeable or not? Quote from the text to back up your point.

Expression écrite (10 points)

● ***Tous les élèves traiteront les questions suivantes.***

1. Do you think Drake paints an accurate picture of the situation or not? If not, why would he do this? (150 words)

2. You're the speaker. Instead of describing an apocalyptic situation, you tell people what they should all do to avoid an environmental catastrophe. (150 words)

● ***Seuls les élèves composant au titre de la LVA traiteront l'une des questions suivantes.***

1. Explain the attitude of the people in the audience. Why do they react that way? Would you behave in the same way under similar circumstances? Why/Why not ? (200 words)

2. Explain what the author is trying to do in portraying Drake as he does. (200 words)

Compréhension écrite

Fiche méthode	Application guidée

Étape 1 Lire le texte et les premières informations

Fiche méthode

→ Lisez attentivement le texte deux fois, sans regarder les consignes, pour identifier les **éléments essentiels** (thème, personnages, époque, etc.) et la **notion** à laquelle se rapporte le texte. Le paratexte peut fournir des informations précieuses.

→ Si vous ne connaissez pas un mot, utilisez le **contexte** pour en déduire le sens.

Application guidée

→ Repérez les éléments qui permettent :
– d'identifier les narrateurs : qui sont-ils et combien ?
– de situer l'action dans le temps : le prétérit suffit-il à situer l'histoire dans un passé lointain ? Quel(s) détail(s) montre(nt) que l'action se déroule dans un contexte contemporain ?
→ Repérez les mots transparents. Attention aux faux-amis ! (ex. : *chandeliers*).

Étape 2 Lire et comprendre les consignes

Fiche méthode

→ Les consignes éclairent le contenu du texte. **Lisez-les toutes** une première fois, puis relisez le texte en surlignant les **informations importantes**.
Soyez attentifs à ce qui est demandé dans les consignes pour répondre avec précision. Apprenez le lexique des consignes !
→ Les questions vont du plus simple au plus complexe.

Application guidée

→ La question **A** attire votre attention sur le lieu *(where)* et les personnes présentes *(people / audience)*. La **B** et la **C** vous amènent à vous concentrer sur le personnage principal ; la **C** permet de faire le lien avec la notion (L'idée de progrès). La **D** évoque ce que pense/ressent le protagoniste (*sound optimistic*), etc.
→ Les **G/H** amènent à parler du but de l'auteur. Quelle image veut-il donner de Drake ? Il faut relire le texte en entier pour répondre.

Étape 3 Répondre aux questions

Fiche méthode

→ Répondez aux questions dans l'ordre, en indiquant les numéros ou les lettres. **Relisez** chaque réponse immédiatement après l'avoir écrite. À la fin, relisez l'ensemble. Attention aux fautes d'inattention (*s* à la 3e pers. sing, etc.).

Application guidée

→ Référez-vous au texte pour vérifier l'orthographe des mots que vous utilisez (*environmental, planet*, etc.). Vérifiez la forme des verbes irréguliers. Pour les citations du texte (**D** et **F**), sélectionnez les passages les plus pertinents.

Expression écrite

Fiche méthode	Application guidée

Étape 1 Lire les sujets

Fiche méthode

→ Lisez attentivement les consignes et soulignez les **termes clés**.
→ Déterminez le **type de production écrite** que l'on vous demande : lettre, discours, essai, récit, dialogue, etc.

Application guidée

Sujet 2
→ *You're the speaker / tell people / avoid an environmental catastrophe*
→ Vous devez écrire un discours.

Étape 2 Préparer la rédaction

Fiche méthode

→ Rédigez **au brouillon** : un plan détaillé, une introduction, un développement, une conclusion.

Application guidée

→ **Exemple de développement pour le sujet 2**
I. Present situation (pollution, global warming, climate change)
II. Possible action (stop wasting energy, use alternative energy, reduce carbon footprint)

Étape 3 Rédiger au propre

Fiche méthode

→ Variez les structures de phrases et le vocabulaire, utilisez la **rhétorique du discours**.
N'oubliez pas les mots de liaison !
→ Aérez votre copie et pensez à vous relire. Attention aux fautes d'inattention !

Application guidée

→ *We have to face the facts:... / There is no getting away from it, we should... / I appeal to every one of you. We must act and act soon. That being said... / We can change things !*
→ Commencez chaque paragraphe par un alinéa et allez à la ligne à chaque changement d'idée.

Are things

1 More or less freedom? B1

Is it funny?

1. Work out what the cartoonist is making fun of and how he does it.
2. Do you find the cartoon funny? Give your reasons.

2 Do we need big data? B1

Listen to the recording MP3 32

1. State briefly what the recording is about.
2. Explain (a) the Prism program, (b) Big Data.
3. Give one example of the possible alternatives to massive data collection. Go into detail. WBT n° 98

Big Data!

3 Worrying news? B2

No longer content to vacuum up, scan, index and sell analytics based on the content of our texts, emails, searches, locations and more, Google now has a new target: tapping, mapping and colonizing the networks wiring our lives.

www.alternet.org.

Write an editorial

You are the editor of your school website and you have just read the piece of news on the left. You decide to write a short editorial as a reaction to it. What are you going to write? (150 words)

4 Is surveillance against the law? B2

Explain and comment

Make sure you understand why the European Commission objects to real-time monitoring of internet use. Then say how you feel about the issue and exchange your views.

New surveillance plans could breach European data protection laws, experts have warned, in a further blow to the Government's controversial proposals. Lawyers said that the European Commission, which previously took the British Government to court over alleged online privacy breaches, would likely object to real-time monitoring of internet use, email and mobile phone calls by the state as it could allow "fishing expeditions" against innocent citizens.

Martin Beckford, *The Daily Telegraph*, April 5, 2012.

getting better?

5 One man's vision of the future B1

Fifty yards of tiptoeing brought them to a door which the Director cautiously[1] opened. They stepped over the threshold into the twilight of a shuttered dormitory. Eighty cots stood in a row against the wall. There was a sound of light regular breathing and a continuous murmur, as of very faint voices remotely whispering.

A nurse rose as they entered and came to attention before the Director.

"What's the lesson this afternoon?" he asked.

"We had Elementary Sex for the first forty minutes," she answered. "But now it's switched over to Elementary Class Consciousness."

The Director walked slowly down the long line of cots. Rosy and relaxed with sleep, eighty little boys and girls lay softly breathing. There was a whisper under every pillow. The D.H.C[2] halted and, bending over one of the little beds, listened attentively.

"Elementary Class Consciousness, did you say? Let's have it repeated a little louder by the trumpet."

At the end of the room a loud-speaker projected from the wall. The Director walked up to it and pressed a switch.

"... all wear green," said a soft but very distinct voice, beginning in the middle of a sentence, "and Delta children wear khaki. Oh no, I don't want to play with Delta children. And Epsilons are still worse. They're too stupid to be able to read or write. Besides they wear black, which is such a beastly[3] colour. I'm so glad I'm a Beta."

There was a pause; then the voice began again.

"Alpha children wear grey. They work much harder than we do, because they're so frightfully clever. I'm really awfuly glad I'm a Beta, because I don't work so hard. And then we are much better than the Gammas and Deltas. Gammas are stupid. They all wear green, and Delta children wear khaki. Oh no, I don't want to play with Delta children. And Epsilons are still worse. They're too stupid to be able..."

The Director pushed back the switch. The voice was silent. Only its thin ghost continued to mutter from beneath the eighty pillows.

"They'll have that repeated forty or fifty times more before they wake; then again on Thursday, and again on Saturday. A hundred and twenty times three times a week for thirty months. After which they go on to a more advanced lesson."

Aldous Huxley, *Brave New World*, 1932.

1. cautiously (adv.) : *prudemment*. 2. D.H.C. : Director of Hatcheries and Conditioning (hatcheries : *[littéralement] couveuses*). 3. beastly (adj.) : *sale, dégoûtant*.

More help WBT n° 99

Read the extract

1. Say where and when the action takes place.
2. Explain what is going on and what methods are being used.
Go into detail. WBT n° 100

Give your point of view

Do you think our society is headed in the direction Huxley imagined so many years ago? Give your reasons.

Grammar

La proposition infinitive WBT n° 101
- *I don't **want to play** with Delta children*

Les relatives p. 140
- *Besides they wear black, **which** is such a beastly colour.*
- *[...] you already have vehicles **that** can do automatic braking, automatic acceleration.*

Your task

Work in pairs: A and B. Prepare and act out the following conversation.
- A: You are either an activist campaigning against cyber-surveillance or a spokesperson for the NSA.
- B: You are a journalist. You interview A. You want to find out about A's arguments for or against cyber-surveillance.

Are we becoming

1 Connected but alone? B1

Brainstorm

Look at the title and the photo and say all the words that come to mind.

Listen to the recording MP3 33

1. Find out what the speaker's job is, say briefly what she is talking about and imagine who she is talking to.
2. Explain what makes this talk different from one she gave many years before.
Go into detail. WBT n° 102

Activity

Divide into two groups.
1. One group supports the idea that when you are connected, you are not alone.
2. The other group believes the opposite: that you can be connected and alone.
Find examples to back up your group's point of view, then organise a debate.

Help
- **heady (adj.)**: *enivrant, grisant*
- **unplug (v.)**: *débrancher*

2 The death of conversation B1

A recent cartoon by Matt Wuerker.

Norman Rockwell, *Thanskgiving*, 1943.

Spot the difference!

The first picture is a modern-day version of Norman Rockwell's iconic painting *Thanksgiving*. What is the "message" conveyed by each picture?

less human?

3 Doctor Smartphone B2

In 200 years we have gone from this... ... to this.

Watch the video DVD MP3 34

1. Say who the people in the video are.
2. Explain what the device is (use the picture) and how it works.
3. Make a list of its advantages.

What do you think?

Do you trust this new way of practising medicine? Say what you think.

Help

- surgery (n.) : (ici) *chirurgie*
- blood stream (n.) : *flux sanguin*
- blood pressure (n.) : *tension artérielle*
- device (n.) : *appareil*

4 Alone together B2

We live in a technological universe in which we are always communicating. And yet we have sacrificed conversation for mere connection.

At home, families sit together, texting and reading e-mail. At work executives text during board meetings. We text (and shop and go on Facebook) during classes and when we're on dates. My students tell me about an important new skill: it involves maintaining eye contact with someone while you text someone else; it's hard, but it can be done. [...]

We've become accustomed to a new way of being "alone together." Technology-enabled, we are able to be with one another, and also elsewhere, connected to wherever we want to be. [...]

A 16-year-old boy who relies on texting for almost everything says almost wistfully, "Someday, someday, but certainly not now, I'd like to learn how to have a conversation."

In today's workplace, young people who have grown up fearing conversation show up on the job wearing earphones. Walking through a college library or the campus of a high-tech start-up, one sees the same thing: we are together, but each of us is in our own bubble, furiously connected to keyboards and tiny touch screens.

Sherry Turkle, *The New York Times*, April 21 2012.

Grammar

Les relatives p. 140

- *We live in a technological universe* ***in which*** *we are always communicating.*
- *A 16-year-old boy* ***who*** *relies on texting for almost everything.*

Read the article

1. Sum up briefly what the article is about. Does the cartoon on page 134 echo the article or not? Give your reasons.
2. Explain what impact technological devices have on our lives, according to the writer. Go into detail. WB n° 103

Discuss

Do you think new technologies have changed human relationships? Why/Why not? Give your reasons.

Your task

Choose one of the people in the *Thanksgiving* cartoon who is using an electronic device. Imagine you are the person and you are thinking aloud about what you are reading, writing, listening to, etc. Listen to each other and comment.

1 Big Mother is watching you! B2

When Apple introduced the Find My iPhone app three years ago, its aim was to help people locate their lost smartphones. But E. J. Hilbert, a 43-year-old former FBI officer, had a better idea – installing the app on his three children's devices, so that he could track them wherever they went.

"They have it on their phone and that's the way it's going to be," says Mr Hilbert, whose day job is investigating cyber crime.

By adapting the Find My iPhone app, Mr Hilbert is part of a wider trend. Until recently technology gave power to the children. Now it is starting to give something back to the parents.

Yesterday's parents did not know how to record their offspring's[1] favourite television programme. Today's parents can record the child's every move, email and purchase[2] – with the help of a variety of new gadgets. [...]

For many parents, however, the priority is protecting their children from online pornography and bullying.

In the UK, all internet customers are to be asked by the end of next year if they want to activate pornography filters. TalkTalk, the first provider[3] to have offered the filters, says that about one in three households activate the filter.

Parents worried about cyber bullying can go further. Dozens of software packages are available to install on desktops and mobiles to check children's browsing history and read their emails and messages. By logging keystrokes[4], the programs can give parents access to sites and passwords.

Henry Mance, *The Financial Times*, August 28, 2013.

1. offspring (n.) : *progéniture*. 2. purchase (n.) : *achat*. 3. provider (n.) : *fournisseur*. 4. keystroke (n.) : *frappe*.

More help WBT n° 104

Read and explain

1. The article mentions new applications and software. Explain what their common aim is.
2. Say what parents' main worries are concerning their children's online activity.
3. Explain the functions of the different pieces of software mentioned.

Go into detail. WBT n° 105

What do you think?

Work in pairs and discuss the following subject: "The kind of software and apps mentioned in the text help to build trust between parents and children."
Report back to the class on your discussion, stating what you agree or disagree on.

2 The driverless car B1

Listen and comment MP3 35

Say (a) what will be happening soon, (b) what has already happened, (c) what happened to Mr Rutherford, (d) what could happen, (e) what is happening at the moment.
Go into detail. WBT n° 106

Activity

Individually, make a list of the benefits and drawbacks of driverless cars. Then discuss the points you have noted with the rest of the class. Does everyone agree?

always better?

3 Safety in the home B1 B2

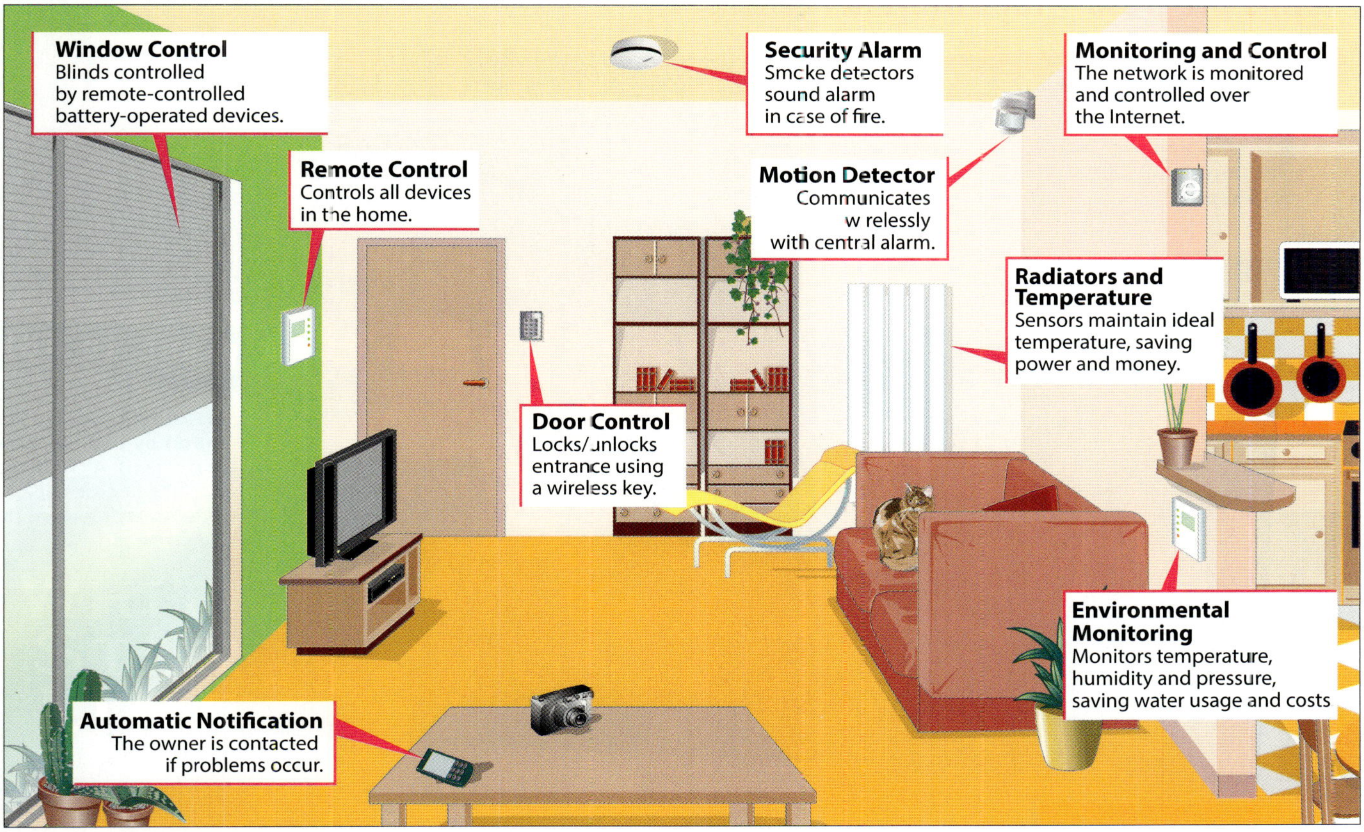

Observe, read and speak

Study the picture.

1. Describe the different devices.
2. Explain what devices make this home safer and why.

Grammar

Whose et dont p. 141
- *"They have it on their phone and that's the way it's going to be," says Mr Hilbert,* ***whose*** *day job is investigating cyber crime.*

Le génitif et la possession WBT n° 107
- *three* ***children's*** *devices*
- ***Yesterday's*** *parents*

Les formes en -ing WBT n° 16
- *The United Kingdom announces it* ***will be testing*** *driverless cars next year.*
- ***installing*** *the app*
- ***investigating*** *the app*

Your task

Go on the internet and find a funny cartoon about one of the topics dealt with on this double page. Prepare your description of the cartoon and your comments on it and present them to the class. The class votes for the funniest cartoon and the best comments.

Les relatives définissantes et non définissantes (PG p. 251)

MÉMO

Ces deux sortes de relatives ont-elles des points communs ?

• Elles sont toutes deux introduites par un pronom relatif et complètent un antécédent dans la proposition qui les précède.

En quoi diffèrent-elles ?

• Comme son nom l'indique, une relative définissante définit l'antécédent de façon précise. Sans elle, la phrase n'a plus de sens : on ne sait plus de qui ou de quoi on parle.

• En revanche, une relative non définissante apporte une information non indispensable, voire superflue, concernant l'antécédent. Un peu comme si l'information était mise entre parenthèses. On peut très bien se passer d'elle sans dommage pour le sens de la phrase et l'identification de l'antécédent.

Peut-on les distinguer simplement ?

• À l'écrit, les non-définissantes sont la plupart du temps précédées d'une virgule, mais ceci n'est pas systématique.

• Par contre à l'oral, leur antécédent est suivi d'une pause, ce qui n'est pas le cas dans les énoncés contenant des relatives définissantes.

Observez et raisonnez

(texte p. 183 et enregistrement p. 136)

• *Fifty yards of tiptoeing brought them to a door which the Director cautiously opened.*

• *Besides they wear black, which is such a beastly colour.*

• *[...] you already have vehicles that can do automatic braking, automatic acceleration.*

1 Isolez les relatives contenues dans ces trois énoncés.

2 Justifiez le choix des relatifs.

3 Identifiez les relatives définissantes et non-définissantes. Justifiez vos réponses.

4 Entraînez-vous à dire ces énoncés à haute voix.

5 Traduisez-les, dites-les et comparez les deux langues.

Entraînez-vous

1 Cartoon fun

Étudiez le dessin. Quel type de relatives contient-il ?

"I'm looking for someone who'll start at the bottom and stay there."

2 Construisez des phrases

Utilisez une relative définissante ou non définissante à chaque fois. Si les deux sont possibles, expliquez la différence de sens entre les deux.

a. Amy, the nurse / on duty / got up when the Director entered

b. The Director walked up to the end of the room / equipped with a loudspeaker

c. The Director walked to the line of cots / eighty little boys and girls lay softly breathing.

d. I don't want to play with children / wear khaki clothes.

3 Dites-le en anglais

Traduisez, et justifiez la ponctuation que vous choisissez.

a. Il y eut une pause après laquelle la voix reprit ...

b. Les enfants Alphas sont ceux qui portent des vêtements gris.

c. Le Directeur, dont tout le monde avait peur, entra dans la salle.

Whose et dont (PG p. 249)

MÉMO

Quelle est la nature de whose ?

- *Whose* est un pronom relatif ou un pronom interrogatif.
- C'est le génitif du pronom *who* : *who* + *'s*.

Comment fonctionne-t-il ?

- En tant que relatif il est toujours suivi d'un nom sans article, comme *'s*.
- En anglais moderne il renvoie à tout type d'antécédent, humain ou non humain.

N.B. : En tant qu'interrogatif, il peut fonctionner seul : *Whose is it?* = À qui est-ce ?

Comment whose relatif (+ nom) est-il traduit ?

- Par « dont » + article + nom.

N.B. : L'inverse n'est pas vrai. Le relatif « dont » peut avoir plusieurs fonctions en français : complément de nom à caractère possessif, complément d'objet indirect, d'adjectif, etc. Seule la première de ces fonctions se traduit par *whose*.

Observez et raisonnez

(texte p. 136)

- *"They have it on their phone and that's the way it's going to be," says Mr Hilbert, whose day job is investigating cyber crime.*

1. Isolez la relative et indiquez comment elle est construite.
2. Quel est l'antécédent de *whose* ?
3. La relative est-elle définissante ou non définissante ? Justifiez votre réponse.

Entraînez-vous

1 Cartoon fun

Expliquez la situation décrite dans ce dessin et dites ce qui le rend amusant.

"*Sold* to the lady whose husband just walked out!"

2 Utilisez *whose*

Reformulez ces phrases en utilisant *whose*.

1. Apple introduced the Find My iPhone app three years ago; its aim was to help people locate their lost smartphones.
2. Today's parents feel much less anxious because their children's every move can now be tracked.
3. Some children may be in great danger when their parents do not check their browsing history.

3 Dites-le en anglais

1. Rebecca, dont la mère se prépare à faire un discours sur l'emploi des SMS, vient justement de lui en envoyer un pour lui souhaiter bonne chance.
2. La conférencière dont le travail avait été salué dans *Wired Magazine*, n'était autre que Sherry Turkle.
3. Le docteur Eric Topol, dont les inventions vont sans doute révolutionner la médecine de demain, travaille pour une société privée.
4. Les médecins dont les patients sont équipés de l'application du Dr Topol peuvent les suivre et les conseiller à distance.

Improve your VOCABULARY

1 Safety

What's the conversation about? MP3 36

Check that you know what these noun groups mean, then listen to six short conversations. Which noun group is concerned in each case? Give reasons for your answers.

a burglar alarm • a crash barrier • a gated community • a pedestrian crossing • a non-slip mat

Complete

Use these components to complete the two-word expressions. The first word is a compound adjective with "proof", the second is a noun.

bullet • child • fool • lock • scheme • watch • water • vest

a. a ......proof ...... = a plan that is sure to work

b. a ......proof ...... = something that can only be opened by adults

c. a ......proof ...... = something worn by policemen

d. a ......proof ...... = something that you can wear on your wrist when swimming

2 Good in company or not?

Opposites

a. Find the four words and expressions in the list that refer to people who get on well with others and enjoy conversation. b. Find their antonyms.

the life and soul of the party • antisocial • a killjoy • gregarious • taciturn • retiring • talkative • outgoing

3 Surveillance

Match and make sentences

a. Match each verb with an appropriate direct object and the corresponding explanation. WBT n° 108

b. Make a sentence of at least ten words with each verb and its direct object.

Verb	Direct Object	Explanation
tap	someone's movements	place a listening device behind a picture, in a lamp, under a desk, etc.
bug	someone's ankle/wrist/etc.	follow someone or something on the move by means of an electronic device
track	a room	listen in to someone's phone conversations by means of an electronic device
tag	a phone	attach an electronic device to someone whose movements are restricted by law

Replace and translate

1. Replace the words in bold type with words from the following list. Change the form of the verbs if necessary.

2. Translate the sentences.

eavesdrop • footage • gather • monitor • person of interest • put a tail on • spy on

a. The secret services **kept a constant watch on** his behaviour for several months.

b. "When he leaves the police station," said the Inspector, "**follow** him."

c. I'm sure she has been **observing** me **secretly** ever since she found out I worked for the embassy.

d. Look outside in the corridor to make sure no one's **listening in** on our conversation.

e. The agency's job is to **collect** information on all foreign nationals living here.

f. The police didn't have any evidence against him in the case, but they regarded him as a **suspect.**

g. She couldn't deny the charge because the police had video **film** of her actually committing the offence.

FINAL TASK

Design an app

**You are design teams working for a company that designs smartphone apps.
You have been asked to come up with a new app and to present it to the Board of Directors.**

Telecommute by remotely controlling your office computer
Work from home – but use the computer in your office – through new remote control apps. View the remote computer, launch and close programs, read e-mail, copy and paste text, and access any files you left behind.

Lose weight and get fit
A new crop of social self-improvement apps help you monitor how much you've eaten and exercised, guide your diet, motivate you and keep you on track.

Baby monitor
The Baby Monitor app for the iPhone is an excellent portable choice. Simply place the phone near baby and you can program it to call you (on another phone, obviously) when baby begins crying.

Need-to-do lists
The key to staying on track with the stuff you need to get done is writing it down and checking it off. The **Remember the Milk** app provides all the bells and whistles you'll ever need in a to-do list on your tablet and your phone.

1 Design an app

- Read the information about new smartphone apps.
- Work in groups of three. You are a design team who have been asked to come up with a new app that improves people's lives. The examples on the page may help you decide which field to choose.
- Prepare to present your idea to your Board of Directors. The three of you (A, B and C) have different roles:
  A: explain what the app is designed to do.
  B: explain who the prospective customers are and why they will want to buy the app.
  C: explain how the app is installed and how to use it.
- Write a presentation, accompanied by a slideshow, to last no more than four minutes.

2 Present the app

- Present your app to the Board (= the rest of the class).
- As a class, vote for the best app!

Science: have we

1 Therapeutic cloning B1

When people think of the word "cloning", they are often hit with frightening images of duplicate human beings being created in somewhat of a mad scientist style experiment. In fact, many members of the public were outraged[1] when "Dolly" the sheep resulted from a cloning experiment in Scotland.

Therapeutic cloning, however, is entirely different and does not involve the creation of a perfectly copied human being. It is reproductive cloning that results in a copy of a specific human being. In therapeutic cloning, no sperm fertilisation is involved nor is there implantation into the uterus to create a child.

Benefits of Therapeutic Cloning

A major benefit of therapeutic cloning is that the cells removed are pluripotent[2]. Pluripotent cells can give rise to all cells in the body with the exception of the embryo. This means that pluripotent cells can potentially treat diseases in any body organ or tissue by replacing damaged and dysfunctional cells.

Ian Murnaghan, October 22, 2014.

1. outraged (adj.) : *scandalisé*. 2. pluripotent (adj.) : *ayant plusieurs potentialités*.

Comment and read

1. Comment on the picture and relate it to the title.
2. Read the text and find out what reaction people have when they hear the word "cloning".
3. Say what you can about (a) Dolly, (b) therapeutic cloning, (c) pluripotent cells.

2 Who should play God? B1 B2

What do you know?

Look at the film poster and say everything you know about Dr Frankenstein. Relate it to the title "Who should play God?"

Listen to the recording MP3 37

1. Say which sciences make up genetic engineering.
2. Find out why genetic engineering is a controversial issue. Go into detail. WBT n° 110

Write an editorial

The first "designer babies" were born yesterday. Write an editorial for the school newspaper in which you highlight the dangers of scientists playing God.

Poster for one of the first Frankenstein movies (1938).

Help

- realm [relm] (v.) : *domaine*
- sensible (adj.) : *(faux-ami) intelligent, raisonnable*
- nightmarish (adj.) ['naɪtmeərɪʃ] : *cauchemardesque*

More help WBT n° 109

gone too far?

3 When is a sheep not a sheep? B2

The Institute was well known to Pierce. An industrial-looking place, but neat and peaceful, out on the County Louth border. In the foreground, a small Georgian farmhouse used for administration standing with an unconvincing serenity, dwarfed as it was by the high flat-roofed constructions around it of corrugated iron in harsh Arctic colours, magenta, mauve, petrol-green. These housed the animals reared with intensive and experimental methods. [...]

This was Missy's birthplace. Progressive, tidy, scientific, more attractive to humans than to animals. Devoted to life certainly, rather than death, in the short term at least, still it reminded me of a progressive concentration camp in some pastoral spot, like Poland. The only honest-to-God agricutural thing about it was the smell of silage[1]. [...]

It was a hearty good-looking farmhand who led us out to the covered pens where the new breed of lamb was kept.

I had had no particular expectations but all the same I was vaguely disappointed. They were the usual woolly little beasts I knew so well. Though with a fine conformation certainly, well shaped, well grown for their age, healthy as snipes[2]. Pierce was impressed. I could tell when Pierce was impressed. Hands in his pockets, head cocked critically for the assistant's benefit, he strolled up and down, looking them over with a barely controlled admiration. Deferentially, I kept my distance. "Explain to me," he said at last to our host, his survey completed, and flattering the man in his inimitable manner, "what's so different about these little fellas. Genetically engineered. Is that it?" [...]

Drawing himself up to his full height, the chap explained.

"You have it there, Mr Hawkins. Genetically engineered is right. You see, what we're at here is experimenting with the genetic makeup[3]..."

There followed then a longish discourse on the genes as the building-blocks of life and DNA and all the rest of it. And about the radical developments in the science, where the genes of one species were being incorporated into another at an early stage of fœtal growth. [...] But the next thing I heard him say gave me a bit of a shock.

"They're very troublesome to manage, sheep are, Mr Hawkins, as you know yourself. But these human genes make them resistant to a lot of the usual ovine infections. Make them that bit less sheeplike, if you follow me. These little fellas here now are a fantastic improvement. They're close enough to what you could nearly call a trouble-free sheep, Mr Hawkins." [...]

Anne Haverty, *One day as a Tiger*, 1997.

1. silage (n.) ['saɪlɪdʒ] : *fourrage ensilé.* 2. snipe (n.) : *bécassine.*
3. makeup (n.) : *constitution, composants.*

More help WBT n° 111

A riddle

The title is a sort of riddle (*énigme*). Relate it to the picture and say what you think the answer to the riddle could be.

Read the extract

1. Say where the scene takes place and identify the various characters.
2. Say why the main character has come to this place and what's going on here.
Go into detail. WBT n° 112

Discuss

What do you think about making animals more resistant to diseases by mixing their genes with human ones?

Grammar

Les adjectifs composés WBT n° 113
• *industrial-looking; flat-roofed*

Your task

You are a scientist. You have just come up with a new theory showing that cloning is the future of mankind. Prepare a 5-minute speech to drive your point home and present it to the class.

A rosy future or

1 The stem cell controversy B2

Ever since her husband had been diagnosed with Alzheimer's disease, Nancy Reagan had come to appreciate the potential of stem cells to expose the mysteries of incurable diseases. Despite her husband's well-known conservatism and antiabortion position, Nancy had been taking ever bolder[1] steps in support of the science that she increasingly believed could help millions of patients, despite its dependence on embryos.

In 2001, she had written a plea[2] to President Bush to support embryonic stem cell studies. Just a few years later, she appealed to Senator Orrin Hatch, another Republican with strong views against abortion, but who favored expanding stem cell research. When Hatch proposed legislation in Congress that would ban reproductive cloning but allow therapeutic cloning in order to generate embryonic stem cells, he was no doubt influenced by Nancy's personal request. In describing her husband's slowly deteriorating mind, Nancy wrote, "Because of this, I am determined to do what I can to save other families from this pain. Orrin, there are so many diseases that can be cured, or at least helped, that we can't turn our backs on this." [...]

But it wasn't until May 2004, as CuresNow was launching its effort to gather enough signatures to put their stem cell initiative on the ballot[3], that Nancy took her appeal public. [...]

When Reagan died barely a month later, Nancy's words took on an added poignancy. Two days before his death, California's stem cell initiative qualified for the ballot in the November election. For the first time, a state would go to the polls to decide whether or not to fund stem cell research.

Alice Park, *The Stem Cell Hope*, 2011.

1. bold (adj.) : *téméraire, audacieux.* 2. plea (n.) : *appel.*
3. on the ballot : *(soumettre) au vote.*

More help WBT n° 114

http://content.time.com/time/nation/article/0,8599,167245,00.html
http://www.foxnews.com/story/2001/08/09/cases-for-and-against-stem-cell-research/

Ronald Reagan and Nancy before he became ill with Alzheimer's.

Describe and comment

1. Describe the picture and comment on it. What do you know about these people?
2. Given the title, the picture and the caption, say what you think the text is about.

Read the extract

1. Say what Ronald Reagan died of.
2. Say what Nancy Reagan fought for before and after her husband's death. Was her fight successful or not? Give reasons.

Go into detail. WBT n° 115

Activity

Work in groups. Use the links to find out more about the stem cell controversy. Take notes and then explain the controversy to the class. You may also take sides and explain your position.

2 On the way to immortality? B1 B2

Watch the video DVD MP3 38

1. Identify the country concerned.
2. Say what new way has been found to produce stem cells.
3. Explain what scientists hope to be able to do in the future.

Go into detail. WBT n° 117

Give a presentation

Give a short oral presentation showing how the video is related to the notion of progress and underlining any risks involved in the breakthrough it deals with.

Help

* breakthrough (v.) : *découverte capitale, grande avancée*
* currently (adv.) : *(faux-ami) actuellement*
* eventually (adv.) : *(faux-ami) à la longue, avec le temps*

More help WBT n° 116

a nightmare?

3 Donor or carer: is this the future? B2

My name is Kathy H. I'm thirty-one years old, and I've been a carer now for over eleven years. [...] But then I do know for a fact they've been pleased with my work, and by and large, I have too. My donors have always tended to do much better than expected. Their recovery times have been impressive, and hardly any of them have been classified as 'agitated', even before a fourth donation. Okay, maybe I *am* boasting now. But it means a lot to me, being able to do my work well, especially that bit about my donors staying 'calm'. I've developed a kind of instinct around donors.

I know when to hang around[1] and comfort them, when to leave them to themselves; when to listen to everything they have to say, and when just to shrug[2] and tell them to snap out of it[3].

Anyway, I'm not making any big claims for myself. I know carers, working now, who are just as good and don't get half the credit. If you're one of them, I can understand how you might get resentful – about my bedsit, my car, above all the way I get to pick and choose who I look after. And I'm a Hailsham* student – which is enough by itself sometimes to get people's backs up[4]. Kathy H., they say, she gets to pick and choose, and she always chooses her own kind: people from Hailsham, or one of the other privileged estates.

No wonder she has a great record. I've heard it said enough, so I'm sure you've heard it plenty more, and maybe there's something in it. But I'm not the first to be allowed to pick and choose, and I doubt if I'll be the last. And anyway, I've done my share of looking after donors brought up in every kind of place. By the time I finish, remember, I'll have done twelve years of this, and it's only for the last six they've let me choose. And why shouldn't they?

Carers aren't machines. You try and do your best for every donor, but in the end, it wears you down. You don't have unlimited patience and energy. So when you get a chance to choose, *of* course, you choose your own kind. That's natural. There's no way I could have gone on for as long as I have if I'd stopped feeling for my donors every step of the way.

Kazuo Ishiguro, *Never Let Me Go*, 2005.

* Hailsham: one of the special schools where people like Kathy were raised and educated.

1. hang around *(v.)* : *rester près (d'eux)*. 2. shrug *(v.)* : *hausser les épaules*.
3. snap out of it *(v.)* : *se secouer, se reprendre*.
4. get people's backs up : *taper sur les nerfs des gens*.

More help WBT n° 118

Grammar

Les subordonnées temporelles p. 156
- ***By the time I finish***, [...] *I'll have done twelve years of this.*

Les degrés de certitude (modaux) p. 157
- *It **may** be possible to grow new organs.*
- *We **might** be able to reach our long-dreamed of goal.*

Never Let Me Go (2010) based on the novel by Kazuo Ishiguro.

Explain the meaning

Explain these words: donor, carer.

Read and imagine

1. Say as much as you can about the narrator and imagine what her job consists in.
2. What sort of world is portrayed in the passage? Use your imagination, and use the links to check your guesses.
Go into detail. WBT n° 119

http://www.theguardian.com/books/2005/feb/26/bookerprize2005.bookerprize
http://www.shmoop.com/never-let-me-go/summary.html

Your task

Access this site:
http://www.bradaiken.com/SF-MedicineArticle.pdf
Work in groups. Work on one of the six parts of the online text and present it to the class. Explain what aspect of medicine it deals with and give examples of books to read or films to see. You may include a short synopsis of one book or film in your presentation.

Into space: but where

1 Space trips to become routine? B1

http://www.spacex.com/dragon
http://www.space.com/26063-spacex-unveils-dragon-v2-manned-spaceship.html

What do you think?

1. Comment on the title.
2. Do you think space flights will become routine any time soon? Give your reasons.

SpaceX and the ISS MP3 39

1. Listen to the recording and say as much as you can about SpaceX and its goals.
2. Would you like to take a trip to the ISS? Why/Why not? Go into detail. WBT n° 120

Help

- souped-up (adj.) : *gonflé (moteur)*
- manned (adj.) : *habité (vol)*
- vie [vaɪ] for (v.) : *être en compétition pour, rivaliser*

2 Space tourism in jeopardy? B1

It has been two weeks since a Virgin Galactic SpaceShipTwo crashed in the Mojave Desert. The crash was a big strike[1] against the company that is trying to create a commercial private space industry. Virgin Galactic CEO George Whitesides told a crowd Thursday that the company will continue pursuing its mission to take tourists to space.

"We have a new spaceship that's going to be ready in a few months," Mr. Whitesides said, according to *The Los Angeles Times*, "so we're going to make sure we get that one as safe as we can and keep going." Virgin Galactic is the brainchild[2] of British billionaire Richard Branson. He is planning to take tourists to space for $250,000 a piece. [...]

Bryan Cronan, *Christian Science Monitor*, November 14, 2014.

1. strike (n.) : *coup dur.* 2. brainchild (n.) : *idée personnelle.*

The remains of Virgin Galactic's SpaceShipTwo.

Tell the story

1. Say what you know about SpaceShipTwo.
2. Read the article and find out when and where the accident happened.
3. Say what Virgin Galactic's aims are now. Go into detail. WBT n° 121

Write about space

Comment on this quote from Richard Branson:
"There are so many exciting things happening now in the world of space. There's risk but there's great reward. So I think being unafraid to try new things is important as we move forward."
(150 words)

will it lead?

3 The final conquest

B2

Trantor, at the beginning of the thirteenth millennium...

Gaal was not certain whether the sun shone, or, for that matter, whether it was day or night. He was ashamed to ask. All the planet seemed to live beneath metal. [...] At first, he had eagerly followed the signs to the 'Sun-Room' and found it but a chamber for basking[1] in artificial radiation. He lingered a moment or two, then returned to the Luxor's main lobby. He said to the room clerk, "Where can I buy a ticket for a planetary tour?"

"Right here."

"When will it start?"

"You just missed it. Another one tomorrow. Buy a ticket now and we'll reserve a place for you."

"Oh." Tomorrow would be too late. He would have to be at the University tomorrow. He said, "There wouldn't be an observation tower – or something? I mean, in the open air?"

"Sure! Sell you a ticket for that, if you want. Better let me check if it's raining or not." He closed a contact at his elbow and read the flowing letters that raced across a frosted[2] screen. Gaal read with him.

The room clerk said, "Good weather. Come to think of it, I do believe it's the dry season now." He added, conversationally, "I don't bother with the outside myself. The last time I was in the open was three years ago. You see it once, you know, and that's all there is to it. Here's your ticket. Special elevator in the rear. It's marked 'To the Tower' Just take it." [...]

He stepped out upon an open terrace bathed in a white brilliance that hurt his eyes. [...] He could not see the ground. It was lost in the ever-increasing complexities of man-made structures. He could see no horizon other than that of metal against sky, stretching out to almost uniform grayness, and he knew it was so over all the land-surface of the planet. There was scarcely any motion to be seen – a few pleasure-craft lazed against the sky – but all the busy traffic of billions of men was going on, he knew, beneath the metal skin of the world.

There was no green to be seen; no green, no soil, no life other than man. Somewhere on the world, he realized vaguely, was the Emperor's palace, set amid[3] one hundred square miles of natural soil, green with trees, rainbowed with flowers. It was a small island amid an ocean of steel, but it wasn't visible from where he stood. It might be ten thousand miles away. He did not know.

Before very long, he must have his tour!

He sighed noisily, and realised finally that he was on Trantor at last; on the planet which was the center of all the Galaxy and the kernel[4] of the human race. [...] He was not aware of a jugular vein delicately connecting the forty billion of Trantor with the rest of the Galaxy. He was conscious only of the mightiest deed[5] of man; the complete and almost contemptuously final conquest of a world.

Isaac Asimov, *Foundation*, 1951.

1. bask (v) : *se dorer*. 2. frosted (adj.) : *(ici) dépoli*. 3. amid (prep.) : *parmi*.
4. kernel (n.) : *noyau*. 5. deed (n.) : *acte, exploit*.

More help WBT n° 122

Read and explain

1. Read the introductory sentence and say where and when the story is set.
2. Describe the unusual sensation Gaal had when he arrived on Trantor.
3. What tour did he intend to go on?
4. Explain what kind of world Gaal has come to.

Go into detail. WBT n° 123

Role play

Gaal goes back to the planet where he lives and is interviewed about Trantor by a journalist. Prepare and act out the interview. Gaal should talk about what he felt, what surprised him and exactly what he saw.

Your task

Some dystopian societies are depicted in books and films you have heard of. Choose one and present it to the class.

Improve your

VOCABULARY

1 Science

1. Verbs or nouns? MP3 40

Listen to the sentences. They are said in an American accent.
Each contains one or more of the following words: experiment, progress, research, test.

– Identify the words and say if they are used as verbs or nouns.

– Comment on the pronunciation of "progress" and "research".

2. British and American MP3 41

Listen to the first three sentences again. This time they are said in a British accent.
Comment on the pronunciation of "progress", "research" and "laboratory".

2 Medicine

1. Match the nouns on the left to their definitions or explanations. WBT n° 124

a disease •	• a problem with blood supply to the brain
a transplant •	• a definitive solution that gets rid of a disease
a pacemaker •	• a sort of photograph that shows the inside of your body
a stroke •	• when blood stops flowing to your heart
a heart attack •	• a device that helps your heart to beat regularly
an X-ray •	• the result of an invasion of the body by agents that cause a disease
a cure •	• the act of replacing one of the body's organs, for example
(an) infection •	• an illness

2. Use the 8 nouns above to complete these sentences.

a. He felt a lot of pain when walking, so he had ...... done. It showed that he had broken a small bone in his foot.

b. She only had a minor ...... but, although there was no long-term brain damage, she couldn't speak properly for some time.

c. Since he's had his ...... fitted, he's been able to walk longer distances without getting short of breath.

d. Malaria is a tropical ...... caused by mosquitoes.

e. Dr Christian Barnard was the first surgeon to do a successful heart ...... in 1967.

f. Everyone hopes that one day soon scientists will find ...... for cancer.

g. If you cut yourself, you should wash the cut with an antiseptic solution in order to prevent ....

h. One of the symptoms of ...... is pain in your left arm.

3 Space

Expressions

a. Check that you know the meaning of the following words and expressions.

b. Use some of the words to describe the picture.

gravity • jet pack • oxygen supply • run out of • spacecraft • spacesuit • stranded • weightless(ness)

A picture based on a scene from the movie *Gravity* (2013).

FINAL TASK

The New Frontier: a slideshow

The US government is developing the concept of founding an American settlement somewhere in outer space. The settlement will be called The New Frontier and must represent the "New American Dream". They have asked different teams of experts to present projects to a government commission, in the form of a slideshow.

1 Choose your role

- Work in groups of four or more.
- You are members of one **team of experts**. The team must be made up of experts on all the different aspects of the project (**scientists, architects, engineers...**). Decide on your individual roles.

2 Prepare your slideshow

- Cover the following points:

• where The New Frontier will be (the moon, Mars, an asteroid, a free-floating space colony, etc.) • access to energy • access to water • food • clothes • means of transportation • means of communication • construction materials and architecture • simulated gravity • life in space in general

- Make sure your project can be considered as the **New American Dream.**
- Be creative! Use **drawings, photos** and **diagrams** in your slideshow.

3 Present your slideshow

- The **commission** (the rest of the class) asks questions and then the whole class votes and chooses **the best project.**

PREPARE FOR THE BAC

Expression orale

FICHE MÉTHODE PAGE 161

Sujet

L'idée de progrès

Modalités de l'épreuve

- **Tirage au sort** de l'une des quatre notions sur lesquelles porte le programme du cycle terminal.
- **Préparation** de l'exposé. **(10 min.)**
- **Exposé oral en continu**, en anglais : présentation de la notion. **(5 min.)**
- **Expression orale en interaction** : conversation entre l'examinateur et l'élève. **(5 min.)**

Série L
- Le candidat apporte ses dossiers constitués dans l'année. L'examinateur choisit la notion.
- Préparation (10 min.). Exposé oral en continu (10 min.). Expression orale en interaction. (10 min.)

Attention : *les citations ci-dessous sont proposées dans le cadre d'un entraînement ; elles fournissent des pistes pour préparer votre épreuve pendant l'année.*
Le jour de l'épreuve, aucun document ne vous sera fourni.

Progress

The best road to progress is freedom's road.

John F. Kennedy (1917-1963), 35th US President.

Progress is a nice word. But change is its motivator. And change has its enemies.

Robert Kennedy (1925-1968), US politician.

There are no constraints on the human mind, no walls around the human spirit, no barriers to our progress except those we ourselves erect.

Ronald Reagan (1911-2004), 40th US President.

The future

For time and the world do not stand still. Change is the law of life. And those who look only to the past or the present are certain to miss the future.

John F. Kennedy (1917-1963), 35th US President.

It is not in the stars to hold our destiny but in ourselves.

William Shakespeare (1564-1616), English poet and dramatist.

It is always wise to look ahead, but difficult to look further than you can see.

Sir Winston Churchill (1874-1965),
British Prime Minister 1940-45 & 1951-1955.

La notion de progrès peut se rapporter à des domaines très différents : l'écologie, la communication, la médecine, la science, etc. Les trois chapitres que vous avez étudiés vous permettent d'avoir différents de points de vue sur la notion. Suivez les étapes ci-dessous pour construire votre présentation.

Fiche méthode	Application guidée
Étape 1 Constituer un dossier	
→ Pour préparer votre présentation orale, créez un **dossier sur la notion**. Attention, seuls les élèves de la série L pourront apporter ce dossier le jour de l'épreuve !	→ Le dossier doit regrouper les différents aspects de la notion traités dans l'année (*solving environmental problems, advances in medicine, space travel*, etc.) et comporter différents supports (images, textes, enregistrements...).
Étape 2 Trouver la problématique et construire le plan	
→ La **problématique** est la question que l'on pose dans l'introduction et à laquelle on répond dans la conclusion. Vous devez toujours vous demander si vous pouvez répondre à votre question avec les arguments et les exemples que vous donnez. → Le **plan** peut être thématique ou binaire (présenter deux points de vue différents). Deux parties suffisent.	→ **Exemples de problématiques** • *Is global warming a myth?* (p. 117) • *What will the cities of tomorrow be like?* (p. 120-121) • *To what extent will machines replace doctors?* (p. 135) → Votre plan peut être thématique (*What effect will advances in genetics have on our lives?*, p. 148-150) ou binaire (*Stem-cells: a chance to cure all diseases or a moral dilemma*, p. 150).
Étape 3 Rédiger l'introduction	
→ L'introduction doit contenir **plusieurs éléments** : – une définition générale de la notion ; – la présentation du sujet choisi ; – l'annonce de la problématique ; – l'annonce du plan.	→ Pour la **définition** de la notion, appuyez-vous sur les mots clés des chapitres étudiés ou sur une citation que vous aurez apprise dans l'année (ex. p. 160). **Exemple :** *Progress: developments in science and technology / an improvement in our quality of life / making the world a better place to live in.*
Étape 4 Rédiger la conclusion	
→ Elle doit être la **synthèse** de tout ce que vous avez dit, mais elle doit aussi permettre d'**élargir votre problématique** de départ. Vous devez donc proposer une ouverture, la plupart du temps sous forme de question. La conclusion est la dernière chose qu'entend votre auditoire. Elle doit donc être soignée.	→ **Élargir la problématique** Exemples : • *How can people be made more aware of environmental problems?* (p. 116-121) • *Will we be living under the sea in 100 years time?* (p. 121) • *Do we trust machines too much?* (p. 135-137)
Étape 5 Mettre au point le développement	
→ C'est la **partie principale** de votre présentation. Entraînez-vous à préparer vos notes sous forme de mots-clés, de façon à ne pas lire votre présentation mot à mot.	→Pour chaque partie, écrivez sur votre plan : les mots-clés (*global warming / greenhouse effect / ice caps / climate change, etc.*), les supports choisis (textes, photographie, etc.), les connecteurs logiques utiles ! (voir p. 226)

Your turn!

Pour améliorer votre aisance à l'oral, entraînez-vous devant un miroir ou une webcam et chronométrez-vous. Essayez de ne pas trop lire vos notes. Faites un effort de prononciation car celle-ci est évaluée au même titre que le contenu de votre présentation.

Cloning the dog

The afternoon before, during her interview – but it wasn't really an interview because the Strikers had already made up their minds and if she'd refused them they would have kept raising the hourly[1] till she capitulated – the two of them, Gretchen and Cliff, had positioned themselves on either side of her and leaned into the bar over caramel-colored scotches and a platter of ebi and maguro sushi to explain the situation. Just so that she was clear on it. "You know what cloning is, right?" Gretchen said. "Or what it involves? You remember Dolly?"

Nisha was holding fast to her drink, her left elbow pressed to the brass rail of the bar in the family room. She'd just reached out her twinned chopsticks[2] for a second piece of the shrimp, but withdrew her hand. "You mean the country singer?"

"The sheep[3]," the husband said.

"The first cloned mammal," Gretchen put in. "Or larger mammal."

"Yeah," she said, nodding. "Sure. I guess."

What followed was a short course in genetics and the method of somatic cell nuclear transplant that had given the world Dolly, various replicated cattle[4], pigs and hamsters, and now Admiral II, the first cloned dog made available commercially through SalvaPet, Inc., the genetic engineering firm with offices in Seoul, San Juan and Cleveland.

Gretchen's voice constricted as she described how they'd taken a cell from the lining of Admiral's ear just after the accident and inserted it into a donor egg, which had had its nucleus removed, stimulated the cell to divide through the application of an electric current, and then inserted the developing embryo into the uterus of a host mother[5] – "The sweetest golden retriever you ever saw. What was her name, Cliff? Some flower, wasn't it?"

"Peony."

"Peony? Are you sure?"

"Of course I'm sure."

"I thought it was – oh, I don't know. You sure it wasn't Iris?"

"The point is," he said, setting his glass down and leveling his gaze on Nisha, "you can get a genetic copy of the animal, a kind of three-dimensional Xerox, but that doesn't guarantee it'll be like the one you, well, the one you lost."

"It was so sad," Gretchen said.

"It's nurture[6] that counts. You've got to reproduce the animal's experiences, as nearly as possible." He gave a shrug, reached for the bottle. "You want another?" he asked, and she held out her glass. "Of course we're both older now – and so are you, we realize that – but we want to come as close as possible to replicating the exact conditions that made Admiral what he was, right down to the toys we gave him, the food, the schedule of walks and play and all the rest. Which is where you come in –"

"We need a commitment here, Nisha," Gretchen breathed, leaning in so close Nisha could smell the scotch coming back at her. "Four years. That's how long you were with him last time. Or with Admiral, I mean. The original Admiral."

The focus of all this deliberation had fallen asleep in Gretchen's lap. A single probing finger of sunlight stabbed through the window to illuminate the pale fluff over the dog's eyes. At that moment, in that light, little Admiral looked like some strange conjunction of ostrich and ape.

Nisha couldn't help thinking of The Island of Dr. Moreau, the cheesy[7] version with Marlon Brando looking as if he'd been genetically manipulated himself, and she would

1. hourly (adj.) = hourly rate (n.) : *tarif horaire.*
2. twinned chopsticks (n.) : *paire de baguettes.*
3. Dolly = name of the first cloned sheep / first name of Dolly Parton, American singer of country music.
4. cattle (n.) : *bétail.*
5. host mother (n.) : *mère porteuse.*
6. nurture (n.) : *éducation.*
7. cheesy (adj.) : *kitsch.*
8. trigger (n.) : *gachette.*

The world's first ever cloned dog.

have grinned a private grin, fueled by the scotch and the thundering absurdity of the moment, but she had to hide everything she thought or felt behind a mask of impassivity. She wasn't committing to anything for four years – four years? If she was still living here in this craphole of a town four years from now she promised herself she'd go out and buy a gun and eliminate all her problems with a single, very personal squeeze of the trigger[9].

That was what she was thinking when Gretchen said, "We'll pay you twenty dollars an hour," and the husband said, "With health care – and dental," and they both stared at her so fiercely she had to look down into her glass before she found her voice. "Twenty-five," she said.

And oh, how they loved that dog, because they never hesitated. "Twenty-five it is," the husband said, and Gretchen, a closer's smile blooming on her face, produced a contract from the folder at her elbow. "Just sign here," she said.

T. Coraghessan Boyle, "Admiral" in *Wild Child*, 2010.

Read and understand

1. Name the three main characters and define their relationships.
2. Who was Admiral and what happened to him?
3. What shows that the Strikers are still moved by that event? (several possible answers)
4. Explain the name Admiral II.
5. Use your own words to explain what SalvaPet, Inc. is.
6. Explain why the Strikers are so anxious to hire the young woman.
7. What is her first reaction to their proposal?
8. How do you explain her answer?

Go further LVA/LELE

1. Reading this passage, what can you deduce about the Strikers' family life?
2. Would you say that the Strikers are rather poor or well-off? Give your reasons.
3. Do you think that the main character will abide by the contract? Why?
4. What category of writing would you place this extract in? Give your reasons.
5. Comment on the way the author treats his characters.
6. How would you link this extract to the notion of progress?

The Thing in the Forest

Still from *The Island of Dr Moreau*, directed by John Frankenheimer, 1996.

The narrator is a man who has been shipwrecked on a strange tropical island.

I strode through the undergrowth[1] that clothed the ridge behind the house, scarcely heeding[2] whither I went; passed on through the shadow of a thick cluster of straight-stemmed trees beyond it, and so presently found myself some way on the other side of the ridge, and descending towards a streamlet that ran through a narrow valley. [...]

I let my eyes wander over this scene for a while, and then began to turn over in my mind again the strange peculiarities of Montgomery's man. But it was too hot to think elaborately, and presently I fell into a tranquil state midway between dozing and waking.

From this I was aroused, after I know not how long, by a rustling amidst the greenery on the other side of the stream. For a moment I could see nothing but the waving summits of the ferns and reeds. Then suddenly upon the bank of the stream appeared Something– at first I could not distinguish what it was. It bowed its round head to the water, and began to drink. Then I saw it was a man, going on all-fours like a beast. He was clothed in bluish cloth, and was of a copper-coloured hue[3], with black hair. It seemed that grotesque ugliness was an invariable character of these islanders. I could hear the suck of the water at his lips as he drank.

I leant forward to see him better, and a piece of lava, detached by my hand, went pattering down the slope. He looked up guiltily, and his eyes met mine. Forthwith he scrambled to his feet, and stood wiping his clumsy hand across his mouth and regarding me. His legs were scarcely half the length of his body. So, staring one another out of countenance, we remained for perhaps the space of a minute. Then, stopping to look back once or twice, he slunk[4] off among the bushes to the right of me, and I heard the swish of the fronds grow faint in the distance and die away. Long after he had disappeared, I remained sitting up staring in the direction of his retreat. My drowsy tranquillity had gone. [...]

I looked around me rather nervously, and regretted that I was unarmed. Then I thought that the man I had just seen had been clothed in bluish cloth, had not been naked as a savage would have been; and I tried to persuade myself from that fact that he was after all probably a peaceful character, that the dull ferocity of his countenance belied[5] him.

1. undergrowth (n.) : *sous-bois.*
2. heed (v.) : *faire attention à.*
3. hue (n.) : *couleur, nuance.*
4. slink (slunk, slunk) (v.) : *se déplacer furtivement.*
5. belie [bɪˈlaɪ] (v.) : *démentir.*
6. hardihood (n.) : *dureté.*
7. scant (adj.) bristly (adj.) : *raides et épars.*
8. gibberish [ˈdʒɪbərɪʃ] (n.) : *charabia.*
9. lank (adj.) : *sans vie.*
10. tangle (n.) : *enchevêtrement.*

Yet I was greatly disturbed at the apparition. I walked to the left along the slope, turning my head about and peering this way and that among the straight stems of the trees. Why should a man go on all-fours and drink with his lips? Presently I heard an animal wailing again, and taking it to be the puma, I turned about and walked in a direction diametrically opposite to the sound. This led me down to the stream, across which I stepped and pushed my way up through the undergrowth beyond. [...]

The vague dread that had been in my mind since I had seen the inhuman face of the man at the stream grew distincter as I stood there. I began to realise the hardihood[6] of my expedition among these unknown people. The thicket about me became altered to my imagination. Every shadow became something more than a shadow, – became an ambush; every rustle became a threat. Invisible things seemed watching me. I resolved to go back to the enclosure on the beach. I suddenly turned away and thrust myself violently, possibly even frantically, through the bushes, anxious to get a clear space about me again. [...]

Before me, squatting together upon the fungoid ruins of a huge fallen tree and still unaware of my approach, were three grotesque human figures. One was evidently a female; the other two were men. They were naked, save for swathings of scarlet cloth about the middle; and their skins were of a dull pinkish-drab colour, such as I had seen in no savages before. They had fat, heavy, chinless faces, retreating foreheads, and a scant bristly[7] hair upon their heads. I never saw such bestial-looking creatures.

They were talking, or at least one of the men was talking to the other two, and all three had been too closely interested to heed the rustling of my approach. They swayed their heads and shoulders from side to side. The speaker's words came thick and sloppy, and though I could hear them distinctly I could not distinguish what he said. He seemed to me to be reciting some complicated gibberish[8]. Presently his articulation became shriller, and spreading his hands he rose to his feet. At that the others began to gibber in unison, also rising to their feet, spreading their hands and swaying their bodies in rhythm with their chant. I noticed then the abnormal shortness of their legs, and their lank[9], clumsy feet. All three began slowly to circle round, raising and stamping their feet and waving their arms; a kind of tune crept into their rhythmic recitation, and a refrain,– "Aloola," or "Balloola," it sounded like. Their eyes began to sparkle, and their ugly faces to brighten, with an expression of strange pleasure. Saliva dripped from their lipless mouths. [...]

I turned as noiselessly as possible, and becoming every now and then rigid with the fear of being discovered, as a branch cracked or a leaf rustled, I pushed back into the bushes. It was long before I grew bolder, and dared to move freely. My only idea for the moment was to get away from these foul beings, and I scarcely noticed that I had emerged upon a faint pathway amidst the trees. Then suddenly traversing a little glade, I saw with an unpleasant start two clumsy legs among the trees, walking with noiseless footsteps parallel with my course, and perhaps thirty yards away from me. The head and upper part of the body were hidden by a tangle[10] of creeper. I stopped abruptly, hoping the creature did not see me. The feet stopped as I did. So nervous was I that I controlled an impulse to headlong flight with the utmost difficulty. Then looking hard, I distinguished through the interlacing network the head and body of the brute I had seen drinking. He moved his head. There was an emerald flash in his eyes as he glanced at me from the shadow of the trees, a half-luminous colour that vanished as he turned his head again. He was motionless for a moment, and then with a noiseless tread began running through the green confusion. In another moment he had vanished behind some bushes.

H. G. Wells, *The Island of Dr Moreau*, 1896.

Read and understand

1. Where is the narrator? In your own words, describe the scene that his eyes wandered over (l. 6).
2. Find all the distinguishing features of the "something" the narrator sees (l. 13).
3. Quote from the text to show that the narrator thinks the thing might be less dangerous than it looks.
4. Compare the "three grotesque human figures" (l. 47) that the narrator next sees with the "something" in line 13. What do they have in common and in what way do they differ?
5. What does the narrator wish to do when he has seen these other strange islanders? Quote from the text.
6. What follows him?
7. Quote from the text and use your own words to show how the narrator's state of mind changes throughout the extract.
8. Who do you think is more scared of the other? Give your reasons.

Go further LVA/LELE

1. This novel belongs to several categories of writing. Which ones? Explain your choices.
2. How does the writer manage to make his character's tale sound real?
3. What gives the story a very modern touch?
4. What suggests that the narrator has landed in a dystopian world?

Chapter 10

Power and influence

Improve your skills

Cross culture

Improve your grammar

Improve your vocabulary

Final task

Prepare for the Bac

1 A campain to boycott KFC because of alleged cruelty to chickens.

3 Crowning the "prom queen" at an American high school end-of-year dance.

2 Online shopping: the supermarket at your fingertips.

React !

1. Describe the pictures in detail. What sort of power or influence is illustrated in each one?
2. Which photos deal with "the American way of life"? Do they show positive or negative aspects? Or both?
3. Do any of the photos reflect your own ambitions, wishes or views? If so, which one(s)? Give your reasons.

Improve your SKILLS

Power at school

1 Having your say

B1

Maggie Atkinson, the children's commissioner for England, says: "A school council is a formal method of taking young people's views into account... This is not about putting children in charge. Rather, it is about listening to their concerns and using their experience as the main users of school services to make improvements."

And yet, in research for Atkinson's office by the National Foundation for Educational Research, just two-fifths of children thought school councils were an effective way of listening to their ideas, and a quarter did not. [...] "Our school made a big fuss about it at the start of the year," says Caroline, a Year 11[1] student in London, "but when they even bother to get us into a council meeting, no matter what we say, nothing happens. It's just a bit pointless." School council elections are the worst face of democracy," says one teacher in Newcastle. "It's just a popularity contest, and the quiet, sensible ones get sidelined[2]." [...]

So why are councils necessary? It's important that people have a say in the way their lives are run – these individuals are policy-makers in training. Treat a child like an adult, they act like an adult.

Tom Bennet, *The Guardian*, March 12, 2012.

1. Year 11 = the fifth year of secondary school in the UK (16-17 year-olds).
2. sideline (v.) : *mettre sur la touche (fig.)*.

More help WBT n° 125

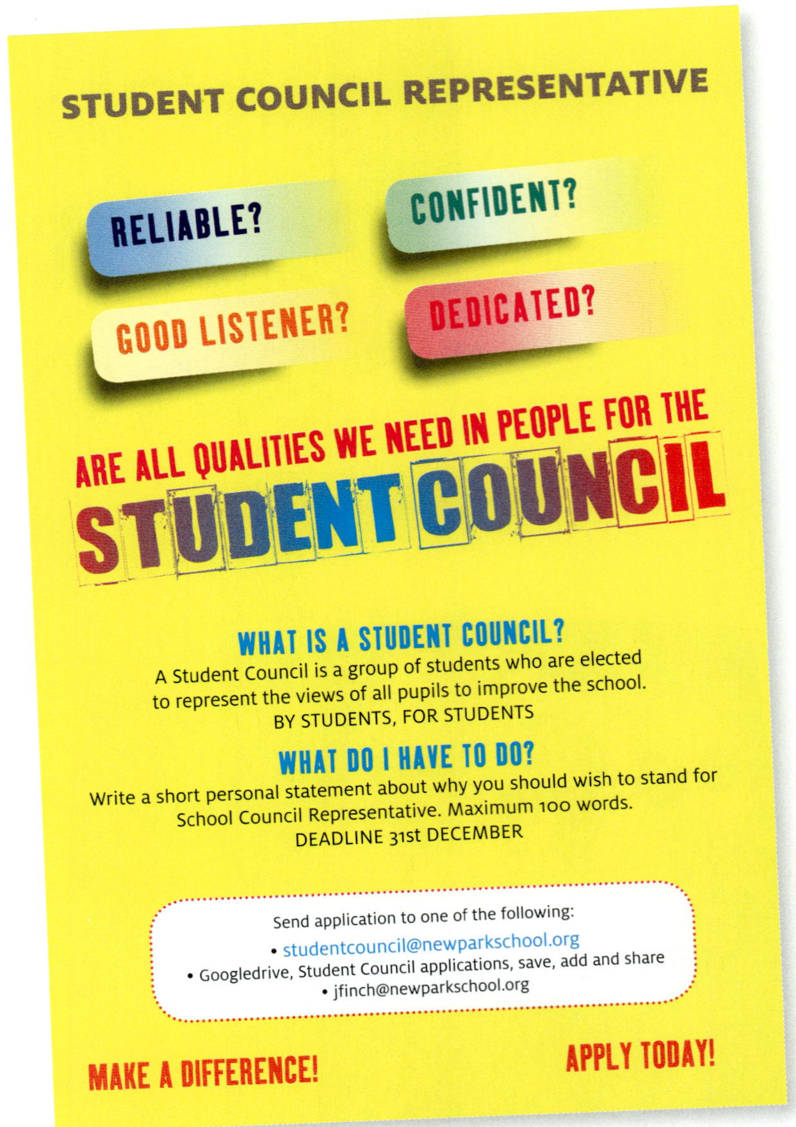

Talk about the poster

Say what the poster tells you about student councils (also called school councils) and the people who are on them.

Read and comment

1. Say what the purpose of a school council is.
2. Does the article present a positive or a negative view of school councils? Give your reasons.
Go into detail. WBT n° 126

What do you think?

Work in groups and look at the four qualities (listed on the poster) required of student council members. What other qualities would you add to the list? Compare your views in a class discussion.

Write an application

You attend the school whose student council put up the poster above. You think you have the right qualities to be on the council. Follow the instructions on the poster and write your personal statement. (100 words)

2 Are you one of us or not? B1

Brainstorm

From the title, the picture and the caption, guess what the movie *Mean Girls* is all about.

Listen and comment MP3 42

1. Link the recording to the picture and the caption. Say how many people are talking and who they are.
2. Say as much as you can about the rules of "Girl World".

Go into detail. WBT n° 127

What do you think?

How is the recording linked to the chapter title (Power and influence) and to the title of this double page?

The Plastics – a group of three girls who "queen" it over the other high school students – and new girl, Cady... From the movie *Mean Girls* based on the book *Queen Bees and Wannabees* by Rosalind Wiseman.

3 Is popularity a good thing? B1

Mitchell J. Prinstein, a professor and director of clinical psychology at the University of North Carolina, outlines[1] the way researchers often look at popularity: there are the students he calls "high status," like the student council president or the captain of the football team.

"Some of the most popular kids are very much disliked by other kids," he said. This may be partly envy, but sometimes these standout[2] teenagers can be bullies or part of the mean-girl clique.

Another kind of popularity is what Professor Prinstein calls "likeability." That is how much a person is liked or preferred by peers – someone other people enjoy hanging out with on a Saturday night. [...]

Surveys estimate that about 20 percent of students in any school are highly liked, about 50 percent are average – having some friends, but not necessarily a lot – and the rest are considered neglected or rejected students. These are either ignored or actively disliked.

Alina Tugend, *The New York Times*, June 18, 2010.

1. outline (v.) : *exposer*. 2. standout (adj.) : *exceptionnel*.

Read and explain

1. Say what you find out about popular kids (status, character...).
2. Say if there is a difference between popularity and likeability.

Go into detail. WBT n° 128

Your task

Work in groups of five or more. You are the members of a student council. You have noticed that a lot of students don't have many friends and don't take part in school activities. You must come up with ways to involve more students in school life. Present your ideas to the class.

Consumer influence

1 Consumer rights B1

The *Which?* mission is to make individuals as powerful as the organisations they have to deal with in their daily lives. We identify where consumers are experiencing problems, and through programmes of research, debate and consumer dialogue we develop effective, practical policy solutions.

Energy and Environment

All consumers should have access to a secure and affordable[1] energy supply and reliable information on the environmental impacts of products and services they use.

Food

All consumers should have access to safe, affordable, nutritious and good quality food that enables healthy lifestyles and informed choices.

Health

Consumers should have access to quality health care and good information about it so that they can make decisions with confidence.

Housing

Buying or letting[2] a home is one of the largest financial transactions many consumers make and also meets[3] a primary need. Consumers need access to clear information to help inform choice and access to protection and redress if things go wrong.

Travel and Transport

Consumers need transport services that provide safety, value for money, choice and information on travel rights and redress.

Public services

Consumers should have access to clear information and advice about public services such as education, health and social care and access to redress when things go wrong.

which.co.uk

1. affordable (adj.) : *abordable*. 2. let (v.) : (ici) *louer*.
3. meet (v.) : (ici) *répondre à*.

Which?, the monthly magazine of the Consumer Association in the UK.

Look and explain

Look at the picture and the caption and explain why the magazine is called *Which?*

Read and comment

1. Read quickly through the text and say what its purpose is.
2. Find all the words that are repeated and say why they are important.

Go into detail. WBT n° 129

2 A victory for consumers? B1 B2

1. soda fountain (n.) : *buvette*.

More help WBT n° 130

Comment

Comment on the visual. What does it show?

Watch and explain DVD MP3 43

1. Say what the video is about and relate it to the title and the visual.
2. Give the arguments for and against the ban.

Go into detail. WBT n° 131

For or against?

In your opinion, who was right: the Board of Health or the judge? If you had been the judge, what would you have done and why? Exchange your views.

3 Online shopping: a consumer paradise? B2

Thanks to the internet, the consumer is finally seizing power. [...] Trading on shoppers' ignorance will no longer be possible: people will know – and soon tell others, even those without the internet – that prices in the next town are cheaper or that certain goods are inferior. [...]

This is changing the nature of consumer decisions. Until recently, consumers usually learned about a product and made their choice at the same time. People would often visit a department store or dealership[1] to seek advice from a salesman, look at his recommendations and then buy.

Now, for many, each of these steps is separate. For instance, Ford is finding that eight out of ten of its customers have already used the internet to decide what car they want to buy – and what they are willing to pay – even before they arrive at a showroom. [...]

But the consumer's choice is about to become even greater. [...] At a touch, consumers will be able to find a local store and then check the offers from nearby outlets even as they browse the aisles, or listen to a salesman. When that happens consumers will truly be kings, and only those firms ready and able to serve these new monarchs will survive.

The Economist, March 31, 2005.

1. dealership (n.) : *concession*.

More help WBT n° 132

Read and explain

1. According to the article, what is the internet doing for consumers?
2. Explain how things are changing and how consumers have gained power.

Go into detail. WBT n° 133

Discuss online shopping

The article was written in 2005. From your own experience, do you think its predictions have come true? Exchange your views.

Grammar

L'auxiliaire modal *should* p. 176

- *All consumers **should** have access to a secure and affordable energy supply*

Your task

Work in groups and choose one of the sectors mentioned in the *Which?* text. Using the criteria laid down by *Which?*, decide if consumers in your own country already have the powers they should have. If not, list the changes that should be made. Present your conclusions to the class.

Improve your SKILLS

The power to say no

1 Bad food? Bad service? Complain! B1

1 Act immediately

The key to successful complaining is to highlight the problem right away, thereby giving the restaurant the opportunity to resolve the problem with minimum fuss.

2 Remain calm and objective

Discreetly call the waiter over, explain the problem, express your disappointment, and ask him or her to resolve the situation. Do not automatically blame the waiter; keep in mind that a long wait for food or a dish that is not cooked to your satisfaction is probably the fault of the chef rather than the server.

3 Suggest a resolution that matches your complaint

Would an apology be enough? Would you like your food replaced? Do you want a discount? Whatever it is, be sure to ask or politely suggest rather than demand.

4 Take it to the next level

If your concerns are not met with an acceptable resolution, ask politely to speak to the manager. Explain the problem to him or her, and state why you are not satisfied with how it has been resolved.

5 Seek outside help

If after complaining to the waiter and the manager you are still dissatisfied, it's time to take your complaints to a higher authority. Contact your local consumer standards body for advice. In the UK, for example, you can try the Citizen's Advice Bureau or the Office of Fair Trading1. In the US, contact your local Better Business Bureau office.

Adapted from http://www.wikihow.com/Complain-in-a-Restaurant.

1. trading (n.) : *commerce.*

More help WBT n° 134

Read and comment

1. Does the picture reflect the advice given in the text? Why/Why not? Give your reasons.
2. Find the two reasons for complaint that are mentioned as well as the possible solutions.
Go into detail. WBT n° 135

Role play

Work in groups of three: a dissatisfied customer, a waiter/waitress who does not manage to provide a satisfactory solution, and a manager/manageress. Imagine the customer's problem and act out the conversation. The rest of the class must decide if you have kept to the guidelines in the text or not.

2 Disobeying the law? B2

Describe and comment

Using the caption to help you, say as much as you can about the picture.

Listen and explain MP3 44

1. Say what happened in 2004 and how Jason felt about it.
2. Give the arguments for and against the ban.
3. Do you think Jason has disobeyed the law? Give your reasons. Go into detail. WBT n° 136

What do you think?

Think about Jason's arguments with regard to disobeying the law. Do you agree with him? In what circumstances might you do the same? Exchange your views.

In 2004, hunt supporters said they would disobey any ban on hunting.

3 The boycott: a tactic of protest B1 B2

Captain Charles Boycott was a landlord's agent a man whose job was to collect rents from tenant farmers[1] on an estate in northwest Ireland. At the time, landlords, many of whom were British, were exploiting Irish tenant farmers, and, as part of a protest, the farmers on the estate where Boycott worked demanded a reduction in their rents. Boycott refused their demands, and evicted some tenants.

The Irish Land League advocated that people in the area not attack Boycott, but rather use a new tactic: refuse to do business with him at all. This new form of protest was effective, as Boycott wasn't able to get workers to harvest crops. And by the end of 1880, newspapers in Britain began using the word the way we know it today, not as a person's proper name, but as a tactic of protest.

Robert McNamara, about.com

1. tenant farmer (n.) : *fermier locataire.*

More help WBT n° 137

Caricature of Charles Boycott by Spy (Leslie Ward) in 1881.

Read and explain

1. Say why Irish farmers protested and how Boycott reacted.
2. Explain how the farmers achieved their objectives.

http://www.theguardian.com/vital-signs/2015/jan/06/boycotts-shopping-protests-activists-consumers
http://listverse.com/2011/09/03/10-famous-boycott

Grammar

La traduction de « il y a » p. 177

- ***There were*** *many people [...] who said they would refuse.*
- ***There have been*** *fox hunts here for hundreds of years.*
- ***There would be*** *a policeman knocking on my door.*

Your task

Since the time of Captain Boycott, there have been numerous campaigns to boycott goods that have been thought to be harmful to humans, to society or to the planet. Work in pairs and find out as much as you can about one such boycott (the links will help you). Present a slideshow, making it clear what happened, why, and whether it was succesful or not.

CROSS CULTURE

The appearance of power

In order to acquire and exercise power, it is often important to take on the appearance of power. This may be in your physical appearance or in the symbols of power around you...

Elizabeth I

The *Armada portrait* by George Gower was painted when the queen was 55. Her hands and face were covered with white make-up to conform to the ideals of beauty of the time.

Queen of England from 1559 to 1603, the "Virgin Queen" became the most powerful monarch in Europe, especially after the defeat of the Spanish Armada in 1588. One of the ways she maintained power was to appear more perfect than any other woman. Official portraits had to portray her as having ageless beauty.

In the film *Elizabeth* (Shekhar Kapur, 1998), the queen (Cate Blanchett) undergoes a de-humanising makeover in order to command the respect of her subjects and of the powerful men who surround her.

Margaret Thatcher

The "Iron Lady", Prime Minister of the UK from 1979 to 1990, was both loved and hated for her right-wing policies. In order to impose her views, she realised that she had to look and sound powerful. She changed her hairstyle, her clothes (notably getting rid of hats) and deepened her voice.

Mrs Thatcher looking her most powerful: a distinctive – and extravagant – hairstyle, a tailored suit and an air of authority.

Kennedy with his wife, Jackie, campaigning in 1960.

When **John F. Kennedy** became President in 1961, he was only 43. He was the first President to use the media to cultivate an image that was closer to that of a singer or a movie star than that of a politician. He knew it was important that he and his family should appear young, attractive, fashionable and accessible.

Sir Winston Churchill

Churchill by Graham Sutherland (1954). Revered statesman or grumpy old man?

In 1954, Parliament commissioned a portrait of Britain's Prime Minister and most revered statesman, Sir Winston Churchill, who had led Britain during World War II. Churchill, aged 80, was furious when he saw it. He said the painter had made him look like a sad, grumpy old man and not someone who had brought victory and peace to his country. The picture was never put on public display and was destroyed by Lady Churchill after her husband's death.

When Roosevelt took the oath on becoming President, the official photograph showed him standing up.

Franklin D. Roosevelt

President of the USA from 1933 to 1945, Roosevelt was a political giant: his "New Deal" got the USA out of the depression and his foreign policy was instrumental in the winning of World War II. However, he suffered from polio and was almost unable to walk. Fearing that he would lose credibility if the public knew of this "weakness", he was never photographed in his wheelchair.

Activities

1. Compare the attitudes of Roosevelt and Kennedy to power. In what way do they reflect changes in American society?
2. Find out more about the symbols of power (a) in portraits of Queen Elizabeth I, and (b) on the Great Seal of the USA (see the links).

What symbols would you use to represent the power of a Head of State or a nation? Give your reasons.

- http://www.rmg.co.uk/explore/sea-and-ships/in-depth/elizabeth/representing-the-queen/symbols-and-emblems-used-in-elizabeth-portraiture
- http://www.statesymbolsusa.org/National_Symbols/USA_Seal.html

Improve your
GRAMMAR

L'auxiliaire modal *should* (PG p.238)

MÉMO

Quelle est l'origine de ce modal ?

- *Should* est la forme passée du modal *shall*.
- Étymologiquement, *shall* est dérivé de l'allemand *sollen* qui exprime le plus souvent le devoir moral, le doute, ou la supposition.

Quelles sont les diverses valeurs de should ?

Selon les contextes, *should* exprime :
- un degré de doute ou de certitude de l'énonciateur ;
- l'éventualité ;
- l'obligation morale, le conseil ou le reproche.

N.B. Plusieurs de ces valeurs peuvent être présentes dans le même *should*.

Comment should est-il traduit ?

Selon les emplois, il se traduit le plus souvent par le présent du conditionnel ou l'imparfait de l'indicatif.

Ex. : *That should make her happy.* → Cela devrait lui faire plaisir.

Should you see her... → Si par hasard tu la voyais...

You should be nicer to her. → Tu devrais être plus gentil *avec elle.*

Observez et raisonnez

(texte p. 170 et vidéo p. 173)

- *All consumers should have access to a secure and affordable energy supply*
- *If it should be the case that a law is unjust [...].*

1 Identifiez le rôle joué par *should* dans ces énoncés (doute, certitude, éventualité, conseil...) et justifiez votre réponse.

2 Quel verbe français permet de traduire ce *should* ? À quel temps et à quel mode ?

3 Traduisez les phrases.

Entraînez-vous

1 Cartoon fun

a. Que fait l'énonciateur dans ce dessin ?
– évalue-t-il les chances qu'une action a de se produire ?
– cherche-t-il conseil ?

b. Imaginez la réponse du porteur de pancarte.

"How much should I put in?"

2 Dites-le en anglais

a. Vous conseillez à un consommateur de lire le magazine *Which?*

b. Vous pensez que logiquement les prix devraient baisser.

c. Vous pensez qu'on devrait faire toutes ses courses en ligne.

d. Vous estimez que dans peu de temps les consommateurs devraient pouvoir trouver la meilleure affaire par un seul clic.

e. Vous pensez que seules devraient survivre les firmes qui répondront aux nouvelles exigences des consommateurs.

3 Traduisez

a. Schoolchildren should be taught about their rights as consumers.

b. The waiter told the customer that it should only take a few more minutes to cook the dish he had ordered.

c. Because of its online subscriptions, the magazine should be able to keep going for many years to come.

d. Football captains are popular? That shouldn't surprise you, should it?

e. Normally the wide choice of goods and prices that the internet offers should benefit the customers.

La traduction de « il y a » (PG p. 250)

MÉMO

De quoi dépend la traduction de « il y a » ?

• La traductiond dépend de la nature du complément qui suit.

De quels types de compléments « il y a » peut-il être suivi en français ?

• « Il y a » peut-être suivi :

– d'un complément d'objet indiquant la quantité.
Ex. : Il y a de nombreux problèmes. → *There are a lot of problems.*

– d'un complément de temps.
Ex. : Il y a trois jours que cela est arrivé. → *It happened three days ago.*

– d'un complément de lieu.
Ex. : Il n'y a que huit kilomètres de chez moi au supermarché. → *It is only five miles from my house to the supermarket.*

Conseil :
Il convient donc de s'assurer de la nature du complément avant de se lancer dans la traduction de cette expression.
Les lignes qui suivent ne traitent que du premier de ces trois cas.

Observez et raisonnez

(enregistrement p. 173)

• *There were many people, you included, who said they would refuse.*
• *There have been fox hunts here for hundreds of years.*
• *There would be a policeman knocking on my door.*
• *There's a pretty good chance you're doing the right thing.*

1 Identifiez les traductions de « il y a » + COD dans les énoncés ci-dessus.

2 Indiquez quel temps grammatical a été utilisé dans chaque cas.

3 Expliquez comment chaque forme est construite.

4 Traduisez les quatre énoncés.

Entraînez-vous

1 Cartoon fun

Traduisez la légende du dessin.

"Now look, men... there may be a god up there, or then again there may not be, but assuming for the moment that there is, then I'm pretty sure he's on your side"

2 Conjuguez

Conjuguez l'exemple : *There are a lot of applicants.*
a. Au prétérit.
b. Au *present perfect.*
c. Au *past perfect.*

3 Traduisez

a. There may be a good reason to disobey the law.

b. There is blood and feathers everywhere. A fox must have got into the chicken house.

4 Dites-le en anglais

Traduisez en utilisant les verbes entre parenthèses.

a. Il va y avoir beaucoup de plaintes. *(be going to)*

b. Si je disais que j'avais enfreint la loi, il y aurait quelques policiers devant ma porte à mon retour à la maison. *(would)*

c. Si la loi n'avait pas été votée, il y aurait eu moins d'agriculteurs mécontents. *(would)*

d. Il ne devrait pas y avoir autant de renards dans cette région. *(should)*

e. Si on ne résout pas le problème, il y aura des dégâts importants. *(will)*

Improve your

VOCABULARY

1 Getting involved

Match the expressions

Match the expressions on the left to their explanations on the right. WBT n° 138

have an axe to grind •	• try to deal with a problem
put forward an action plan •	• write out the list of items to be dealt with in a meeting
be committed to doing something •	• have something to complain about that affects you personally
get on your high horse •	• suggest a possible course of action
draft an agenda •	• take an arrogant attitude
tackle an issue •	• be willing to give your time and energy to something

Identify the expression MP3 45

Listen to the sentences. Which of the above expressions is concerned in each case?

2 Consumer power

Complete the sentences WBT n° 138

Use the expressions below to complete the sentences. Use each expression only once.

a bargain • damaged • demand a refund • faulty • make a complaint • overpriced

1. The crystal bowl was ...... in the post, so I sent it back.
2. If you ...... it means you ask for your money back.
3. Your products are ...... – your competitors' products are much cheaper.
4. The flat-screen TV was a ...... – it was £25 less than any other on the market.
5. If an electrical device is ...... it means that it doesn't work properly.
6. If you aren't satisfied, you can always ...... by writing to customer service department.

Make a complaint

a. Match the nouns and adjectives to make seven complaints. Use each noun and adjective only once.

b. Translate each complaint.

	bread		bitter.
	coffee		corked.
	fish		off.
This	orange	is	stale.
	pasta		tough.
	steak		undercooked.
	wine		undrinkable.

3 Popularity

People or things?

Make sure you know what all of the words and expressions in the following table mean. Check in a dictionary if necessary. Then say which can apply to people, which to things, and which to both people and things.

popular	unpopular
all the rage	unsellable
cool	disliked
trendy	friendless
in great demand	ignored
highly sought-after	unloved
well-liked	unwelcome

Imagine a conversation

1. You are really excited because you have just been given something that all your friends will be jealous of. Imagine what it is.

2. Work in pairs and act out a conversation. You tell your partner what you have been given and he/she reacts. Use at least two expressions from the table above.

FINAL TASK

Decide who are the most powerful

You work for a magazine. The owner of the magazine wants to devote the next issue to the three most powerful people in the world. Some of them are shown on this page. Their decisions and opinions can determine what you buy, what you wear, what you think, whether you are rich or poor...

1 Choose 3 people

- Choose the three people who you think are the most powerful and influential in the world today. They can be anyone – not necessarily people mentioned in this chapter or shown on this page.

2 Make decisions

- Work in groups. Each group is the editorial committee of the magazine. The committee has to choose:
– the three powerful people who will figure in the magazine;
– which one of the three will figure on the front cover.

3 Report back

- Report back on your decisions to the other groups, giving the reasons for your final choice, and compare your results.

Mark Zuckerberg, inventor of Facebook.

Jim Yong Kim, President of the World Bank.

Angela Merkel, German Chancellor.

Cristiano Ronaldo, footballer.

US President **Barack Obama**.

Susan Wojcicki, Senior vice-president of Google

Beyoncé, singer.

PREPARE FOR THE BAC

FICHES MÉTHODE PAGE 181

Compréhension de l'écrit (10 points)

Sujet The Hunger Games

Just as the town clock strikes two, the mayor steps up to the podium and begins to read. It's the same story every year. He tells of the history of Panem, the country that rose up out of the ashes of a place that was once called North America. He lists the disasters, the droughts, the storms, the fires, the encroaching seas that swallowed up so much of the land, the brutal war for what little sustenance remained.

The result was Panem, a shining Capitol ringed by thirteen districts, which brought peace and prosperity to its citizens. Then came the Dark Days, the uprising of the districts against the Capitol. Twelve were defeated, the thirteenth obliterated. The Treaty of Treason gave us the new laws to guarantee peace and, as our yearly reminder that the Dark Days must never be repeated, it gave us the Hunger Games.

The rules of the Hunger Games are simple. In punishment for the uprising, each of the twelve districts must provide one girl and one boy, called tributes, to participate. The twenty-four tributes will be imprisoned in a vast outdoor arena that could hold anything from a burning desert to a frozen wasteland. Over a period of several weeks, the competitors must fight to the death. The last tribute standing wins.

Taking the kids from our districts, forcing them to kill one another while we watch – this is the Capitol's way of reminding us how totally we are at their mercy. How little chance we would stand of surviving another rebellion.

Whatever words they use, the real message is clear. "Look how we take your children and sacrifice them and there's nothing you can do. If you lift a finger, we will destroy every last one of you. Just as we did in District Thirteen."

To make it humiliating as well as torturous, the Capitol requires us to treat the Hunger Games as a festivity, a sporting event pitting every district against the others. The last tribute alive receives a life of ease back home, and their district will be showered with prizes, largely consisting of food. All year, the Capitol will show the winning district gifts of grain and oil and even delicacies like sugar while the rest of us battle starvation.

"It is both a time for repentance and a time for thanks," intones the mayor.

Suzanne Collins, *The Hunger Games*, 2008.

Questions

- ***Tous les élèves traiteront les questions suivantes.***

A. When do the events mentioned take place? In the past or the future? Give your reasons.

B. What words prove that what is happening is a sort of ritual ceremony?

C. In your own words, sum up what happened before the Hunger Games were established. (80 words)

D. Explain why the Hunger Games came to be.

E. What is a "tribute"?

F. What shows the absolute power of the Capitol over the districts?

- ***Seuls les élèves de l'option LVA traiteront les questions G et H.***

G. How does the mayor really feel about the situation and the Hunger Games? Justify your answer with quotes from the text.

H. Explain why the games are called Hunger Games.

Expression écrite (10 points)

- ***Tous les élèves traiteront les questions suivantes.***

1. *The Hunger Games* may remind you of some current reality shows on TV. Say how you feel about reality TV shows in general. Do you like/dislike them? Which ones? Give reasons for your answer. (150 words)

2. Many science-fiction novels or films describe nightmarish worlds. Choose one of the following:

a. If you have read or seen works of this type, summarise what happened in one of them. (200 words)

b. Why do you think writers and film-makers give such a pessimistic vision of mankind's future? (200 words)

- ***Seuls les élèves de l'option LVA traiteront la question suivante.***

3. Explain how the author illustrates the notion of absolute and ruthless power in this passage. What feeling does he wish to impress on the reader? (200 words)

Compréhension écrite

Fiche méthode	Application guidée

Étape 1 Lire le texte et les premières informations

Fiche méthode

➜ Lisez attentivement le texte deux fois, sans regarder les consignes, pour identifier les **éléments essentiels** (thème, personnages, époque, etc.) et la **notion** à laquelle se rapporte le texte. Le paratexte peut fournir des informations précieuses.
➜ Si vous ne connaissez pas un mot, utilisez le **contexte** pour en déduire le sens.

Application guidée

➜ Repérez les éléments qui permettent :
– d'identifier le narrateur : sait-on qui il est ?
– de situer l'action dans le temps : l'emploi du prétérit suffit-il à situer cette histoire dans un passé lointain ?
➜ Repérez les mots transparents (*podium*, *obliterated*, etc.). Attention aux faux-amis !

Étape 2 Lire et comprendre les consignes

Fiche méthode

➜ Les consignes éclairent le contenu du texte. **Lisez-les toutes** une première fois, puis relisez le texte en surlignant les **informations importantes**.
Soyez attentif à ce qui est demandé dans les consignes pour répondre **avec précision**. Apprenez le lexique des consignes !
➜ Les questions vont du plus simple au plus complexe, du global au plus détaillé.

Application guidée

➜ La question **A** attire votre attention sur le moment de l'action (*future*) ; la **B** évoque un élément important du texte, le rite (*ritual ceremony*), etc. Dans la question **B**, il faut citer des mots du texte (*What words prove*... ?) ; dans la **G**, il faut décrire (*How*), mais aussi justifier (*justify*) en citant le texte (*quotes*), etc.
➜ Pour la question **H**, par exemple, il est nécessaire de relire le texte entièrement.

Étape 3 Répondre aux questions

Fiche méthode

➜ Répondez aux questions dans l'ordre, en indiquant les numéros ou les lettres. **Relisez** chaque réponse immédiatement après l'avoir écrite. À la fin, relisez l'ensemble. Attention aux fautes d'inattention (*s* à la 3e pers. sing., etc.).

Application guidée

➜ Référez-vous au texte pour vérifier l'orthographe des mots que vous avez utilisés (*encroach*, *defeat*...). Vérifiez les verbes irréguliers (*rose*, *brought*, *frozen*...). N'oubliez pas les guillemets lorsque vous citez le texte (**B** et **H**, par exemple).

Expression écrite

Fiche méthode	Application guidée

Étape 1 Lire les sujets

Fiche méthode

➜ Lisez attentivement les consignes et soulignez les **termes clés**.
➜ Déterminez le **type de production** écrite que l'on vous demande : lettre, discours, essai, récit, dialogue, etc.

Application guidée

➜ **Sujet 1**
reality shows / TV reality / how you feel / like/dislike / Give reasons
➜ Vous devez exprimer une opinion : dire si vous aimez ou pas les *TV shows*, en expliquant pourquoi. N'hésitez pas à citer un exemple précis d'émission !

Étape 2 Préparer la rédaction

Fiche méthode

➜ Rédigez **au brouillon** :
- un plan détaillé ;
- une introduction ;
- un développement ;
- une conclusion.

Application guidée

➜ **Exemple de développement pour le sujet 1**
I. Definition (observing/judging people in amusing/difficult/embarrassing situations – Examples)
II. I dislike them (reasons: people seeking celebrity, humiliating, voyeurism, seeing others in trouble/stressed, etc. – Examples)

Étape 3 Rédiger au propre

Fiche méthode

➜ Variez les **structures de phrases** et le **vocabulaire**. N'oubliez pas les mots de liaison !

➜ Aérez votre copie et pensez à vous relire. Attention aux fautes d'inattention !

Application guidée

➜ *Whereas documentaries aim to inform, producers of reality shows only want... / In my opinion,... / Some of the participants are chosen because audiences will dislike them. As a conclusion, I would say...*
Commencez chaque paragraphe par un alinéa et allez à la ligne à chaque changement d'idée.

Chapter 11 Who controls our lives?

1 A model on the runway at a fashion show.

2 Mark Zuckerberg, founder of Facebook, explaining how Facebook works.

3 A newspaper rack in a British newsagents'.

React !

1. The three photos deal with three very different subjects: three aspects of modern life. What are they? How are they related to the title of this chapter ("Who controls our lives?")?

2. Do any of the three subjects play an important part in your life? Why/Why not? Exchange your views.

Improve your SKILLS

Who decides

1 Is fashion important? B2

A scene from *The Devil Wears Prada* (2006). Meryl Streep (centre right) plays Miranda, the tyrannical editor of *Runway*, the most influential fashion magazine in the world.

Anne Hathaway as Andy Sachs, Miranda's new assistant and not yet a fashion victim...

Describe and comment

1. Describe the photos (who, where, doing what?).
2. Say what the photos and captions reveal about the personalities of Miranda and Andy.

Listen to the recording MP3 46

1. Say where you think the conversation takes place and what the characters are doing.
2. Explain the difference between Miranda and Andy with regard to fashion. Go into detail. WBT n° 140

Discuss fashion

Are people influenced by fashion more than they think? Discuss as a group. The links will help you.

Write

Imagine an interview between a famous couturier and a journalist who thinks that the fashion industry simply encourages people to waste their money. Write 100 words.

http://fashionandpower.blogspot.fr/2011/02/power-of-fashion-new-look.html
http://www.examiner.com/article/fashion-shapes-our-identity
http://www.brainyquote.com/quotes/keywords/fashion.html

Help

- stuff (n.) : *truc(s)*
- lumpy (adj.) : *(ici) qui n'a pas de forme*
- blithely unaware : *parfaitement ignorant*
- Casual Corner : *chaîne américaine de magasins bas de gamme (1850-2005)*
- fish out (v.) : *sortir*
- clearance bin (n.) : *bac « fin de séries »*

More help WBT n° 139

Grammar texte p. 185

Rejet de la préposition WBT n° 141
- *Kathy Kuriakis was the name I worked under.*

Cause, conséquence, but WBT n° 192
- *I was making so much money I could afford to rent a flat in Holland Park; The love of money forced people into the paths of evil in order to feed their inflamed appetites.*

Structure causative WBT n° 61
- *I had it done out by an interior designer.*

how we look?

2 Fashion and money

B2

Money is like a comfort blanket. It wraps you up and keeps you warm. It insulates you. It gives you a deep, babyish pleasure. I made so much of it because I was the best. Absolutely the best. No one can ever deny that. [...] My image filled the top shelves of newsagents. I sold men's jeans with that heart-jerking picture in the ripped vest. I sold cars and ketchup. I was more famous as Kathy Kuriakis than I could ever have been trotting up and down the catwalks of Paris like a pedigree heifer[1] in the auction ring[2].

Kathy Kuriakis was the name I worked under. Those of you who've been asleep for the last eighteen months will at last be able to put a face to me now. Or at least a body.

Sammy Rubin invented the name. He was good at names. Kathy, he said, had a homely ring to it. Kuriakis added an exotic edge.

I was making so much money I could afford to rent a flat in Holland Park. It had two balconies overlooking some garages. I had it done out by an interior designer. I spent as fast as I earned. [...] I loved money. I am not ashamed to say so.

'The love of money is the root of all evil.' I remember that from RE lessons at the Sacred Heart. Sister Carmel once spent a whole period[3] on the morality of making money as opposed to the immorality of enjoying it. It was the love of money, she said, that was the dangerous and corrupting passion, not the creation of it. The love of money forced people into the paths of evil in order to feed their inflamed appetites.

I said I thought poverty was far more corrupting.

"You've misunderstood my point, Sandra," Sister Carmel said. "I am not talking about fifty pence for the gas meter[4]. I am talking about large sums of money, the kind of money that equals power. Let us not forget that money is the fuel on which the whole world runs."

I remember that I was shocked by this pragmatism. She was not supposed to say that. She was supposed to say that religion was the fuel which turned the engines.

Anyway, I don't think the love of money is necessarily evil. I think it's just good fun. Money poured into my account with the generosity of a summer garden. It grew like vines. I handed out ten-pound notes to people begging in the street. I bought extravagant presents for my friends.

Valerie Windsor, *Saint and Warrior*, 1996.

1. heifer ['hefə] : *génisse*.
2. auction ring : *endroit où le bétail mis aux enchères est parqué.*
3. period : *a class (usually of one hour).* 4. gas meter : *compteur à gaz.*

More help WBT n° 142

Comment and imagine

Comment on the photo. Imagine what is going through the fashion buyer's mind.

Read the text

1. Say what sort of text this is (newspaper article, advertisement, essay, novel, etc.).
2. Identify the narrator. Give both her names and explain why there are two.
3. Find out about the character's job.
4. Explain her relationship with money.

Go into detail. WBT n° 143

Write

What do you think of the way she spends her money. What would you do in her position?

A fashion buyer taking notes at the presentation of a haute couture collection. Retail chains like Nieman Marcus make millions of dollars out of fashion.

Your task

You are a celebrity and have decided to "go natural" (no make-up, no slavish following of fashion). You have been invited to a talk show to state your point of view. Act out the interview.

Who decides how

1 Addicted to Facebook? B1

"Dear Andy: How have you been? Your mother and I are fine. We miss you. Please sign off your computer and come downstairs for something to eat. Love, Dad."

Help

- quip (v.) : *plaisanter*
- be hooked on : *être « accro » à*
- mind-boggling (adj.) : *stupéfiant*
- boast (v.) : *(ici) compter*
- withdrawal (n.) : *(ici) manque*
- mood (n.) : *humeur*

Comment

1. Give your definition of "addiction".
2. Describe the picture and explain what the cartoonist is suggesting or making fun of.

Listen to the recording MP3 47

1. Say what main point the speaker is making. Give your reasons.
2. Explain what researchers have recently found regarding the power of social media.
3. Go into detail. WBT n° 144

Discuss privacy

Work in groups.
1. Compare the amount of time you and your classmates spend on social network sites and your reasons for doing so.
2. Discuss the impact that spending time on social networks has on your school performance and your social life.
The links will help you.

http://www.hongkiat.com/blog/facebook-addiction-signs/
www wikihow.com/Defeat-a-FacebookAddiction

2 Controlling our privacy B1

Explain and comment

1. Define the word "privacy".
2. Describe the cartoon and explain the message it conveys.

Watch the video DVD MP3 48

1. Sum up what the video is about.
2. Explain what the team of researchers have developed and why.
3. What does Mark Zuckerberg think?
4. Give details about the research project.
Go into detail. WBT n° 145

Discuss privacy

What information do you (a) willingly share, (b) never share on Facebook or other social media? Explain why.

3 Cyberbullying

B2

A change to the criminal justice bill would target abuse on the internet or via mobile phones in England and Wales.

People convicted[1] of cyber-bullying and text message abuse could face up to two years in prison, under plans backed by the government. The justice secretary, Chris Grayling, has backed an amendment to the criminal justice bill that would target new rules at combating trolls[2] that sexually harass and verbally abuse[3] people on the internet or via mobile phones in England and Wales.

The amendment, due to be discussed in parliament on Thursday, was proposed by the Conservative MP for Ealing Central and Acton Angie Bray, after one of her constituents said her 14-year-old daughter had been "verbally raped" by 2,000 obscene texts sent by an older man, who escaped conviction.

"Just tabled amendment to criminal justice bill to make life just a bit harder for cyber-bullies and sex pests using texts to harass victims," said Bray on Twitter.

The amendment would allow for greater penalties of up to two years in prison and extend the period of time made available to authorities attempting to build difficult cases against offenders. Offences such as internet trolling fall under the Malicious Communications Act, which can only be tried in a magistrates' court[4].

Bray's tabled amendment comes after a string of high-profile abuse cases involving Twitter and text messages. Two abusers of the feminist campaigner Caroline Criado-Perez were jailed in January for subjecting her to threats of violence and rape on Twitter after Criado-Perez launched a campaign for more women to be represented on banknotes.

The Labour minister for culture, media and sport, Helen Goodman, called for "a clear legal framework" to tackle the problem of cyber-bullying and the suicides of vulnerable young people in January, after the deaths of the teenagers Tallulah Wilson and Hannah Smith. [...]

A committee will discuss the tabled amendment in parliament on Thursday, which will be added to the changes to laws to be voted on this year.

Samuel Gibbs *The Guardian*, March 26, 2014.

1. convict [kənvɪkt] (v.): *juger coupable*. 2. troll (n.) : *en argot Internet, une personne qui vise à générer des polémiques*. 3. abuse (v.) : *(faux-ami) insulter*. 4. magistrates' court (n.) : *tribunal de première instance*.

Grammar

Le passif + be + V-ing p. 193

• *[...] what information **is being shared** with external services.*

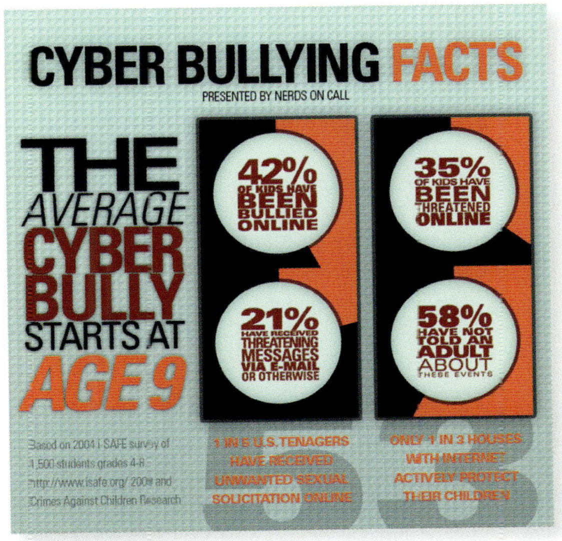

Explain and comment

1. Define "cyberbullying".
2. Describe what information the picture gives and comment on it.

Read the text

1. Sum up what the MP's amendment is about and what its aim is.
2. Explain what the new bill would change compared to the present situation. Go into detail. WBT n° 146

Discuss cyberbullying

Have you or people that you know, ever been bullied or threatened online? Explain what happened

Write

1. What can we do to prevent and/or stop cyberbullying?
2. Do you agree with what Parliament is about to do to fight and deter cyber-bullies? Give your reasons.

Your task

Prepare questions for a quiz aimed at finding out what sort of people are addicted to social media and to what degree. Ask students, teachers and members of your family about it. Then discuss your answers with the class.

Improve your SKILLS

Who decides

1 Mass media influence on society B1

Comment on the cartoon

1. Explain what the cartoon is suggesting. Find out what idiomatic expression it illustrates.
2. Do you agree with the cartoonist?

Discuss

Discuss the way you use the media. Do you think you're being manipulated in any way? Give your reasons.

2 How free is the press? B1 B2

Freedom of the press worldwide in 2014

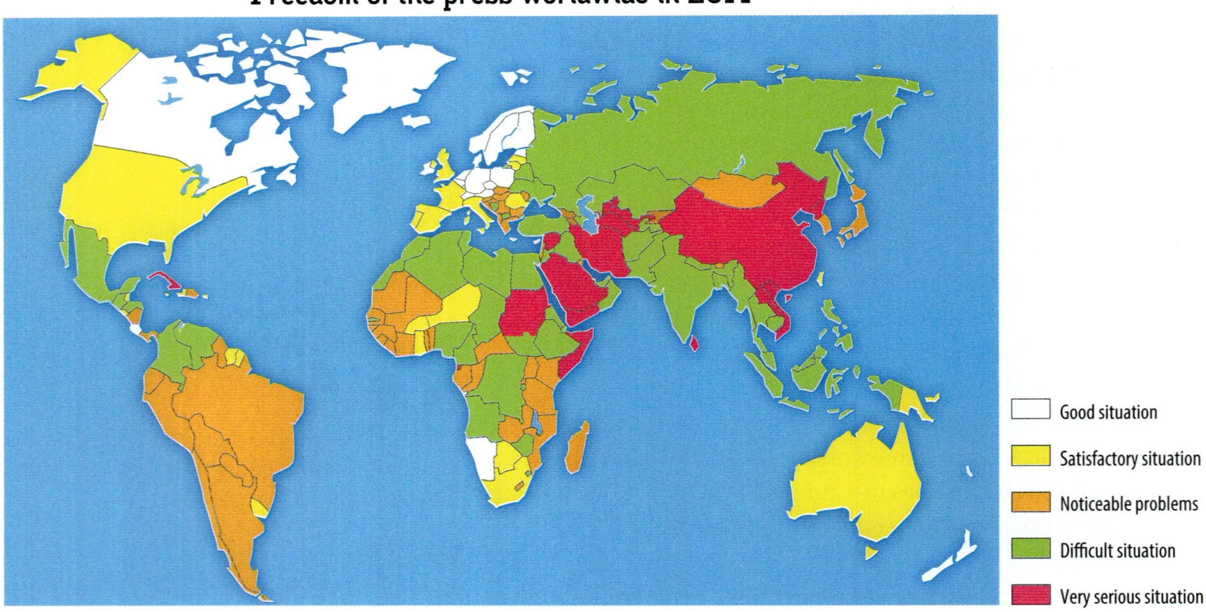

"I am a journalist because I believe that if all the world had all the facts about everything, it would be a better world." (Andrew A. Rooney, *Pieces of My Mind*, 1982.)

Explain and comment

1. Explain what the map shows.
2. Comment on Andy Rooney's quote.

Watch the video DVD MP3 49

As a class, report back on the video. Include the following information:
- the country concerned;
- how Globovision was (a) protected, (b) intimidated;
- the reporter's conclusion.

Help

- **alleged** *(adj.)*: *présumé*
- **share** *(n.)*: *(ici) action (en bourse)*
- **beat** *(n.)*: *(ici) territoire*

More help WBT n° 147

what we read?

3 What front page sells a paper? B2

"I'm serious," said Hilary. "Who wants to read about a bunch of civil servants and whether they can join a union or not? I mean, big deal[1]. On top of that, why should we run a story that's damaging to the government?"

"I don't care who we damage," said Peter, "as long as it sells papers."

"Well you're not going to sell many like that." She looked at her watch. "I can get you a better front page in twenty minutes. Maybe less."

"I beg your pardon?"

"I'll write it and give you the picture."

Hilary went back to her desk and dialled the home number of her Cambridge friend. Among the subjects they had discussed after their interview was a mutual acquaintance – another actress – who had just given birth to her third child. Her body was no longer looking its best, but this had not prevented her, apparently, from doing nude scenes for a television film to be broadcast in a few months' time. Hilary's friend, who happened to be living with the film's editor, had mentioned in passing that she had access to some of the footage[2], which made for interesting viewing.

"Listen, be a darling, would you, and bike some stills[3] over?" said Hilary. "We'll have a bit of fun."

In the meantime she sat down and typed:

IT'S BOOBS[4] AT TEN!

> Saucy BBC bosses have got a raunchy treat in store for us this autumn, with a hot new play so sexy that it won't be screened until well after the nine o'clock watershed.
>
> The torrid drama stars __________, whose three young children will certainly be in for a surprise when they see their Mum cavorting in an outrageous three-in-a-bed romp with American heartthrob _____ ______.

It didn't take long to make up the rest. Hilary's story dominated the next day's front page, with the High Court's decision relegated to a small paragraph in the bottom corner.

Jonathan Coe, *What a Carve Up!*, 1994.

1. big deal : *et alors ?* 2. footage (n. sing.) : *séquence(s).*
3. still (n.) : *(ici) cliché, photo.* 4. boob (n. fam.) : *sein.*

More help WBT n° 148

Grammar

Le génitif p. 245
- *the next day's front page.*

Describe and comment

1. Describe the front page illustrated. What do we call this sort of newspaper?
2. What does it tell you about the tastes of its readers?

Read the text

1. Say in which country the scene takes place. Give your reasons.
2. Talk about the editor: his priorities, his opinion of Hilary, his view at the end of the extract.
Go into detail. WBT n° 149

What do you think?

1. Do newspapers aim to inform readers or to increase their readership?
2. Oscar Wilde said: "The public have an insatiable curiosity to know everything, except what is worth knowing." Do you agree? Write 150 words.

Your task

Work in groups of three and choose three current news items. Then write three short front-page articles in tabloid style. Choose a punchy headline and a photo for each item.

CROSS CULTURE

Momentous Media Moments

Important, controversial and funny moments in media history...

The power of a cartoon

This famous cartoon was published in 1754 in *The Pennsylvania Gazette*. The owner of the newspaper was **Benjamin Franklin**, who was already writing "revolutionary" articles. He was one of the first to realise that a cartoon could have as much, if not more impact than a piece of writing.

Find out what the abbreviations mean and what the cartoon's message is.

Don't believe everything you see on TV!

The BBC has a reputation for truth and integrity, so when a much-respected BBC news progamme featured a report on the **Swiss spaghetti harvest** on 1st April 1957, thousands of people believed it was true. It showed a Swiss family pulling pasta off spaghetti trees and placing it into baskets. It is the most famous TV hoax in history!

When a newspaper changed history

FINAL

DAILY NEWS

NEW YORK'S PICTURE NEWSPAPER

10¢

NIXON BLASTS 'FALSE CHARGES'

Asks Public to End 'Obsession,' Get On With Nation's Business

'Time to Let Watergate Go to Courts'

The 1972 Watergate scandal, which led to President Nixon's resignation, was the result of investigations by two journalists on *The Washington Post*. Nixon stated, "I am not a crook", but people trusted *The Washington Post* more than him...

THE Sun

QE2 IS SET TO SAIL FOR WAR

We told you first

GOTCHA

Our lads sink gunboat and hole cruiser

SUNK

CRIPPLED

BATTLE FOR THE ISLANDS

UNION BOYCOTTS WAR

£50,000 BINGO! Today's lucky numbers are on Page 20

Shocking!

Rarely has **a tabloid headline** created so much controversy. "Gotcha" (= Got you") is the phrase used when catching someone you have been chasing and thereby winning a game or arresting a criminal. Used to announce a major victory in the Falklands War in 1982, it shocked a lot of people because so many men died in the attack.

The day facebook Went Down

With increasing numbers of Facebook addicts, each **"outage"** affects more and more people. In 2014, there were several "outages". On each occasion, emergency services in the US (911) received panic calls. It was as if a national emergency had been declared!

Activities

- Compare the motivations of the editor of the *Washington Post* in 1972 (when it began the disclosures about Nixon's role in the Watergate affair) and the editor of *The Sun* in 1982. Do you think they were both justified in what they allowed to appear on their front pages?
The links will help you.
- Which recent "media moment" sticks in your memory the most? The Oscar Pistorius trial? Scandals involving politicians or celebrities? Choose a news story, find out how it was reported in the English language media and present the story to the class.

http://www.bl-uk/onlinegallery/features/frontpage/gotcha.htm/watergate.info/

Improve your **GRAMMAR**

Cause, conséquence, but (PG p. 251)

MÉMO

Comment introduire la cause en anglais ?

- Le plus souvent, à l'aide des conjonctions de subordination *as, because, for, since* qui introduisent des subordonnées conjonctives.
- Mais on utilise également de nombreuses locutions prépositives : *because of, owing to, due to*, etc., suivies d'un nom.

Comment introduire la conséquence ?

- Le plus souvent, à l'aide des conjonctions de subordination *so* et *that*.
Cette notion suit souvent des expressions exclamatives introduites par *so* + adjectif ou *such* + nom.
- On peut également utiliser des adverbes comme *consequently, therefore*, etc.

Comment introduire la notion de but ?

- On utilise soit la locution conjonctive *so that*, soit la préposition *to* ou des locutions prépositives comme *in order to*.
N.B. : • *so that* est souvent réduit à *that*.
Ex. : *I gave the man £10 (so) that he might buy himself some lunch.*
- Ne pas confondre ***so that*** + but et ***so (adj. / adv.) that*** + conséquence !

Observez et raisonnez

(texte p. 185)

- *I was making so much money I could afford to rent a flat in Holland Park.*
- *The love of money forced people into the paths of evil in order to feed their inflamed appetites.*

1 Dans le premier énoncé, distinguez la partie qui exprime la cause et celle qui exprime la conséquence.
Une partie de la conjonction introduisant la conséquence a été omise. Quelle est-elle ?
Reformulez en commençant par (a) la conséquence, (b) une conjonction introduisant la notion de cause.

2 Dans le second énoncé, isolez la partie de la phrase qui exprime le but.

3 Traduisez les deux énoncés.

Entraînez-vous

1 Cartoon fun

Imaginez ce qui s'est passé lors de cette scène de ménage (cause, conséquence, but), en utilisant les bonnes conjonctions. Expliquez à quoi sert le tapis. Vous pouvez aussi imaginer un dialogue entre le mari et la femme.

"Well, I'm sorry. But your mother criticized my chicken casserole one too many times."

2 Expression

Complétez les phrases en vous appuyant sur le texte p. 185 ou sur vos propres idées.

Consequence

1. Money is such a comfort blanket …… .
2. Kathy was so famous …… .
3. She made so much money …… .

Purpose

4. Her agent chose the name Kathy Kuriakis …… .
5. She had her flat done out by an interior decorator …… .
6. They used the image of Kathy's body …… .

Cause

7. Kathy was very surprised at what Sister Carmel said …… .
8. …… she could afford to buy expensive clothes, perfume, anything she liked.

3 Dites-le en anglais.

1. Kathy était tellement belle qu'ils utilisaient sa photo pour vendre toutes sortes de choses.
2. Comme elle était très belle, la photo de Kathy était utilisée pour vendre toutes sortes de choses.
3. La publicité utilise souvent la beauté des femmes pour inciter les gens à acheter toutes sortes de choses.

Le passif + *be* + V-*ing* (PG p. 236)

MÉMO

En quoi le passif anglais diffère-t-il du passif français ?

- En français, seuls les verbes transitifs directs, ceux qui ne peuvent fonctionner qu'avec un complément d'objet direct, peuvent être utilisés à la forme (voix) passive.
- En anglais, tous les verbes peuvent être utilisés au passif. Le passif peut également être « combiné » avec la forme en *be* + V-*ing*, dite « continue ».

Comment former un passif en be + V-ing ?

Ex. : *build* → *be built* → *be being built* = construire → être construit → être en cours de construction.

À quoi sert le passif en be + V-ing ?

À insister sur l'aspect **inachevé** d'une situation ou d'une action subie.

Observez et raisonnez

(vidéo p. 186)

- *[...] because they will know they have a sort of firewall that precisely tells them what information is being shared with external services*

1 Isolez la voix passive dans cette phrase.

2 Indiquez lequel des deux *be* est celui de la voix passive et lequel est celui de la forme en *be* + *V-ing*.

3 Traduisez la phrase.

Entraînez-vous

1 Cartoon fun

Utilisez le passif pour expliquer ce qui se passe dans ces deux dessins. Utilisez des verbes suivants : *shout at* (premier dessin), *rob* et *insert* (second dessin).

"Your behavior is unacceptable!
You are a disgrace to this school!"

2 Dites-le en anglais.

a. Andy se voit donner une leçon sur le fonctionnement de la mode.

b. Elle se fait également un peu ridiculiser.

c. Les actrices sont payées des fortunes pour vendre des parfums, des voitures, des montres...

d. Je me moque de la façon dont cet argent est dépensé.

e. La couverture du magazine n'est pas encore prête. On est en train de retoucher les photos.

Improve your

VOCABULARY

1 The media

Television: the right definition MP3 50

1. Listen to the eight definitions and match them to the words and expressions below.

a. an anchorman/woman: *un(e) présentateur/trice (des informations télévisées)*

b. a chat show: *un talk-show*

c. a commercial: *un spot publicitaire*

d. prime time: *heure(s) de grande écoute*

e. a serial: *un feuilleton*

f. a series: *une série*

g. a sitcom: *une comédie de situation (série)*

h. a special correspondent: *un envoyé spécial*

2. Give your own definitions for the following types of TV programme.

a. a documentary

b. a game show

c. a reality TV show

The print media: complete the sentences

Use the folllowing words to complete the sentences.

deadlines • editor • features • glossy • gutter • magazine • meet • press • quality

1. *Vogue* is a .... aimed at women who are interested in fashion.

2. A journalist's job can be very stressful because they have to ...... very strict ....

3. The .... is the person who is in charge of long articles about subjects of general interest.

4. The *Times*, the *Guardian* and the *Daily Telegraph* are ...... newspapers.

5. Newspapers and magazines that deal in scandal and gossip are often called the ....

Headlines

Newspaper headlines can be difficult to understand because of compound words and "compacted" verb forms. Can you work out what these headlines mean? Explain each one in one sentence.

PRINCE'S AID IN LEAK SCANDAL

WALKOUT DASHES PEACE HOPES

CLUB FIRE VICTIM CLAIMS EXITS LOCKED

BANKERS TO LOSE BONUSES WARNS PM

2 Money

Find the right words

Make sure you know the meaning of the words in the following table. Then find all the synonyms and antonyms in each column. WBT n° 150

Nouns	Verbs	Adjectives
expenditure	afford	bankrupt
income	buy	broke
mortgage	earn	generous
rent	make ends meet	mean
salary	purchase	penniless
spendthrift	save	prosperous
wages	spend	well-to-do

Use the words

Make sentences of not less than 10 words using the following words from the table. Then translate the sentences.

a. income/make ends meet

b. afford/rent/broke

c. mortgage/expenditure

Complete the text

Complete the paragraph with words from the table on the left. There may be more than one possible answer for some of the blanks. WBT n° 150

My godmother was very ...... because she owned a very ...... business, but she never gave me more than £10 for my birthday. She said she couldn't ...... to ...... expensive presents. I thought the real reason was because she was ...... but Mum said I was wrong. She said it was because my godmother's father, who had died before I was born, had been a ...... and was ...... when he died. As a result, she lived in constant fear of being ...... and ...... as little as possible of her ....

FINAL TASK

Launch a new smartwatch!

A smartwatch is one of the latest "connected" devices.
There are many producers worldwide, including Android, Sony and Samsung.

1 Study your role

- Work in groups.

a. You are in charge of organising **the launch of a new French smartwatch** on the US market. It has been produced in association with a famous French fashion designer (you choose which designer).

b. Both the manufacturer and the designer have a lot of power and influence. The watch could therefore be a "must" – both a **fashion accessory** and a **high-tech device**.

c. You have to come up with **a product launch** and **media campaign** that **will persuade** people to buy the watch.

2 Choose your weapons!

- In order to launch the smartwatch, you need **to do several things.**

a. **Design a telephone survey** (10 questions) to obtain a profile of the Americans most likely to buy a smartwatch (age, sex, occupation, socio-economic bracket, etc.)

b. **Write press releases** that two magazines will print: a **fashion** magazine and a **high-tech** magazine. Choose a **slogan** and think carefully about how you describe the product (particularly adjectives that will attract potential buyers).

c. Decide what sort of **event** would be best to launch the product: a press conference, a party, a fashion show... ? Who will you invite?

d. Decide on how you will use **other media** to launch the watch (TV, Facebook, Youtube...).

3 Present your launch plan

- Present your **plan** to the rest of the class.
- Decide whose plan is the best!

The smartwatch:
how can you live without one?

PREPARE FOR THE BAC

Compréhension de l'oral (10 points)

FICHE MÉTHODE PAGES 196-197

Modalités de l'épreuve

• Un **enregistrement** audio ou vidéo en lien avec une notion du programme. **(1 min. 30)**
• Le **titre** vous est communiqué avant la première écoute.
• **Trois écoutes/visionnages** espacés chacun(e) d'une minute, durant lesquels vous pouvez prendre des **notes**.
• Un **compte-rendu** en français, par écrit. **(10 min)**
Attention *! Il ne vous est pas demandé d'écrire le script de l'enregistrement, ni de commenter ce qui est dit, ni de prendre parti mais uniquement de* ***rendre compte de ce que vous avez compris***.

Sujet d'entraînement

Cyberbullying

Lisez attentivement la fiche méthode en cachant la partie « application guidée », puis reportez-vous à l'aide, au fur et à mesure des difficultés rencontrées.

Fiche méthode	Application guidée
Étape 1 Anticiper à partir du titre donné	
➔ **Analysez le titre** pour préparer votre écoute. Cela vous guidera dans la compréhension du texte. ➔ Mobilisez le **vocabulaire** utile à ce document. Vous serez ainsi plus apte à comprendre certains termes utilisés.	➔ Repérez le thème abordé et la notion à laquelle il se rattache (Lieux et formes du pouvoir). ➔ Listez tous les mots et expressions que vous connaissez et que vous êtes susceptible d'entendre dans cette vidéo (*bully / online / social networks / texting / messaging*, etc.).
Étape 2 Écouter et noter au brouillon	
➔ **Première écoute** Valorisez une compréhension globale **:** – **repérez** le type de support, la nature du document, le nombre d'intervenants, etc. ; – **relevez** quelques mots ou expressions sans noter de phrases entières. (Les images peuvent vous aider à comprendre, mais attention elles peuvent aussi n'avoir qu'un rôle illustratif.)	➔ **Première écoute** – Type de support : enregistrement / nature du document : interview / intervenants : un homme et une femme (psychologue) / sujet : harcèlement en ligne. – Mots et expressions : *not limited / playground / physical action / offline / online / parents / mobile phone / report /*
➔ **Deuxième écoute** • **Notez un maximum** de mots et expressions compris, accentués et répétés.	➔ **Deuxième écoute** *school / study / online / psychologist specialising in social networks / age 9 to 16 / 88 minutes a day online / parental control / not only websites, social media/ hard to monitor, etc.*
➔ **Troisième écoute** • Concentrez-vous sur les **informations manquantes**. Relevez des informations plus précises (noms, dates, lieux, données chiffrées, etc.).	➔ **Troisième écoute** *not only physical / Catherine Mason / 50% online + offline / 75% use internet for social contact / mobile phone calls, texting and video clips or photos / 5% report / keep it to themselves / 54% of European parents are worried*, etc.

Étape 3 Rédiger le compte-rendu

→ Détachez-vous de l'anglais et pensez maintenant uniquement **en français**. Réutilisez toutes vos **notes** pour rédiger votre compte-rendu et n'oubliez pas de faire une **introduction**.
Si le support est une vidéo, ne décrivez pas les images mais concentrez-vous sur ce que vous avez entendu.
→ Écrivez des phrases courtes et simples.
Utilisez des verbes **introducteurs** et variez le vocabulaire.

→ Aérez votre copie et pensez à vous relire !

→ Pensez en français pour faire un compte-rendu cohérent. Utilisez vos notes (étapes 1 et 2) pour la rédaction.
Dans l'introduction, présentez la nature du support et le contexte : qui ? où ? quand ? quoi ? (interview entre un journaliste et une psychologue / harcèlement chez les jeunes, etc.)

→ Pensez aux verbes introducteurs (*Le journaliste présente le sujet... / La psychologue explique...*). Utilisez un vocabulaire riche et précis (*contrôle parental*, étude spécialisée dans les réseaux sociaux *dénoncer, assistance téléphonique, etc.*).
→ Commencez chaque paragraphe par un alinéa et allez à la ligne à chaque changement d'idée.

À votre tour !

Twitter ban in Turkey DVD

À présent, appliquez la méthodologie à cette vidéo.

Voici une grille de notation sur 10 correspondant aux attentes du baccalauréat pour essayer de vous situer selon que vous êtes en LV1 ou LV2.

CONTENT	LEVEL	LV1	LV2
COMPRÉHENSION TRÈS INSUFFISANTE **Vous n'avez repéré que des mots isolés (peut-être uniquement basés sur les images ou le titre) mais sans établir de liens entre eux.**		1	2
COMPRÉHENSION SUPERFICIELLE **Vous avez relevé des mots isolés, des expressions courantes et des phrases simples. Votre compréhension reste superficielle.**	A1	3	4
COMPRÉHENSION PARTIELLE **Vous avez su identifier le thème majeur de la discussion et identifier chaque locuteur sans comprendre toutes les informations.**	A2	5	7
COMPRÉHENSION SATISFAISANTE **Vous avez su relever les points principaux (contexte, objet, sentiments des interlocuteurs, conclusion de l'échange) et les mettre en relation.**	B1	8	10
COMPRÉHENSION FINE **Vous avez su relever les points principaux et un nombre suffisant de détails significatifs vous permettant de rendre compte du point de vue.**	B2	10	

Chapter 12

Taking control

1 Parent-child relationships can sometimes be difficult...

2 The CEO chairs a meeting of directors.

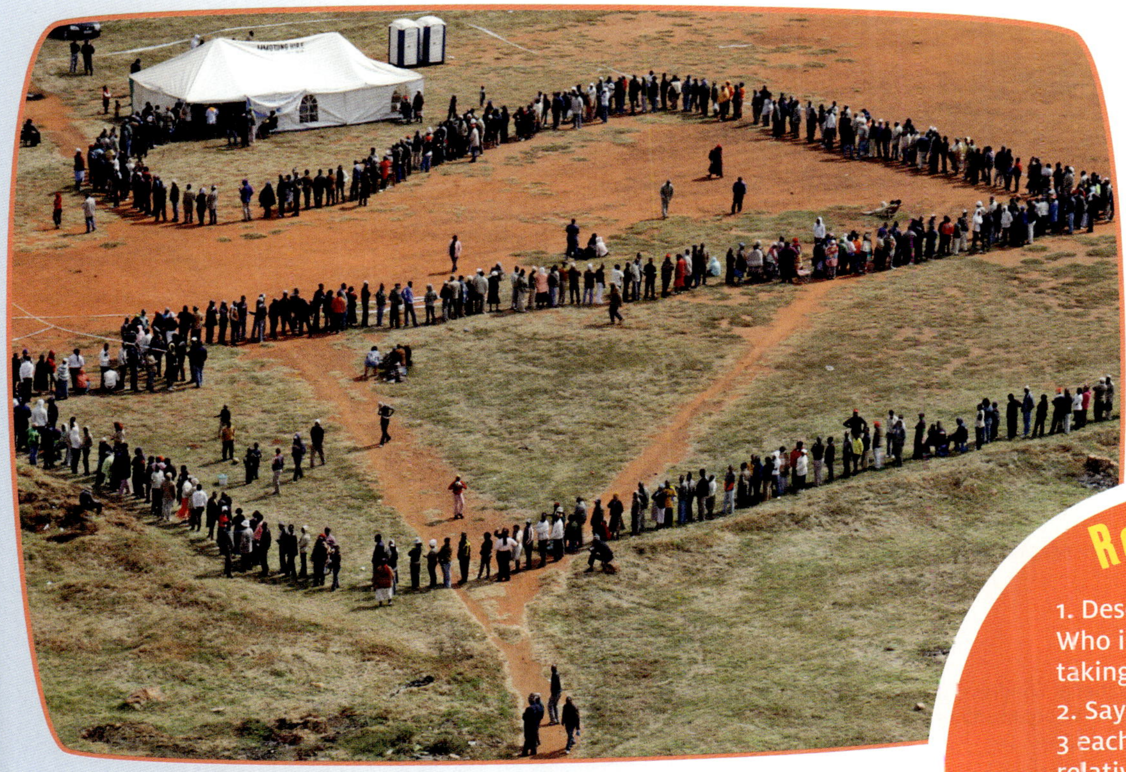

3 Seen during the 2009 South African general election.

React !

1. Describe the photos. Who is exercising power or taking control in each one?
2. Say how photos n° 2 and 3 each reflect specific – and relatively recent – social or political changes.

Multi-cultural countries:

1 More power to a neglected minority? B1

Tony Abbott, the Australian Prime Minister, on a visit to Arnhem Land, one of the largest Aboriginal reserves in Australia.

http://siekman.tripod.com/
http://www.indigenousaustralia.info/
http://www.aboriginalculture.com.au/
http://www.culture.gov.au/articles/indigenous/

Comment on the photo

1. Say what the photo tells you about the Aborigines of Australia.
2. Does the photo give you a favourable impression of the Australian Prime Minister or not? Give your reasons.

Listen to the recording MP3 52

Say what the Australian Prime Minister is intending to do and why.
Go into detail. WBT n° 152

What do you think?

Do you approve of what the Prime Minister is trying to achieve? Discuss.

Help

* **grim (adj.)**: *dur, sinistre*
* **plight (n.)**: *triste sort*
* **outback (n.)**: *brousse de l'arrière pays australien*
* **strive (v.)**: *lutter, faire de rudes efforts/tout son possible*

More help WBT n° 151

2 The first post-Mandela election B1

Brainstorm

Say what you know and what you think about Nelson Mandela and South Africa. Exchange your views.

Watch the video DVD MP3 51

1. Explain why this election is so important.
2. Who is expected to win?
3. Say what you now know about South Africa's economic and political situation. Go into detail. WBT n° 154

Choose a quote

Choose a quote from Nelson Mandela (see the links) that appeals to you and say why you like it.

Help

* **ANC (African National Congress) (n.)**: *parti politique qui a débuté comme organisation révolutionnaire*
* **dogged (adj.)**: *empêtré*
* **shed (v.)**: *(ici) se débarrasser de, se défaire de*

More help WBT n° 153

http://www.sahistory.org.za/elections-post-apartheid-south-africa
http://www.bbc.com/news/world-africa-27321171
http://www.goodreads.com/author/quotes/367338.Nelson_Mandela

who holds the power?

3 Seven rules to abide[1] by B1

"Sit down on your behind, Minny, because I'm about to tell you the rules for working in a White Lady's house." [...]

I was about to quit school and start my first real job. Mama wanted me to stay on and go to ninth grade – she'd always wanted to be a schoolteacher instead of working in Miss Woodra's house. But with my sister's heart problem and my no-good drunk daddy, it was up to me and Mama. I already knew about housework. After school, I did most of the cooking and the cleaning. But if I was going off to work in somebody else's house, who'd be looking after ours? [...]

"Rule Number One for working for a white lady, Minny: it is nobody's business. You keep your nose out of your White Lady's problems, you don't go crying to her with yours – you can't pay the light bill? Your feet are too sore[2]? Remember one thing: white people are not your friends. They don't want to hear about it. And when Miss White Lady catches her man with the lady next door, you keep out of it, you hear me?

Rule Number Two, don't you ever let that White Lady find you sitting on her toilet. I don't care if you've got to go so bad it's coming out of your hairbraids. If there's not one out back for the help, you find yourself a time when she's not there in a bathroom she doesn't use. [...]

"Rule Number Three: when you're cooking white people's food, you taste it with a different spoon. You put that spoon to your mouth, think nobody's looking, put it back in the pot, might as well throw it out.

Rule Number Four: you use the same cup, same fork, same plate every day. Keep it in a separate cupboard and tell that white woman that's the one you'll use from here on out[3].

Rule Number Five, you eat in the kitchen.

Rule Number Six: you don't hit on her children. White people like to do their own spanking.

Rule Number Seven: this is the last one, Minny. Are you listening to me? No sass-mouthing[4]."

"Mama, I know how –"

"Oh, I hear you when you think I can't, muttering about having to clean the stovepipe, about the last little piece of chicken left for poor Minny. You sass a white woman in the morning, you'll be sassing out on the street in the afternoon."

Kathryn Stockett, *The Help*, 2009.

1. abide by (v.) : *respecter (loi, règlement...)*. 2. sore (adj.) : *douloureux*.
3. from here on out : *dorénavant*. 4. sass-mouthing (n. fam.) : *impertinence, culot*.

More help WBT n° 155

A scene from *The Help* (2011).

Read the extract

1. Say where and when you think this scene takes place. Use the photo to help you.
2. Rephrase the seven rules briefly and in your own words.
Go into detail. WBT n°156

Activity

Work in pairs.
Imagine what happens next. Does Minny argue with her mother or not?
Prepare and act out the next part of the conversation.

Grammar

Les pronoms possessifs. WBT n° 12
- *But if I was going off to work in somebody else's house, who'd be looking after **ours**?*

Your task

Work in groups and choose one aspect of Aboriginal life (art, culture, beliefs, way of life, etc.). Using the links (p. 200), prepare a five-minute presentation and deliver it to the class.

Power on the job:

1 Lucky to be a woman? B1

- **Name:** Sheryl Sandberg (b. 1969)
- **Occupation:** COO of Facebook.
- **Fascinating facts:** Facebook has nearly 2 billion users and a turnover of 7 billion dollars a year.

- **Name:** Oprah Winfrey (b. 1954)
- **Occupation:** TV chat show host and businesswoman.
- **Fascinating facts:** One of the richest and most influential women in the USA.

- **Name:** Indira Gandhi (1917-1984)
- **Occupation:** Prime Minister of India
- **Fascinating facts:** The only woman PM of India, she was named "Woman of the Millennium" by the BBC in 1999.

Who do you admire?

1. A lot of people admire the three women in the photos. Say why you think this is.
2. Think of one prominent woman that you particularly admire (dead or alive). In 1 minute, note down your reasons and then present the person to the class.

Listen and explain MP3 53

1. Listen to the speaker and say what she is talking about.
2. Explain what makes her (a) happy and optimistic, (b) pessimistic.
Go into detail. WBT n° 157

Give your opinion

Do you think that men are "luckier" than women? Write 150 words, giving reasons for your answer.

Help

- C-level (n., adj.) : *au niveau de* CEO (Chief Executive Officer : *directeur général) ou* COO (Chief Operating Officer : *directeur d'exploitation)*
- top out (v.) : *culminer*
- non-profit (adj.) : *à but non lucratif*

2 Women who work for men B1

Surprised?

Comment on the facts in the box. Do they surprise you? Give your reasons.

Discuss

Who would you prefer to work for – a man or a woman? Why?

60% of women prefer working for men because men are:

- better managers and decision-makers
- less moody
- more authoritative
- more straight-talking
- tougher
- better at delegation
- more likely to give praise

Adapted from *The Daily Telegraph*, November 27, 2014.

who's in charge?

3 The CEO calls a board meeting B2

"I called the meeting today," Fiona said quietly, sitting up straight in her chair. Despite her calm voice, she had a delivery style that people listened to, and she could electrify every person in the room, when she shared some of her more innovative ideas. "Because I want to discuss the recent leak[1] in the press." They all knew about it, and every member of the board was concerned.

"I think we all agree that it puts us in an awkward[2] position. The closing of the Larksberry plant[3] is going to impact thousands of our employees, who will be laid off. It's an announcement that will need to be made with extreme caution. How we deliver that message, and how we handle it thereafter, if managed badly, could have a very serious negative effect on our stock[4], and could even cause panic in the market. And there's no question, even though we voted on it in our last meeting, that announcing it to the public, our stockholders, or our employees is still premature. Now we need time to put damage control measures in place, and I've been working on that full time since we last met.

I think we have some very good plans to take at least some of the sting out of it. We *have* to close that plant, for the health of the company, but the last thing any of us wanted was for that to be leaked to the press before we had the details settled. And as you all know, it came out two weeks ago in *The Wall Street Journal* and then *The New York Times*. I've been doing nothing but clean up ever since.

And I think we're all in agreement that the most disturbing thing about this is not just the timing, but that clearly, it was leaked by someone on the board. The information that appeared in the press is only known by us, in this room. Some of it has never been in writing, and there is just no way for the press to know any of it, unless someone in this room talked."

There was a heavy silence, as Fiona looked from one to the other with an intense and serious gaze. Her expression let no one off the hook. "It's unthinkable that that should happen here. It's the first time in my six years at NTA, and I have never had a leak from the boardroom in my entire career. I know it happens, but this is a first for me, and probably for some of you too." She looked at each of them again, and they all nodded.

Danielle Steel, *Power Play*, 2014.

1. leak (n.) : *fuite*. 2. awkward ['ɔːkwəd] (adj.) : *(ici) inconfortable, délicate*.
3. plant (n.) : *usine*. 4. stock (n., US) : *actions d'une société*.

More help WBT n° 158

http://www.nidirect.gov.uk/discrimination-at-work
http://www.hg.org/employment-discrimination-law.html
http://everydaylife.globalpost.com/female-discrimination-workplace-2736.html

Your task

Work in pairs and find out about job discrimination because of gender in either the USA or the UK (history, the law, solutions to problems...) and write a short report. The links will help you.

Fortune magazine publishes an annual list of the most powerful women in the world and holds a "summit". This is Nora O'Donnell, an influential CBS journalist, at the 2013 summit.

Brainstorm

Look at the picture and the caption. In what way has *Fortune* (an important US business magazine) decided to reflect changes in society? Exchange your views.

Read the extract

Say what position you think Fiona occupies in the company.
Say why Fiona called the meeting (the problem, its cause, possible consequences, Fiona's authority...). Go into detail. WBT n° 159

Give your opinion

Write 150 words, giving your reasons:
– If you are a young woman, would you like to lead a life like Fiona's?
– If you are a young man, what do you think of Fiona?

Grammar

Le *present perfect* + *be* + V-*ing* p 208
• *[...] and I've **been working** on that full time since we last met.*

Le subjonctif WBT n° 160
• *It's unthinkable that that **should happen** here.*

Families: who lays

1 A special sort of contract B1

Explain

1. From the information in the comic strip, work out what a curfew is and explain it.
2. If a curfew exists in your home, talk about it. If not, how would you react if there was one?

Role play

In groups of four, prepare and act out a role play. You are a family: mother, father and two teenagers. The parents want the children to sign a contract that sets up curfew rules. The children may agree or object. You must come to a collective decision at the end of the role play.

2 Who should run my life? B1 B2

Describe and comment

1. Say what you can about the ad. (when? message? social background?)
2. Explain how things have changed since the ad was published.

Listen to the recording MP3 54

1. Describe Suzanne's relationship with her husband.
2. How does she feel at this moment in time?
3. Say what you know about Suzanne's life and her plans. Go into detail. WBT n° 162

Write a conversation

After talking to her friend, Suzanne decides to talk to her husband about the business she wants to start. Imagine their conversation. (150 words)

Help

- boil down to (v.) : *se résumer à*
- catering (n.) : *service traiteur*
- barely (adv.) : *à peine*
- trick-or-treat : *expression utilisée par les enfants pour Halloween*

More help WBT n° 161

down the law?

3 Family power play B2

Irie wants to take a year off before she goes to university, but her parents object…

On the 25th of October 1991, 01.00 hours, Irie embarked upon a late-night attack. She knew from experience that her mother was most vulnerable when in bed; late at night she spoke softly like a child, her fatigue gave her a pronounced lisp; it was at this point that you were most likely to get whatever it was you'd been pining[1] for: pocket money, a new bike, a later curfew. It was such a well-worn tactic that until now Irie had not considered it worthy of this, her fiercest and longest dispute with her mother. But she hadn't any better ideas.

"Irie? Wha –? Iss sa middle of sa nice… Go back koo bed…"

Irie opened the door further, letting yet more hall light flood the bedroom.

Archie submerged his head in a pillow. "Bloody hell, love, it's one in the morning! Some of us have got work tomorrow."

"I want to talk to Mum," said Irie firmly, walking to the end of the bed. "She won't talk to me during the day, so I'm reduced to this."

"Irie, pleaze… I'm exhaushed… I'm shrying koo gesh shome shleep."

"I don't just *want* to have a year off, I *need* one. It's essential – I'm young, I want some experiences. I've lived in this bloody suburb all my life. Everyone's the same here. I want to go and see the people of the world… that's what Joshua's doing and his parents support him!"

"Well, we can't bloody afford it," grumbled Archie, emerging from the eiderdown. "We haven't all got posh jobs in science, now have we?"

"I don't *care* about the money – I'll get a job, somehow or something, but I do want your permission! Both of you. I don't want to spend six months away and spend every day thinking you're angry."

Zadie Smith, *White Teeth*, 2000.

1. pine for (v.) : *désirer ardemment.*

More help WBT n° 163

Read the text

1. Identify the characters in this scene, and say how they are related.
2. Say where the action takes place and what the problem is.
3. Find out why Irie wants to take a year off.

Go into detail. WBT n° 164

What do you think?

Do you think parents should interfere with their children's plans? Exchange your views.

Grammar

Les valeurs du *would* p 209

- *He **would** think of something else for me to do.*
- *He **wouldn't** let me put them in day care.*

Your task

Organise a TV talk show. Work in groups. Choose the host and the guests. Under the host's guidance, the guests discuss the following point: What makes a "good" parent?

CROSS CULTURE

The cost of independence

Self-determination – the right for a country to govern itself – is something we rarely question these days, but taking control of one's own destiny can cost thousands of lives, and not everyone wants it...

Most Canadians are very attached to their own flag and their own values.

From Empire to Commonwealth

The vast majority of **British colonies** – including the huge territories of Canada and Australia – achieved independence from the UK without a shot being fired. They remain members of the Commonwealth and, in many cases, retain the British monarch as their Head of State.

1947. Trains taking Moslems from India to the new state of Pakistan.

It was a different story in 1947 when India obtained independence. The subcontinent was partitioned into India, Pakistan and Bangladesh. Half a million people died in riots and 14 million people were displaced.

Secession

In 1948, **southern Ireland** finally became a republic after centuries of conflict with England, which had ruled the whole island on and off for about 800 years. Unlike the USA, whose fight for independence was based on "no taxation without representation", the main issues involved were national identity and religion.

Northern Ireland still remains part of the UK but it is a divided community where republicanism is still strong, as seen in this demonstration during the "Troubles".

We don't want independence!

Britain still possesses 14 "overseas territories", former colonies that have chosen not to be independent. Two of them – the Falkland Islands and Gibraltar – are fiercely British and have been the cause of conflicts with Argentina and Spain.

The Barbary macaques of Gibraltar are the only wild monkeys living in Europe. Gibraltarians say that if ever the monkeys leave the rock, the British will leave Gibraltar too!

Photos taken during the campaign before the 2014 Scottish independence referendum.

Both Scotland and Wales have had their own parliaments for over 15 years but, in 2014, Scotland had the chance to become independent – Scottish nationalists had forced a referendum. However, 55% of Scots voted to stay in the UK.

Activities

1. Work in groups and choose one of these topics for research:
- The reasons why the USA and Ireland wanted independence.
- The reasons why some former British colonies have preferred not to be independent.
- Events in India, Pakistan and Bangladesh when they were separated. What went wrong? Present-day effects?

2. Report back to the class.

Le present perfect en *be* + V *-ing* (PG p. 233)

MÉMO

À quoi sert cette forme verbale ?

• Le *present perfect* associé à *be* + *ing* permet, au moment où l'on parle (le présent) :
– d'insister sur le fait qu'une action ou une situation commencée dans le passé n'est pas achevée ;
– de commenter ses résultats ou ses conséquences (approbation, critique, moquerie, etc.) présentes.

Comment traduit-on cette forme ?

• La plupart du temps par un simple présent.
N.B. Contrairement à une croyance répandue, cette forme verbale ne sert pas à mesurer la durée de l'action : ce sont aux compléments de temps que revient cette tâche.

Observez et raisonnez

(texte p. 203)

• *Now we need time to put damage control measures in place, and* ***I've been working*** *on that full time since we last met.*

1. Décrivez la construction de la forme en gras.
2. Reportez-vous au texte p. 203 et identifiez qui parle.
3. Dites quand l'action a commencé et si elle est terminée.
4. Que faudrait-il savoir pour en mesurer la durée ?
5. Quel mot renvoie au début de l'action ?
6. Laquelle des deux valeurs rappelées dans l'encadré Mémo cet énoncé exprime-t-il ?
7. Trouvez un autre exemple d'emploi de cette forme verbale dans le texte p. 203.
8. Traduisez les deux phrases.

Entraînez-vous

1 Cartoon fun

Associez chaque phrase au dessin correspondant.
• L'homme parle de la durée de l'action.
• L'homme commente la situation.

"HE'S BEEN HOLDING THAT SIGN FOR FIFTEEN YEARS!"

'I see you've been talking to the plants again.'

2 Dites-le en anglais

Utilisez le *present perfect* en *be* + *-ing* pour traduire les verbes en gras.

1. La question, c'est qui **révèle** à la presse des informations confidentielles concernant notre société ?
2. Nous pouvons mener une carrière parce que nous vivons maintenant dans un monde qui **change** depuis quelques années.
3. Certaines d'entre nous **atteignent** l'échelon supérieur de notre profession.
4. Dans le domaine caritatif, seules 20 % des femmes **dirigent** une ONG.
5. Cela fait des années que Suzanne **rêve** de lancer sa propre entreprise.

Les valeurs du modal *would* (PG p. 237)

MÉMO

Quelle est l'origine de ce modal ?

- *Would* est la forme passée du modal *will*. À ce titre, il en a toutes les valeurs.
- Étymologiquement, *will* exprime la volonté.

Quelles sont les diverses valeurs de would ?

- Selon les contextes, *would* exprime :
  – la certitude absolue de l'énonciateur ou l'absence de celle-ci ;
  – la volonté, l'intention de l'énonciateur ou du sujet grammatical ;
  – l'habitude et les caractéristiques de l'énonciateur ou du sujet grammatical.
- Notez que plusieurs de ces valeurs peuvent être présentes dans le même *would*.

Comment would est-il traduit ?

- Selon les emplois, il est traduit le plus souvent par l'imparfait de l'indicatif ou le présent du conditionnel.

Observez et raisonnez

(enregistrement p. 204)

- *"...every single time I said I was ready to start my catering business, he would think of something else for me to do with the kids that would usurp my time."*
- *"He wouldn't let me put them in day care, because he thought those places were dangerous."*

1. Repérez les occurrences de *would* dans ces énoncés.
2. Qui parle ?
3. À qui *he* renvoie-t-il ?
4. En quoi les deux premiers *would* diffèrent-ils du troisième ?
5. Traduisez les énoncés.
6. Laquelle des trois valeurs rappelées dans le Mémo n'est pas représentée dans ces deux énoncés ?

Entraînez-vous

1 Cartoon fun

Dites quelle est la notion véhiculée par le *would* dans ce dessin.

"IT WOULD NEVER WORK, GEROME. YOU'RE MICROSOFT AND I'M NETSCAPE."

2 *Would* au cinéma

Dans le film *Places in the Heart* (1985), une mère, dans les années 30, est obligée de punir son jeune fils en l'absence de son défunt père. Lisez l'échange entre mère et fils et indiquez la valeur de chacun des *would* utilisés.

Mother: Well, young man, what **would** your Pa do, if he were here?

Son: He'**d** spank me, I reckon. (= I suppose)

Mother: When your Pa did this, how did he do it?

Son: Most times, I'**d** lean on the table, grab hold and he'**d** let me have it.

Mother: How many times?

Son: Pa **would** be mad over something like this. I reckon he'**d** give me ten good licks.

3 Dites-le en anglais

a. Il n'y a pas si longtemps, les hommes prenaient le volant et les femmes s'asseyaient à l'arrière !

b. D'ordinaire, je passais mes journées à conduire les enfants ici et là.

c. Mais qu'aurait-il fait si tu avais décidé de lancer ta propre affaire ?

d. Il n'aurait jamais voulu me laisser faire ça.

Improve your

VOCABULARY

1 The world of work

Explain the abbreviations MP3 55

1. These are some common abbreviations used in the workplace. What do they stand for? Use the words in the list.

a. HR, **b.** CEO, **c.** PA, **d.** R&D, **e.** IT, **f.** PR.

and • assistant • chief • development • executive • human • information • officer • personal • public • relations • research • resources • technology

2. Now listen to the definitions and match them to the abbreviations.

Complete the sentences WBT n° 165

Check that you know the meaning of these words and expressions. Then use them to complete the sentences. Change the verb forms when necessary.

• apply for • clock in • make redundant • take on staff • unemployment • work in shifts • work overtime

1. The factory operates 24 hours a day, so the staff have to ...... : three teams work eight hours each.

2. When the company went bankrupt, 200 people were ......

3. Because of the huge demand for our products, we are all ...... at the moment – an hour or two every day.

4. We need to ...... to work in our new Hong Kong branch. We'll need about 25 people.

5. When you ...... a job, you have to include your CV.

6. Every morning I have to ...... by 8.30. If I'm late, I may get a reprimand from the supervisor.

7. There is still a high level of ...... in some European countries because of the financial crisis.

Match the words

Match the words and expressions with their explanations.
WBT n° 165

blue-collar worker •	• the employees, the people who work for a company
bonus •	• a person with responsibility for a department
director •	• remuneration that is not in the form of money (i.e. a company pension, a company car...)
fringe benefits •	• a committee composed of people who represent all the employees and the management
immediate superior •	• an organisation that defends the rights of specific groups of employees
manager •	• a person who does manual work
staff •	• someone who is learning his/her job
trade union •	• the person who you are responsible to
trainee •	• a person in charge of a large sector of company operations and takes part in forming company policy
white-collar worker •	• extra money you receive for good work
works council •	• a person who doesn't do manual work

2 Giving and taking orders

Classify the expressions WBT n° 165

Put these expressions into two categories:

a. giving orders;

b. taking orders.

abide by the law • call the shots • carry out instructions • conform to the regulations • keep to the rules • lay down the law • put your foot down • submit to authority • take charge • withdraw permission

Use the expressions

1. Describe the situation in this picture. Use at least one expression from the above list.

2. Choose three more of the above expressions (that you didn't use in question 1) and put each one into a sentence.

FINAL TASK

"See you in court!"

**Three different cases are being heard in court today.
What will the outcome be?**

Case A: A minority group is suing the government. They are demanding to be given their rightful place in society.

Case B: A woman is suing her employer for discrimination at work.

Case C: A teenager is suing her/his parents for their refusal to let him/her leave home.

1 Choose your role

Work in groups of 5. Choose one of the cases and choose your role:

- the plaintiff: the person representing the tribe (A), the woman (B), the teenager (C)
- the defendant: a government representative (A), the employer (B), one of the parents (C)
- the lawyer for the plaintiff
- the lawyer for the defendant
- the judge

2 Prepare the background and the arguments

- As a group, prepare for the court hearing. Give names to all the participants and cover the following details:

– Case A: the claim (land, permits, special rights...)

– Case B: the company name and business, the plaintiff's job, the company representative's job, specific reasons for suing...

– Case C: reasons and justification for wanting to leave home, reasons for the parents' refusal

- The lawyers prepare their arguments and the judges prepare questions.

3 Act out the hearing

- The lawyers put their cases; the judge asks questions and takes notes. The plaintiff and the defendant can object to what is being said.
- The judge gives a ruling and explains his/her decision.
- The rest of the class assess each group's performance (you will get an assessment sheet from your teacher).

The First Day

Elizabeth put on her black sunglasses. She said goodbye to her parents, kissed them and walked to the public bus stop where she waited quietly for the bus that would take her to her new school. But when she got off at the bus stop closest to Central High she didn't see any of the other eight black children who were meant to be starting at the school with her that day. She didn't see any black people at all. She saw a sea of white people, thousands of them from all over the state and, judging from the out-of-state license plates, from other states as well. She saw hundreds of soldiers in full battle dress: boots, helmets. The soldiers were armed. She saw bayonets, too many to count.

She looked at the guards lined up along the road leading to the school building and she looked at the white crowd. The day before, she had been told to go to the school's main entrance. It was a block away from where she was standing. It occurred to her that when walking the block to the front of the school she might be safer if she walked it from behind the guards so that for the length of the block there would be a line of guards between her and the crowd. It was at the corner of the block that she chose to try to pass through the line of guards in order to stand on the other side of them. She was wearing sunglasses and the black-and-white pleated dress she had made with her mother. It was her first day at a new school. She was fifteen and she chose a soldier at random[1].

The soldier didn't speak but pointed across the street in the direction of the crowd. She tried not to look frightened and walked as the random soldier had directed her. What might another soldier have done? Elizabeth had always achieved high grades, always been an excellent student.

Elizabeth Eckford walked toward the crowd and, at least at first, that section of it closest to her moved back, away from her, almost as though afraid of her, as though afraid they might catch something from her. If you stood too near her perhaps you could *become* her. People would look at you. You would stand out[2] simply by being in that part of the crowd nearest to her. You hadn't gone there expecting to stand out. That wasn't why you were there. But now you might stand out through no fault of your own. So you had better make sure that everybody around knows where you really stand. You hate her. You hate her as much as anyone else in the crowd hates her. You might even hate her more. By standing near you, she's making you especially uncomfortable, more uncomfortable than she makes everybody else feel, and how *they* feel is only how you felt moments ago before she chose you to make especially uncomfortable. Why did she have to choose you? She brings trouble with her wherever she goes. You can see it. You've been told this all your life, known it all your life, but now you can actually feel it. She's making you sweat. She's making your heart race. Everybody's looking as she stands near you. Oh Christ, you hate her. Why did she have to make you feel like this? You hate her so much.

"Here she comes. Get ready!" someone shouted.

Elizabeth moved away from the crowd and closer to the guards. She walked briskly[3] but she didn't run. The noise of the crowd was everywhere. All she had to do, she told herself, was make it to the main entrance at the end of the block.

Elizabeth managed to reach the front of the school. She approached another guard. This one wouldn't meet her eyes. He stared out beyond her, over her head like she wasn't there. The noise was all around her as though attached to the air. The guard wouldn't let her pass. She saw that there was a path which led directly to the front entrance a little farther on. She turned and took it. She hadn't realized the school was so big. White students were walking up to the guards at the front door and were being let through.

1. at random : *au hasard.*
2. stand out (v.) : *se démarquer.*
3. briskly (adv.) : *d'un bon pas.*
4. clutch (v.) : *serrer fortement.*

Little Rock, Arkansas, 1957. Elizabeth Eckford in the episode recounted in the passage.

Still with the feeling that her legs could give way at any moment, she walked toward the guard who was letting the white students through. He didn't move. Again it was like she wasn't there. She tried to get in between him and the guard next to him. He raised his bayonet to block her. Then the other guards moved in. They raised their bayonets too. As though sensing something, some change or new phase, a quiet descended on the crowd for a moment. Elizabeth didn't know what to do. She turned away from the guards and just stood there, between them and the crowd. Now the crowd moved toward her, closer, and she heard, "Lynch her! Lynch her!"

She turned around to face the guards again but they remained impassive and impassable. The noise of those thousands of angry white people was like nothing she had ever heard before. She had always got good grades. She had always been very polite, always been a good girl, been no trouble to her teachers, always paid attention. These people didn't know her. Where in her fifteen years of life was the thing she had done that was so bad they should hate her this much? There were so many of them and they all hated her. They appeared to feel this so strongly even though none of them knew her. It was hard to think but she found and clutched[4] at the thought that somehow it might be better for her if she could make it back to the bus stop from where she'd arrived. It was a new plan, to make it back to the bench at the bus stop. She turned around and started the journey back, flanked by the crowd on each side. Still she didn't run but her legs felt as though they might buckle at any time. When she finally got to the bench at the bus stop her legs did buckle slightly but she propped herself up on the back of the bench.

Elliot Perlman, *The Street Sweeper*, 2011.

Read and understand

1. How old is Elizabeth and what is she trying to do?

2. What problem is she facing?

3. Are the guards there to help her?

4. What does the crowd want? Why?

5. Compare the crowd's behaviour with the way Elizabeth has been brought up and the way she behaves.

6. What does Elizabeth decide to do at the end of the passage?

Go further LVA/LELE

1. Who do you think holds the power in this extract? Why?

2. Is the event seen from just one point of view? Is the author an objective observer or not? Give your reasons.

3. What does the author want us to think? How does he get his message across? Is he successful?

4. This extract is based on a real event. Do you think it is an accurate portrayal of what happened? What are your feelings and impressions after reading the text?

The power of money

Money. I never gave it much thought. Until I started making real, proper grown-up money, its existence was something that I largely ignored[1]. As I now realize, how you deal with money – how you control it and how it controls you (and it inevitably ends up doing that) is something you learn very early on. My adolescence was a frugal one, as Dad paid Mom a very nominal amount of alimony[2] and child support. At high school I was always known as 'the librarian's daughter'.

Unlike most other teenagers in Old Greenwich, I didn't have my own personal car, let alone membership of a country club – Old Greenwich being the sort of place where boys get their first set of golf clubs on their eleventh birthday. As I began to understand, *not* having a car and *not* spending the weekends at some white-bread enclave was no bad thing. But I still wished I could have had some of their fringe benefits – most of all, not having to worry about asking Mom for certain things, as she was constantly embarrassed about her small salary and the fact that she couldn't do more for me, even though I kept reassuring her that I needed no more than I had.

It's extraordinary how patterns of behavior develop without either you or those closest to you ever realizing that they are being formed. Mom felt guilty about not having much money. I felt guilty about Mom feeling guilty, and also felt hurt and confused about my father being so parsimonious. Simultaneously I wanted to win scholarships (and hold down assorted part-time jobs) to relieve my mom of certain financial burdens and show my father that I could hold my own in the world.

So while at college, I did work fifteen hours a week in the library to earn basic pocket money During grad school at Harvard, I taught an introductory freshman course in English composition to augment the fellowship stipend[3]. And because everything had to be so carefully budgeted in my life, I became very adept at living on very little. [...] I cooked most of my meals at home. I bought clothes at discount outlets. I could easily afford to see two movies a week. The T got me around Cambridge and into Boston. I never felt I wanted for anything because I wasn't really longing for[4] anything.

1. ignore (v.) : (*faux ami*) not pay attention to something or someone.
2. alimony (n.) : money paid regularly to a former spouse.
3. stipend (n.) : money paid regularly to somebody, as wages or money to live on.
4. long for (v.) : want something very much.
5. heady (adj.) : having a strong effect on your senses.

That's the thing about not having a great deal of money. You learn that you actually require very little to keep things interesting. It's only when you begin to make money that you find yourself thinking you need things you never dreamed of needing before. And once you get those things, you start ruminating about everything else that you don't have. Then aspirational despair sets in. [...]

Money. The trickiest substance in life – as it's the way we keep score, measure our worth, and think we can control our destinies. Money: the essential lie.

But in those first crazy months when I started working at Freedom Mutual, money seemed like a great new crazy lover who was determined to show me a fresh way of looking at the world. Out with the drab, narrow economies of a frugal life. In with the pleasures of living well and not having to pay a vast amount of attention to the price tag attached.

Money. Much to my continued surprise, I found myself becoming a fast convert to its heady[5] pleasures and the sense of possibility that it engendered.

Money. It was also a game.

Or, at least, that was how Brad Pullman looked upon it.

Brad Pullman was the CEO of Freedom Mutual. He was in his late thirties – a dentist's son from Long Island and a self-described 'one-time geek' who had been settling scores with the world from the moment he discovered Money. He went to Middlebury, then to Harvard Business School, after which he found his way into the 'secure, low-stress world of mutual funds'.

"Everything I did in the first thirty years of my life was predicated on risk aversion. I tell you, Jane, fear is Life's Big Roadblock." (Those were his caps, by the way.) "It's the one and only thing that will keep you from achieving all that you want to achieve, or living the life you deserve. And the truly insidious thing about fear is – it's completely self-perpetuated. We create the dread that clogs up our lives." [...]

"I am happy to admit that, in my 5.4 million-dollar townhouse on Beacon Hill, I have fifty designer suits. Does any man need fifty suits and one hundred and fifty shirts? Don't be absurd. Fifty suits and one hundred and fifty shirts in a 5.4 million-dollar townhouse is a sign of futile over-consumption... until, of course, you do the math. Fifty suits and one hundred and fifty shirts – let's say the outlay was around 100k over a five-year period, so 20k per annum. Now if you are some mid-level exec pulling down one hundred and 50k per annum before taxes, 20k a year on suits... well, it's virtually a crack-cocaine habit, right? But if you're pulling down eight million per annum, as I did last year..."

That was another thing about Brad Pullman. He not only announced the cost of everything "Like my new watch? Jaeger LeCoultre. Bought at European Watches on Newbury Street. Fifty-four hundred dollars – actually a steal" – but also let it be known – all the time – how much he was making, how much the firm was making, how much you, his minion, *should be* making, but aren't because... well, "Do you have the juice to Overcome the Negatives and score the big bucks?"

I met Brad Pullman at my interview. I'd found out about the job courtesy of the Harvard Placement Office. After turning down the post in Wisconsin I asked Ms Steele if there were any openings in the world of Big Bucks.

"Plenty, of course – but you have a PhD in English, so why would you want to—?"

"It's a career change," I said.

"Even before your career has started," she said.

Douglas Kennedy, *Leaving the World*, 2009.

Read and understand

1. What do you learn about the narrator's social background?
2. What do you find out about her family?
4. What shows she was a sensible and brilliant student?
5. How did she manage when on a tight budget?
6. When and why did her attitude to money change?
7. What do we learn about Brad Pullman?
8. How is the futility of his life portrayed?
9. Has the narrator learned a lesson regarding money? If so, which one?

Go further LVA/LELE

1. How does this extract illustrate the title it has been given?
2. Through whose eyes is Brad Pullman seen?
3. Look at the way the author and the narrator describe the characters. Are they the same?
3. Where in the text do we learn that something changed radically in the narrator's life? Why does the author introduce it at this point?
4. What shows that all this is said in retrospect?

Méthodologie

1 La perspective « actionnelle »

- **L'objectif**

  Dans chaque chapitre, il est de prolonger et de faire aboutir le travail fait en cours en vous impliquant concrètement et personnellement à travers une série de tâches d'expression (écrite ou orale), qui mènent à une tâche finale d'ampleur (communément appelée « action » ou « projet »).

- **Les moyens et la mise en œuvre**

  Ces tâches sont préparées en classe, à la maison ou au CDI en utilisant Internet, des dictionnaires, etc.

« Produire » un résultat final

Après un travail sur un document ou une série de documents, le professeur vous demandera de réfléchir, individuellement ou en groupe, à un prolongement : votre tâche sera de préparer un projet lié à ce que vous avez appris en classe dans le but de développer votre autonomie langagière.
Vous serez guidés par des consignes de départ précises ; vous devrez expliquer votre projet au professeur afin qu'il vous donne le feu vert ; l'exposé de votre projet sera fait soit oralement soit à l'écrit, et bien évidemment en anglais.

Exemples de projets actionnels

- Préparer un jeu de rôles, le mettre en scène, jouer la comédie en classe.
- Présenter un film ou un extrait de film comme le ferait un critique cinématographique ou un spectateur.
- Faire une revue de presse détaillée et argumentée sur un sujet précis.
- Réaliser une enquête ou un sondage.
- Rédiger un article de journal, une lettre, un journal intime, un blog, etc.
- Réaliser et exposer une affiche.
- Présenter un projet scientifique, commercial, etc.
- Produire une brochure informative, commerciale, touristique ou un diaporama.
- Interviewer vos camarades jouant eux-mêmes un rôle précis.
- Réaliser une vidéo (vraies, fausses actualités, séquence de film, etc.).

Comment s'impliquer ?

- Réfléchissez précisément à ce qui vous est demandé : résultat final, limites, contraintes imposées par les consignes, but poursuivi envers les autres élèves.
- Validez chaque étape du projet avec votre professeur : conception, résumé ou scénario écrit en anglais, mise en œuvre, réalisation.
- Donnez libre cours à votre imagination et à votre créativité dans le cadre des consignes données : apportez des objets personnels choisis spécialement pour le projet, déguisez-vous si c'est justifié, adoptez un ton humoristique, dramatique, ironique selon les circonstances... Toutes choses à faire valider par votre professeur, bien sûr.

2 Interagir

- Votre professeur vous demandera souvent de travailler en petits groupes de trois ou quatre ou de faire du *pairwork*.
- Votre **objectif** est de vous faire comprendre, de communiquer avec conviction et efficacité, mais toujours en anglais !

Travailler en groupe

- Le travail en groupe est un travail aussi sérieux et exigeant que le travail individuel. En partageant et en répartissant un travail complexe, vous pourrez partager des connaissances avec vos camarades et apprendre les uns des autres.
- Essayez de ne parler qu'en anglais, vous avancerez beaucoup plus vite.
- À tour de rôle, rapportez à l'oral une partie des informations que vous aurez trouvées avec votre équipe.

Parler devant la classe

- Ne pensez pas aux éventuelles erreurs que vous allez commettre (si vous aviez déjà un anglais parfait, vous n'auriez pas besoin d'être en cours d'anglais !) ; le plus important est de **faire passer** votre message.
- Ne « collez » pas à vos notes – mais gardez-les à portée de main en cas de besoin.
- Parlez fort, à ceux qui sont au fond de la classe, et non pas uniquement au professeur.
- Soignez le débit. Laisser le temps à vos camarades de prendre des notes sans pour autant leur dicter l'information.
- Soignez votre prononciation. Articulez bien en ouvrant bien la bouche et n'oubliez pas les 's' en fin de mots.
- Il est normal d'hésiter de temps à autre (voir la fiche méthode « Expressions utiles – *Gap-fillers* », p. 227.)
- Vérifiez que votre public vous suit.

Écouter et prendre des notes

- Habituez-vous à prendre des notes à chaque fois que quelqu'un intervient (voir la fiche « Prendre des notes », p. 220).
- N'hésitez pas à demander à l'intervenant de répéter et de parler. *(Can you repeat that please? / Please speak up! / I didn't catch what you said after...)*
- Encouragez l'intervenant en faisant signe que vous suivez ; cela fait partie de la communication.

Méthodologie

Converser naturellement

- Converser implique de poser des questions et d'écouter les réponses pour pouvoir réagir. Vous devez être le plus spontané possible (voir le précis grammatical « Questionnement, négation, réponses courtes et *tags* », p. 241).
- N'oubliez pas qu'une conversation ne consiste pas seulement en des questions et des réponses ; il faut aussi réagir (voir fiche méthode « Expressions utiles – Réactions », p. 227).
- Pensez à solliciter plus de précisions en formant une deuxième question basée sur la réponse de votre interlocuteur.
- N'oubliez pas que nous communiquons aussi avec des gestes.

3 Prendre des notes

- Au lycée, pour gagner en rapidité et en efficacité, il est indispensable de développer des **stratégies de prise de notes**, et ce quelle que soit la matière enseignée.
- La prise de notes est le premier stade de la **compréhension** et de l'**assimilation**. C'est aussi une aide précieuse pour **prendre la parole plus aisément**.

Les principes de la prise de notes

Objectif
Écrire **l'essentiel** avec un maximum de **rapidité**.

À éviter
- Attendre que celui/celle qui parle (professeur ou élève) dicte ou écrive au tableau.
- Se précipiter pour écrire et vouloir tout prendre en note sans sélection préalable.
- Prendre des notes illisibles, donc inutilisables par la suite.

La préparation matérielle

- Préparez une fiche de prise de notes, des stylos de différentes couleurs et un/des surligneur(s).
- Lisez la fiche de prise de notes pré-renseignée que votre professeur vous distribuera pour avoir des repères préalables.
- Aérez les notes :
  – allez à la ligne à chaque idée nouvelle, à chaque thème nouveau ;
  – laissez des blancs entre les différents points évoqués ;
- Mettez des repères, toujours aux mêmes endroits (dates, sujet, numérotation, etc.).

À supprimer dans les notes

- Les articles.
- Les verbes dont la disparition ne gêne pas la compréhension.
- Les éléments de commentaire, de digression, non indispensables à la compréhension de l'ensemble.

Les abréviations

- Ayez recours à des abréviations.
- En voici quelques exemples ; vous pouvez bien sûr les modifier et créer vos propres abréviations.

with	w
without	w/o
because	bec
for example	ex. *ou* e.g.
between	betw
people	peop
British	Brit
American	Am
Australian	Austr
possible	poss
impossible	imposs
first, second, third	1st, 2nd, 3rd
and	&
more than less than	> <
approximately	±
as soon as possible	asap
also known as	aka
at	@
to be continued	tbc
means, is, are	=
in addition	in +
increase decrease	↑ ↓
compared with	compd w/
different from, is not	≠
woman	♀
man	♂

4 Comprendre un document écrit

1 Avant de lire le texte

- Étudiez le paratexte – tout ce qui se situe autour du texte : une éventuelle image, un titre, la source (journal, roman… avec date et le nom de l'écrivain ou du journaliste).
- À partir du paratexte vous pourrez commencer à émettre des hypothèses sur l'éventuel thème que le texte traite.
- Vérifiez que les lignes sont numérotées, ce qui vous aidera à en repérer la structure et à faire référence, ensuite, à des passages ou expressions-clés.

2 Première lecture

- Lisez assez rapidement le texte et essayez de relever :
  – les personnages – ***who?*** (faites attention aux pronoms et aux noms propres – faciles à repérer par les majuscules) ;
  – les lieux mentionnés – ***where?*** (aussi grâce aux majuscules) ;
  – les éventuelles dates ou les indications de temps pour déterminer ***when?*** ;
  – identifiez de quoi il est question – ***what?*** (repérez les mots répétés et les champs lexicaux).

  Surtout, **ne vous focalisez pas** sur les mots ou expressions que vous ne connaissez pas !

3 Deuxième lecture

- Lisez le texte très attentivement. Essayez de repérer les groupes nominaux (souvent précédés d'un déterminant (*the, this, that, those, these*, l'article *a/an* ou le génitif *'s*) et les groupes verbaux (étudiez bien leurs formes).
- Concentrez-vous sur les mots que vous connaissez et les mots transparents (ceux qui ressemblent à des mots en français) mais méfiez-vous des faux-amis.
- Si vous devez répondre à des questions précises sur le texte, c'est maintenant le moment de les lire, avant de relire le texte pour une troisième fois. Les questions peuvent souvent vous aider à comprendre le texte ou à diriger votre lecture.

4 Troisième lecture

- Avec tout ce que vous avez pu comprendre du paratexte, des deux premières lectures ainsi que de la lecture des questions, utilisez le contexte pour essayer de déduire le sens des mots inconnus. Vérifiez aussi que vous comprenez à qui ou à quoi renvoie chaque pronom.
- À ce stade, vous serez capable de répondre aux questions ou de résumer le texte.

5 Comprendre un document oral

- Il est normal de ne pas tout entendre ou tout comprendre d'emblée.
- À la différence du discours écrit, qui peut être relu autant de fois que nécessaire, il n'y a pas de trace du discours oral car il est spontané et plutôt constitué de phrases courtes, parfois incomplètes, souvent reprises et reformulées après une pause ou une hésitation.
- L'intonation et/ou la gestuelle viennent souvent éclairer le sens du message, le nuancer, parfois même le contredire.

Marche à suivre

1. PREMIÈRE ÉTAPE

- Essayez d'anticiper ce que vous allez entendre à partir du titre donné au support audio/vidéo.
- Pensez au vocabulaire que vous connaissez et qui correspond au champ lexical du thème annoncé par le titre.

2. DEUXIÈME ÉTAPE

Première écoute

- Repérez la nature du support (publicité, extrait de discours, flash radio, extrait de roman, dialogue extrait d'un film, etc.) et portez votre attention sur une compréhension globale.
- Notez quelques informations objectives :
  – les intervenants, le ton des échanges, et les indices sonores non langagiers ;
  – les lieux, le moment.

  Notez quelques mots accentués qui vous permettront de définir le thème principal dont il est question.

Écoutes suivantes

- Essayez de repérer :
  – les mots les plus accentués et les plus répétés ;
  – les actions ou les sentiments auxquels ils renvoient ;
  – les relations entre les personnages, leur état d'esprit ;
- Formulez des hypothèses pour les recouper avec ce que vous avez repéré et compris et en déduire le sens de ce qui vous a échappé.

Méthodologie

6 Présenter une image

Stagecoach Attack,
by Charles Marion Russell (1864 -1926).

Le genre

This is a cartoon strip, a caricature, a painting, a drawing, a portrait, an advertisement / advert / ad, a still from a film, a poster, a photo ...

Par qui ? Issu de...

It was created / drawn by… and printed in ...
It was painted by / taken by / designed by ...
The cartoonist / caricaturist / painter / artist / designer / photographer ...
It can be found in ...

Sa forme

The cartoon is made up of four / five /... frames
The painting measures ... and is painted in oils / water-colours / pastels ...
The ad consists of ... with the caption / title ...
As for the layout of the poster, there's a photo in the middle ...
It's a black and white / colour photo ...

Les personnages et la mise en scène

It features three / four characters.
The scene takes place / is set in ...
The man looks ... *(+ adjectif)*
The girl is ... *(+ V-ing; utilisez la forme -ing pour décrire les actions que vous voyez)*

La mise en relief

The family is highlighted / brought to our attention.
The cartoonist focuses on ...
It illustrates / portrays / depicts ...
The artist captures ...

Le message et le ton

The artist wants to point out that ...
He/She draws our attention to
He/She wants to make us aware of / make us realise that…
It may have been painted to show ...
The cartoonist is satirising ...
He/She attempts to make ... look ridiculous.
It's ironic /humorous / comic / exaggerated / underplayed / ...
It's a cruel depiction of ... / a flattering portrayal of ... / a funny illustration.

Le point de vue personnel

I identify with ...
The situation is very familiar to me.
I do not share the artist's vision at all.
I do not think the cartoonist has gone far enough.

7 Présenter un texte

1 Parler du genre et de la date de publication

- *Pour un extrait de roman, (auto)biographie, nouvelle, essai, livre* :

This extract / passage is taken from / is an excerpt from the novel / (auto)biography / short story / essay / book (written) by ... and published in 1980.
It is written / narrated in the first / third person and there is a lot of / some dialogue / description.

- *Pour un article de presse :*

This is an article by / written by ... from the ... newspaper / magazine published on the third of February 2015. Its headline is...

- *Pour un poème ou une chanson :*

This poem / sonnet / song was written by ... in 1652. It has / is made up of ... verses, each verse having ... lines. Its rhyme scheme is ABAB.

- *Pour un journal intime :*

Here are a few extracts from the diary of ... / ...'s diary written on the second, third and fourth of February, 1950.

2 Parler du sujet pricipal

It is principally about...
It deals with...
Its main theme is...
It tackles the subject of...
It explains / illustrates / describes / depicts...

3 Parler des personnages

Three characters are present and another four are just mentioned.
The main / central characters in this passage are...
We are introduced to three characters:...

4 Dire où et quand

The scene is set / takes place during the winter of 1980.
Most of the action happens / takes place in the street.

5 Citer

...and I quote, in line...
As we read in line...

8 Rédiger un dialogue

CHOIX 1 : vous pouvez choisir de présenter votre dialogue **comme une pièce de théâtre**.

PRÉSENTATION : écrivez les énoncés de chaque énonciateur :

- sans utiliser de guillemets ;
- en ajoutant des indications scéniques, si vous le souhaitez.

PAUL *(sits down with his head in his hands) I can't go on any more.*
JANE *What's the matter, Paul? (She comforts him by putting her arm around him.)*

CHOIX 2 : vous écrivez votre dialogue **à l'intérieur d'une narration**. Il faut alors respecter la **ponctuation anglaise**.

PRÉSENTATION : pour chaque nouvel énonciateur :

- allez à la ligne et ouvrez les guillemets (**pas de tirets**) ;
- fermez les guillemets à la fin de l'énonciation et ajoutez votre narration pour expliquer qui parle, comment, et ce qu'il fait.

"..........," said Paul angrily, banging his fist on the table.
"...............?" he went on to ask.
"......................," replied Jane in a condescending tone.

Méthodologie

VOCABULAIRE POUR RÉDIGER UN DIALOGUE

INTRODUCTORY VERBS

- **1. speak**
  add, answer, break in, declare, interrupt, point out, repeat, reply, say
- **2. speak loudly**
  call (out), cry, scream, shout, yell
- **3. speak softly**
  mumble, murmur, mutter, whisper
- **4. speak emotionally**
  boast, complain, confess, groan, insist, laugh, moan, object, scoff, sigh, sob, stammer

GESTURES

bang one's hand, clench one's fist, frown, gaze at, look at, pull a (long) face, put one's head in one's hands, shrug (one's shoulders), stare at, throw one's arms in the air

ADVERBS

abruptly, angrily, calmly, excitedly, forcefully, helpfully, ironically, joyfully, lamely, lovingly, nervously, sadly, sarcastically, strangely, suddenly, sympathetically

9 Rédiger un article de presse

L'objectif

Écrire quelque chose de captivant et structuré qui transmet de l'information sur la base d'éléments précis.

Le titre

- Il peut être :
  – informatif (il répond à la question *what?* ou *who?*) ;
  – incitatif (il sous-entend le contenu par des mots clefs, un jeu de mots, etc. ; soyez créatifs !).

L'introduction

- Il faut éveiller la curiosité du lecteur ; soignez la première phrase !
- Il faut présenter les faits : *what? who? where? when?*

Le développement

- Il peut prendre plusieurs formes :

  – la pyramide inversée (le premier paragraphe apporte l'information clef ; la suite de l'article apporte des informations secondaires en ordre décroissant d'importance) ;

  – le sablier (le premier paragraphe apporte l'information clef ; la suite de l'article apporte des précisions, mais on garde des informations marquantes pour les placer en fin d'article) ;

  – l'organisation chronologique (elle respecte le déroulement des événements rapportés).
- Chaque paragraphe doit apporter une information nouvelle.

Le style

- Il faut écrire dans un style qui met en avant les informations à transmettre et non pas l'avis du journaliste !

> **CHILDREN SOLD GUNS IN SCHOOL**
>
> Kids have been selling guns to each other in a school playground – for as little as £5 each.
> Teachers uncovered the illicit trade when a lad fired one of the air guns in class, narrowly missing another pupil.
> An 11-year-old boy is thought to have brought the pellet-firing weapons into Dellmer High School, Blackpool.
> One parent said: "It's terrifying that children are carrying guns in class." A police spokeswoman said: "These ball-bearing guns are not toys – they can be very dangerous."
> What can parents, teachers and adults in general do to prevent kids from playing with guns? Join our net forum!
>
> Stan Jennings, March 21, 2010

- En anglais, on utilise souvent la voix passive :
  – *A meeting was held to discuss…*
  – *A UFO has been spotted close to …*
- Utilisez le prétérit pour raconter les événements passés.
- Utilisez un vocabulaire riche et évitez la répétition de vocabulaire ou l'utilisation d'adjectifs pauvres comme *good, bad, interesting.*
- Évitez des phrases trop compliquées ; n'oubliez pas que l'objectif est de transmettre l'information de façon simple et claire.

La conclusion

- Elle peut :
  – élargir le thème ;
  – relancer le débat ;
  – décrire sous un angle différent la situation ou le personnage mentionnés dans l'introduction.
- Il faut bien soigner la dernière phrase – la « chute » – qui va laisser le lecteur sur une impression générale (bonne, mauvaise, à méditer…).

10 Écrire une lettre

1 The writer's address: top right.

2 The date: under the writer's address.

3 The addressee's address *(for business letters)*: on the left, after the date.

4 The greeting
- if name unknown: Dear Sir / Madam
- if surname known: Dear Mr / Mrs *(married woman)*/ Miss *(unmarried woman)* / Ms *(any woman)* Smith
- if first name known: Dear John / Mary …

5 The introduction *(examples)*
- I'm writing to tell you / to ask you …
- Thank you for your letter of 8th May.
- Further to your telephone call today, …

6 The main body of letter

7 Signing off
- Yours faithfully *(very formal)*
- Yours sincerely *(business and acquaintances)*
- (with) Best wishes *(friends)*
- (with) Love from *(very good friends)*
- Best regards *(business emails)*

8 Signature

1 25, Grange Rd
Williamstown
AB1 C23 Kent

2 4th June 2015

Mr H. Williams
3 Harry's Pizza Place
25 High Street
Williamstown
AB2 C95 Kent

4 Dear Mr Williams,

5 I would like to apply for the job of part-time pizza chef as advertised in the Kent Messenger.
6 I am…
[..]

I look forward to hearing from you very shortly.

7 Yours sincerely,

8 Jack Cook

11 Débattre

Donner son avis / *Stating an opinion*

I think / believe / reckon
Je pense / crois / suppose

In my opinion / to my mind / from my point of view, …
À mon avis / Pour moi …

The way I see it, … / My feeling is that …
Mon sentiment est que …

If you want my honest opinion / If you ask me, …
Si vous voulez savoir ce que je pense vraiment / mon avis, …

According to Yasmine, …*
Selon Yasmine, …

As far as I'm concerned, …
Pour/en ce qui me concerne …

What I'm trying to say is that …
Ce que j'essaie de dire, c'est que …

*Attention ! *According to me* n'existe pas.

Demander l'opinion / *Asking for an opinion*

What's your opinion? / How do you feel about that?
Qu'en pensez-vous ?

What are your thoughts on all of this?
Que pensez-vous de tout ça ?

Do you have anything to say / add?
Avez-vous quelque chose à dire / à ajouter ?

Wouldn't you say that…?
Ne diriez-vous pas que … ?

Exprimer son accord / *Expressing agreement*

I agree with you 100 percent. / I totally agree with you.
Je suis 100 % / totalement d'accord avec vous.

I couldn't agree with you more.
Je ne pourrais pas être plus de votre avis.

That's so true.
C'est tellement vrai.

That's undeniable.
C'est indéniable.

You're absolutely right.
Vous avez tout à fait raison.

That's exactly how I feel.
C'est exactement ce que je ressens.

I have to side with Mary on this one.
Je suis obligé(e) d'être d'accord avec Marie sur ce point.

There's no doubt about it.
Il n'y a aucun doute là-dessus.

You have a point there.
Vous marquez un point ici.

I was going to say (exactly) the same thing.
J'allais dire exactement la même chose.

Exprimer son désaccord / *Expressing disagreement*

I don't think so.
Je ne (le) pense pas.

I'm afraid I disagree. / I totally disagree.
Je crains de ne pas être d'accord. / Je suis en total désaccord.

I beg to differ.
Permettez-moi de ne pas être d'accord.

I'd say the exact opposite.
Je dirais tout le contraire.

I object to that.
J'ai une objection.

That's not always true / not always the case.
Ce n'est pas toujours vrai / le cas.

I have my doubts about that.
J'ai mes doutes sur ce point.

You're talking nonsense / rubbish.
Vous dites n'importe quoi.

Interruptions / *Interrupting*

Can I add something here?
Puis-je ajouter quelque chose ?

Is it okay if I jump in for a second?
Est-ce que je peux intervenir une minute ?

If I might add something, ...
S'il m'est permis d'ajouter quelque chose, ...

Sorry to interrupt, but ...
Désolé(e) de vous interrompre, mais ...

Sorry, go ahead. / Sorry, you were saying?
Désolé(e), continuez ... / Vous disiez ... ?

You didn't let me finish.
Vous ne me laissez pas terminer.

Mettre fin à un désaccord / *Settling an argument*

Let's just move on, shall we?
Passons au point suivant, voulez-vous ?

Let's drop it.
Laissons cela. / Restons-en là.

Let's agree to differ.
Prenons acte de notre désaccord.

12 Organiser et lier son discours

Les mots de liaison, les expressions et tournures idiomatiques servent à rendre votre discours fluide et cohérent. Ils permettent au lecteur de mieux suivre vos propos.

Ils vous aident à :
– introduire et conclure ;
– justifier vos propos ;
– apporter des précisions et des nuances ;
– exprimer votre point de vue.

Ordonner ses pensées logiquement

First of all / to begin with / firstly, ...
Tout d'abord, ...

Secondly, thirdly, ...
Deuxièmement, troisièmement, ...

Then / next / after that, ...
Puis / Ensuite, Après, ...

Finally / Last of all, ...
En dernier / Pour finir ...

Commencer par une généralité

As a general rule, ...
En règle générale, ...

It is generally agreed that ...
Tout le monde s'accorde à dire que ...

As a matter of fact, ...
En fait, ...

It cannot be denied that ...
Force est de constater que ...

Clore une argumentation

As a / In conclusion, it may be argued that ...
En conclusion, on peut arguer que ...

To conclude, ...
À conclure, ...

All things considered, ...
Tout bien considéré, ...

After weighing up the pros and cons of the matter, ...
Après avoir pesé le pour et le contre, ...

It must be acknowledged that ...
On doit bien reconnaître que ...

Compléter ou préciser son argumentation

Moreover / Furthermore, ...
En outre, ...

Besides / What's more / In addition (to that) / On top of that, ...
De plus, ...

It could also be said that ...
On pourrait aussi ajouter que ...

Exprimer la cause et la conséquence

Consequently / As a result (of this) / As a consequence, …
Par conséquent / En conséquence, …

Therefore / Thus / So / Hence, …
Donc / Ainsi / De là / D'où …

That's why … / For this reason, …
C'est pour cela que … / Pour cette raison, …

Exprimer une contradiction, une opposition

Alternatively / On the contrary / Conversely, …
Alternativement / Au contraire / À l'inverse

Contrary to / Unlike …
Contrairement à

Despite / In spite of …
Malgré / En dépit de …

Although / Even though / Even if …
Bien que / Même si …

However / Nevertheless / Nonetheless, …
Cependant / Néanmoins, …

(and) yet	*(et) pourtant*
instead of	*au lieu de*
whereas	*tandis que*

Mettre deux éléments en parallèle, comparer et contraster

on the one hand … on the other …
d'un côté, … de l'autre …

The flip side of the coin is that …
Le revers de la médaille est que …

The bright side is that …
Le côté positif est que …

The down side is that …
Le côté négatif est que …

in comparison
en comparaison

In the same way / Similarly / Equally, …
De la même manière / Également, …

Donner un exemple

for example / for instance, …
par exemple …

As we can see in the case of …
Comme nous pouvons voir dans le cas de …

Conclure

In conclusion / As a conclusion / To conclude, …
En conclusion / Comme conclusion / Pour conclure, …

To summarise / In summary, …
Pour résumer / En résumé, …

overall
dans l'ensemble

Vérifier la compréhension

Shall I repeat?
(Voulez-vous que) je répète ?

Am I making myself clear?
Est-ce que je m'exprime clairement ?

You seem lost. Are you following?
Tu sembles perdu(e). Tu suis ?

Should I speak louder?
Devrais-je parler plus fort ?

Well done! That's great!
Bien joué ! C'est fantastique !

Which point would you like me to go over again?
Sur quel point voulez-vous que je revienne ?

Expressions utiles

Pour rendre votre parole plus naturelle et pour vous donner le temps de réfléchir à comment vous allez poursuivre, il est nécessaire de maîtriser les *gap-fillers* et les expressions qui permettent de réagir.

Gap-fillers

Um … Er …	*Euh.*
So …	*Donc …*
Well, …	*Eh bien, …*
OK then.	*Bon, d'accord.*
Let's see.	*Voyons.*

I'm not quite sure how to say/put this, but …
Je ne suis très sûr(e) de comment formuler ceci, mais …

In other words, …	*En d'autres termes, …*
What I mean is …	*Ce que je veux dire c'est …*
That's to say …	*C'est-à-dire …*
in fact	*en fait*
obviously	*évidemment, de toute évidence*
If you see what I mean.	*Si vous voyez ce que je veux dire.*
indeed	*en effet*

Réactions

Me too.	*Moi aussi.*
Me neither / Nor me.	*Moi non plus.*
Oh no, not me.	*Ah non, pas moi.*
It's the same for me.	*C'est la même chose pour moi.*
Lucky you!	*Veinard !*
Poor you!	*Pauvre de toi !*
Wow, that's amazing!	*Waouh, c'est époustouflant !*
You're kidding!	*Tu plaisantes !*
That's absolutely terrible!	*C'est absolument affreux !*

No way!
Pas moyen. / Tu plaisantes ! Pas question.

I can('t) imagine.
J'imagine / Je ne peux pas imaginer.

13 Les procédés de traduction

Conseils généraux

- Avant de vous lancer dans la traduction, il convient de bien explorer le texte et le passage que vous allez traduire. Essayez :

  – d'en évaluer le contenu (est-il descriptif, affectif, intellectuel… ?) ;

  – de reconstituer la situation ;

  – de repérer le niveau de langue (écrite, orale, formelle, familière, vulgaire…) ;

  – d'identifier les effets stylistiques.

Procédés de traduction les plus courants

1. L'EMPRUNT

- On l'utilise quand le français ne possède pas de mot équivalent au mot à traduire pour des raisons culturelles ou de nouveauté scientifique :

  She handed me a glass of sherry.
  Elle me tendit un verre de sherry.

  Click to download the plug-ins.
  Cliquez pour télécharger les plug-ins.

  Certains emprunts (ex: plug-ins) sont faits pour créer des effets (stylistiques, savants, etc.) alors qu'une recherche approfondie montre que le français possède des équivalents :
  Cliquez pour télécharger les greffons.

- Le traducteur qui veut créer un effet « couleur locale » aura souvent recours à des emprunts alors que des mots français équivalents existent :

  Corridas ? He loved them! He was a real aficionado!
  Les corridas ? Il adorait ! C'était un vrai aficionado.

  Notez que l'anglais lui-même a emprunté des mots espagnols :
  Bullfights ? He loved them. He was a real fan.

  Notez les variantes françaises possibles selon l'effet que l'on veut créer :
  Les courses de taureaux ?
  Il adorait. Il en était fan.
  Les courses de taureaux ?
  Il adorait. Il en était vraiment féru.

- Emprunts abusifs passés dans la langue courante :

  I've just bought a laptop.
  Je viens de m'acheter un laptop/un ordinateur portable/un portable.

  « Portable » est un emprunt abusif (un anglicisme) puisque le mot « portatif » est sa traduction littérale.

2. LE CALQUE

- À éviter aussi souvent que possible. Il fait souvent sursauter les correcteurs de versions :

  the man in the street
  l'homme dans la rue/l'homme de la rue

  Alors que la meilleure traduction est :
  le Français (le citoyen) moyen

3. LA TRADUCTION LITTÉRALE

- Elle consiste à traduire d'une langue dans l'autre, mot à mot :

  She fell off the stepladder.
  Elle est tombée/tomba de l'escabeau.

  The plane took off on time.
  L'avion a décollé/décolla à l'heure.

- Mais les différences culturelles ou linguistiques interdisent souvent ce procédé. Parfois, la traduction littérale n'a pas de sens :

  Elle m'a posé un lapin.
  *She put me a rabbit. She stood me up.

- Les différences syntaxiques obligent aussi à abandonner la traduction littérale :

  The dog was run over.
  **Le chien a été roulé dessus.*
  Le chien s'est fait écraser.

- Les trois procédés décrits ci-dessus relèvent de la traduction « directe » ; ceux qui suivent de la traduction dite « oblique ».

4. LA TRANSPOSITION

- Ce procédé consiste à utiliser dans la langue d'arrivée des mots d'une autre nature que ceux employés dans la langue de départ :

  Ring me up as soon as they arrive.
  Appelez-moi dès leur arrivée.

  « Dès qu'ils arrivent » est tout à fait recevable, mais l'inverse n'est pas possible : **Ring me up as soon as their arrival.*

- Le célèbre « chassé-croisé » est un exemple de transposition :

  The children groped their way across the room.
  Les enfants traversèrent la pièce (obscure) à tâtons.

5. LA MODULATION

- On recourt à ce procédé lorsque la langue d'arrivée n'a pas d'équivalent littéral à la tournure de la langue de départ :

  I will always remember the day when we met.
  Je n'oublierai jamais le jour où nous nous sommes rencontrés.

  Il s'agit ici de modulation obligatoire. Mais la traduction proposée ci-dessus montre un autre exemple de modulation, facultative, celle-ci :

  I will always remember. *Je n'oublierai jamais.*
  (opposition affirmatif/négatif et dans le domaine grammatical et dans le domaine lexical)

  Notez que la traduction de l'énoncé anglais de départ pourrait très bien se faire avec une transposition :
  Je n'oublierai jamais le jour de notre rencontre.

6. L'ÉQUIVALENCE

- Les exclamations produites par des situations similaires dans des cultures différentes donnent un bon exemple d'équivalence :

  Ouch! *Aïe !* Peek-a-boo! *Coucou !*

- Le cas des expressions idiomatiques figées ou des proverbes en donnent un autre exemple :

  straight from the horse's mouth
  de source sûre

  He drinks like a fish.
  Il boit comme un trou.

  strong as an ox
  il a une force de cheval

  as good as gold
  sage comme une image

  Every cloud has a silver lining.
  À quelque chose malheur est bon.

7. L'ADAPTATION

- Ce procédé consiste à trouver l'équivalent français d'une tournure étrangère intraduisible littéralement pour des raisons essentiellement culturelles :

  He bolted down his meal before you could say Jack Rabbit.
  Il avala/engloutit son repas en un clin d'œil.

8. L'ÉTOFFEMENT ET L'AMPLIFICATION

- Ce procédé est aussi appelé « expansion ».
- On rencontre des cas où il est indispensable d'ajouter une précision dans la langue d'arrivée afin d'obtenir le même effet que celui obtenu dans la langue de départ.
- C'est souvent ce qu'on est obligé de faire pour traduire les prépositions anglaises ou plus généralement lorsque la traduction littérale ne se suffit pas à elle-même :

  To the trains / planes
  accès au quai/aux avions

  Passengers to Waterloo
  les passagers à destination de la gare de Waterloo

  Don't forget to stop at the bakery for the bread.
  N'oublie pas de t'arrêter à la boulangerie pour prendre le pain.

- On traduit souvent les prépositions en ajoutant un adjectif :

  the plot against the king
  le complot ourdi contre le roi

- Il faut aussi très souvent étoffer la traduction des pronoms démonstratifs et des conjonctions :

  This in itself would turn out to be a rather dangerous option.
  Ce choix en lui-même devait se révéler plutôt dangereux.

  The murderer, as was expected, came back to where he had left his victim.
  L'assassin, comme il fallait s'y attendre, revint à l'endroit où il avait laissé sa victime.

- En fait, l'étoffement est un cas particulier de l'amplification, qui consiste à pallier un manque de mots dans la langue de départ :

  The girl cried herself to sleep.
  À force de pleurer, la fillette finit par s'endormir.

  She talked him out of his scheme.
  Elle le persuada de renoncer à son plan.

  She sweet-talked herself into the job.
  À force de belles paroles, elle a réussi à se faire embaucher.

  He worked himself to the top.
  Il a gravi les échelons à force de travail.

9. L'ELLIPSE

- Il s'agit le plus souvent de l'omission d'un pronom personnel dans une langue ou l'autre :

Watch it!	*Attention !*
Tell him.	*Dis-le lui.*
You made it!	*Tu as réussi !*

  When is he getting married ? He didn't say.
  Quand se marie-t-il ? Il ne l'a pas dit.

10. LA DILUTION

- Le phénomène existe dans les deux langues, anglais et français. Il arrive que la même idée dans une langue requière moins de mots que dans une autre :

  I smoked for ten years but I never inhaled.
  J'ai fumé durant dix ans mais je n'ai jamais avalé la fumée.

  The rabid dog was frothing at the mouth.
  Le chien enragé écumait.

11. LA COLLOCATION

- Ce procédé concerne des mots de nature différente dont l'usage favorise l'association. On est là, le plus souvent, dans le domaine de la traduction d'expressions idiomatiques :

  Her eyes were heavy with sleep.
  Elle tombait de sommeil.

Précis grammatical

1. LE GROUPE VERBAL

2. LE GROUPE NOMINAL

A. Le nom

B. Les déterminants du nom

3. LA PHRASE ET LE DISCOURS

A. La phrase

B. Le discours

Une grammaire communicative

L'approche des spécificités grammaticales de l'anglais adoptée dans ce précis est celle de la **grammaire communicative**, c'est-à-dire que nous donnons autant d'importance à la réflexion sur l'intention de **communiquer** qu'à celle qui porte sur la forme que prennent les messages langagiers et à l'**effet de sens** que celle-ci produit.

Quelques définitions

Énonciateur La personne qui s'exprime (oralement ou par écrit). On dit parfois « locuteur ».

Co-énonciateur La personne destinataire du message délivré par l'énonciateur. On dit parfois « interlocuteur ».

Énoncé Le message oral ou écrit produit par l'énonciateur ; on parle aussi dans ce cas de « phrase ».

Intention de communiquer Le sens que l'énonciateur veut donner à son message.

Effet de sens La façon dont ce message est perçu par le co-énonciateur.

Abréviations des renvois :

GV : voir partie « Le groupe verbal »

GN : voir partie « Le groupe nominal »

Phr. : voir partie « La phrase et le discours »

1. LE GROUPE VERBAL

Il existe en anglais deux types de verbes :

– les verbes lexicaux comme *run, sleep, think, sleep, rest...*

– les verbes auxiliaires qui servent à conjuguer les verbes lexicaux : *be, have, do*
dont les modaux font partie : *can/could, may/might, must, shall/should, will/would.*

N.B. Certains auxiliaires ont pour origine des verbes lexicaux : *be* (= exister), *have* (= posséder), *do* (= faire).

1 Les verbes lexicaux

• Les verbes lexicaux sont :
– simples (*fall, write, swim*) ;
– prépositionnels (*wait for sb., stare at sb., look for sth.*) ;
– à particule (*look up, sit down, go away*) ;
– à particule et prépositionnels (*come back from, look up to*).

• Ils sont soit **transitifs** (ils nécessitent un complément d'objet [direct ou indirect]), soit **intransitifs** (ils fonctionnent sans complément d'objet).

Comme en français certains verbes peuvent être transitifs et/ou intransitifs :

He did nothing but talk, talk, talk, and he talked nonsense.
Il n'a rien fait d'autre que parler encore et encore,
et il n'a dit que des âneries.

• Il existe aussi des verbes de **sens attributif** : ils permettent d'introduire un attribut pour le sujet ou le COD, selon les emplois :

I'm sick.
Je suis malade.
He seemed/looked worried.
Il a semblé/avait l'air soucieux.
She made me angry.
Elle m'a vraiment fâché(e)/mis(e) en colère.

Verbes prépositionnels

• Un grand nombre de verbes prépositionnels anglais se traduisent par des verbes sans préposition en français : *look **at** sb* = regarder **Ø** qqn ; *wait **for** sb* = attendre **Ø** qqn, etc.
À l'inverse, certains équivalents anglais de verbes français nécessitant une préposition fonctionnent sans préposition :

Will you remember Ø me? Tu te souviendras **de** moi ?

• À la forme interrogative, la préposition est généralement rejetée à la fin de la phrase :

What are you looking for? Que cherchez-vous ?

Verbes à particule (*phrasal verbs*)

• Ne pas confondre les verbes prépositionnels et les verbes à particule. Les premiers sont toujours suivis de leur complément :

He put his coat over the chair. He put his coat over it.
Il a posé son manteau sur la chaise./Il l'a posé dessus.

• Les seconds, qu'on appelle aussi des *phrasal verbs*, intercalent parfois leur complément entre le verbe et sa particule, et celui-ci doit impérativement être intercalé si c'est un pronom :

He put on his coat/he put his coat on. He put it on.
Il a mis son manteau. Il l'a mis.

• La difficulté à les différencier parfois tient au fait que, selon les emplois, un grand nombre de particules (adverbes) sont aussi des prépositions. (Voir La phrase 2 et 3.)

2 Les verbes auxiliaires

Be

• À l'origine, comme « être » en français, *be* veut dire « exister » :

To be or not to be, that is the question.
Être ou ne pas être, telle est la question.

Il perd ce sens lorsqu'il est employé comme auxiliaire ou verbe de sens attributif.

• Quand il est auxiliaire, *be* est suivi soit d'un participe présent (forme dite « continue ») soit d'un participe passé (forme passive). Dans ces emplois, l'énonciateur parle de la nature du sujet ou de la situation dans laquelle il se trouve :

The dog was running across the street.
Le chien traversait la rue en courant.
It was run over by an oncoming bus.
Il fut écrasé par l'autobus qui arrivait.

• C'est *be* auxiliaire qui prend la marque du temps.

Have

• À l'origine, comme « avoir » en français, *have* veut dire « posséder ». Il perd ce sens lorsqu'il est employé comme auxiliaire.

• Comme *be*, il est intercalé entre le sujet et le participe passé dont il est suivi. Il est l'auxiliaire des temps grammaticaux appelés *present perfect* et *pluperfect*.

• *Have* + participe passé sert à l'énonciateur qui exprime un bilan par rapport au moment de parole (le présent) :

I've been here before. Je suis déjà venu/passé par là.

• *Had* + participe passé sert à l'énonciateur qui exprime un bilan par rapport à un moment passé :

I hadn't seen her for at least ten years.
Cela faisait au moins dix ans que je ne l'avais pas vue.

• C'est *have* auxiliaire qui prend la marque du temps.

N.B. Aux temps composés du français (passé composé, plus-que-parfait, passé antérieur, futur antérieur) on utilise soit l'auxiliaire « avoir » soit l'auxiliaire « être » (ce dernier s'il y a changement de lieu, mouvement, ou changement d'état).En anglais on n'utilise que l'auxiliaire *have* :

He has gone upstairs to study.
Il est monté étudier.
They had left long before we arrived.
Ils étaient partis longtemps avant notre arrivée.

Do

• À l'origine, *do* veut dire « faire ». Il a ce sens lorsqu'il est verbe lexical et prend alors les formes *do, did, done, doing* suivant le temps et la forme que l'énonciateur emploie :

I do that every day at the same time.
Je fais cela tous les jours à la même heure.
I did it myself. J'ai fait cela moi-même/tout seul.
Have you done that before? As-tu déjà fait ça ?
What were you doing? Que faisiez-vous ?

• Quand il est auxiliaire, *do* ne peut prendre que deux formes : présente et passée (comme presque tous les modaux).

• *Do* auxiliaire est suivi de la base verbale du verbe conjugué (comme les auxiliaires modaux).

• C'est *do* auxiliaire qui prend la forme du temps grammatical utilisé.

• *Do* est l'auxiliaire qui permet à l'énonciateur de :

– demander si une action est/a été réalisée :

Do you always put milk in your tea?
Tu mets toujours du lait dans ton thé ?
Did you do that all by yourself?
Est-ce que tu as fait cela tout/toute seul(e) ?

– nier qu'une action est/a été réalisée :

I don't go to school by bus every day.
Je ne prends pas toujours l'autobus pour aller à l'école/au lycée.
She didn't want to talk to me.
Elle ne voulait pas/n'a pas voulu me parler.

– demander confirmation :

Didn't they get divorced last year?
N'ont-ils pas divorcé l'an passé ?
Doesn't she have a job?
Elle n'a pas de travail ?/Est-elle sans travail ?/N'a-t-elle pas de travail ?

– confirmer l'existence d'une action ou d'un fait :

OK, OK, I did tell them. I know it was a mistake.
D'accord, d'accord, je le leur ai (bien) dit/c'est moi qui le leur ai dit. Je sais que c'était une erreur.

3 La conjugaison : généralités

La conjugaison des verbes anglais est relativement simple.

- À la forme affirmative du présent, on utilise la forme de la base verbale à toutes les personnes sauf à la troisième où l'on ajoute un « -s » que l'on prononce (voir Le groupe verbal 17 pour la prononciation de cette désinence).
- Aux formes interrogative, négative et interro-négative du présent, on utilise l'auxiliaire *do* [duː] ; c'est lui qui prend la marque de la troisième personne : *does* [dʌz].
- Au prétérit, le verbe – qu'il soit régulier ou irrégulier – ne change pas de forme quelle que soit la personne du sujet.
- Le participe passé est lui aussi invariable.
- Aux formes interrogative, négative, et interro-négative du prétérit, c'est l'auxiliaire *did* (passé de *do*) qui sert à conjuguer le verbe.

La notion de temps

Bien différencier le temps chronologique (passé, présent, avenir) et les temps grammaticaux.

- L'anglais n'a que deux temps simples : le présent et le passé. Même la référence à l'avenir s'exprime avec des formes « présentes » d'auxiliaires – *will, shall, is/are* (voir Le groupe verbal 7, Futurité ou référence à l'avenir).
- Les verbes anglais sont :

– « réguliers », auquel cas leur prétérit et leur participe passé se forment en ajoutant *-ed* à la base verbale (*V-ed*). Voir Le groupe verbal 17 pour la prononciation de cette désinence.
– « irréguliers », et dans ce cas il convient de mémoriser les formes du prétérit et du participe passé. (Voir les tableaux des verbes irréguliers p. 254-255.)

La notion d'aspect

- Les formes verbales « composées » de l'anglais sont construites à partir de :

– *be* + participe présent
(forme dite continue, ou *be* + V-*ing*) ;
– *have* + participe passé.

- Les linguistes les appellent des « aspects ».
- Lorsque l'énonciateur se contente de dire les faits, il emploie une forme simple.
- Il emploie les aspects lorsqu'il essaie de faire comprendre sous quel angle il envisage les choses : début, continuité de l'action, expression d'un bilan et/ou d'un commentaire sur les faits dont il est question.

4 La conjugaison : temps et aspects

Les temps se combinent aux aspects selon la récapitulation suivante.

Présent simple

- Utilisé pour donner de simples informations ou énoncer des vérités générales :

She works hard. Elle travaille dur.
Oil floats on water.
L'huile flotte sur l'eau/est plus légère que l'eau.
I hate liars. Je déteste les menteurs.

Présent en *be* + V-*ing* (forme dite continue)

- Utilisé pour commenter les faits relatés, donner une opinion, un sentiment, dire dans quelle situation ou quel état se trouve le sujet :

Be quiet! I'm driving. I need to concentrate.
Du calme ! Je conduis. J'ai besoin de me concentrer.
He's always making fun of me.
Il est toujours en train de se moquer de moi./
Il faut toujours qu'il se moque de moi.

Prétérit simple

- Utilisé pour rapporter des faits révolus, coupés du présent :

She took her car keys, opened the door and walked to her car without a word.
Elle prit les clés de sa voiture, ouvrit la porte, et se dirigea vers son véhicule sans un mot.

Prétérit en *be* + V-*ing*

- Utilisé pour renvoyer à la situation dans laquelle se trouvait le sujet :

They were (busy) watching the soccer game when the power went out.
Ils étaient en train de/étaient occupés à regarder le match de foot quand la coupure de courant se produisit.

Present perfect

- Utilisé pour exprimer un bilan au moment de parole (le présent) :

Look! He's [has] painted the kitchen blue.
Regarde ! Il a peint la cuisine en bleu.

Present perfect en *be* + V-*ing*

- Utilisé pour commenter le bilan que l'on fait de la situation dans laquelle se trouve le sujet :

Good heavens! You've been drinking again!
Juste ciel ! Mais tu as encore bu, toi !

Pluperfect (plus-que-parfait)

- Utilisé par l'énonciateur pour faire un bilan par rapport à un repère passé, ou marquer l'antériorité de certains faits par rapport à d'autres faits passés :

I arrived late. They had finished dinner.
Je suis arrivé en retard. Ils avaient fini de dîner.

Pluperfect en be + V-ing

- Utilisé pour faire un bilan commenté par rapport à des repères passés :

  They had been gorging themselves with fast food.
  Ils s'étaient empiffrés de fast food.

N.B. Prudence quand on passe du français à l'anglais : si le plus-que-parfait français peut le plus souvent se traduire par le *pluperfect*, il n'en va pas de même pour le passé composé qui se traduit soit par un prétérit (narration de faits révolus) soit par un *present perfect* (bilan par rapport au moment de parole).

I saw it last year. Je l'ai vu l'an passé.
I have never seen it. Je ne l'ai jamais vu.

5 L'aspect be + V-ing : valeurs et remarques

- La valeur la plus courante de cette forme verbale, quel que soit le temps grammatical avec lequel on la combine, est l'accent que l'énonciateur met sur la situation ou l'état dans lesquels se trouve le sujet (action dite inachevée) :

  Be quiet, children, Dad's driving. (action en cours)
  Du calme, les enfants, papa conduit.
  "What are you drinking?" "Just water please, I'm driving."
  – Que prenez/prendrez-vous ? – Juste un verre d'eau s'il vous plaît, je conduis. (pas d'action en cours ici, donc pas de « en train de... »)
  "What kind of car do you own, Mr Brown?"
  "Oh, I'm driving an old Bentley." (pas d'action en cours ici non plus)
  – Quel genre de voiture avez-vous, Mr Brown ?
  – Oh, je conduis une vieille Bentley.

- L'énonciateur fait référence à des décisions déjà prises, à des projets déjà établis :

  "How are you going to Morocco? By plane?"
  "No. We're driving through France and Spain this year."
  – Comment allez-vous au Maroc ? En avion ?
  – Non, nous traversons la France et l'Espagne en voiture cette année.

- L'énonciateur utilise cette forme pour marquer son refus ou sa volonté :

  I'm not marrying that jerk! No way!
  Pas question que j'épouse ce demeuré !

- Il l'utilise également – avec des expressions de fréquence – pour porter un jugement sur le sujet ou dire ce qu'il en pense :

  Careful! Mary is always borrowing money.
  Fais attention, Marie est toujours en train d'emprunter de l'argent.

- L'énonciateur reprend une idée ou une situation déjà mentionnée :

  When you said that, you weren't telling the truth.
  Quand vous avez dit cela, vous ne disiez pas la vérité.

Ce qu'il ne faut pas perdre de vue

- L'énonciateur qui emploie une forme en *be* + V-*ing* au lieu d'une forme simple emploie deux verbes au lieu d'un. Il est donc logique d'en déduire qu'il essaie d'en dire plus qu'avec une forme simple. Le travail du non-anglophone est donc d'utiliser le contexte, et la façon dont le message est délivré, pour bien en identifier le sens.

Point commun aux formes en *be* + V-*ing*

- Tous les exemples ci-dessus montrent que les énoncés en *be* + V-*ing* font référence à un moment qui précède le moment de parole ou le moment repère : dans tous les cas, l'action a commencé, a été décidée, déjà pensée voire vécue avant le moment repère.

6 Les formes passées et le renvoi à l'irréel (le prétérit « modal »)

Le prétérit «modal»

- Le français emploie souvent l'imparfait de l'indicatif pour faire référence à l'irréel : ce qui est envisagé, supposé, souhaité ou regretté. En anglais l'énonciateur utilise le prétérit dit «modal» dont les formes sont les mêmes que celles du prétérit « chronologique » à une exception près : toutes les formes de *be* sont *were* quelle que soit la personne : *If I were you,...* Si j'étais vous...

- Les expressions les plus courantes qui entraînent l'emploi du prétérit modal sont *if, if only, I wish, it's time/high time, I would rather*, (si, si seulement, je souhaite/regrette que, il est temps/grand temps que, je préfèrerais que...), expressions qui marquent le regret créé par une situation particulière :

  I wish we had a bigger house.
  Si seulement nous avions une plus grande maison/
  Je souhaiterais avoir une plus grande maison/
  Je regrette de ne pas avoir une plus grande maison.

It's high time you did your work.
Il est grand temps que tu fasses ton travail.
I'd rather she didn't come.
Je préfèrerais qu'elle ne vienne pas.

N.B. Notez quand même la différence entre :
I wish he spoke English. (Il ne sait pas parler anglais.)
Je voudrais bien qu'il parle anglais/sache parler anglais.
I wish he would speak English. (Il sait parler anglais mais il ne veut pas.)
Je voudrais bien qu'il fasse un effort pour parler anglais.

• Pour bien maîtriser la construction et l'emploi de ces tournures, il convient de comprendre que la réalité ne donne pas satisfaction à l'énonciateur qui souhaite donc qu'elle soit différente, d'où le « jeu » forme affirmative/forme négative ou forme négative/forme affirmative (ou celui des adjectifs et/ou adverbes contraires) que l'on constate dans les exemples du tableau ci-dessous.

Réalité qui déplaît	Réalité souhaitée	
I'm too tired to go out.	*I wish/if only I weren't so tired.*	présent affirmatif → prétérit négatif
Sorry, I don't have enough time to help you.	*I wish/if only I had more time to help you.*	présent négatif → prétérit affirmatif
I backed my car into hers.	*I wish I hadn't backed my car into hers.*	prétérit affirmatif → pluperfect négatif
I was not rich enough at the time to marry her.	*I wish I had been rich enough to marry her.*	prétérit négatif → pluperfect affirmatif
I'm too small to reach the top shelf.	*I wish I were tall enough to reach the top shelf.*	adj. « négatif » *small* → adj. « positif » *tall* adv. *too* → adv. *enough*

7 Futurité ou référence à l'avenir

• Sens des énoncés qui font référence à l'avenir (l'après-moment de parole). Ils expriment :

– soit la volonté, l'intention de l'énonciateur ou du sujet :

She says she won't marry him, ever.
Elle dit qu'elle ne l'épousera jamais, au grand jamais.
They are not going to accept that.
Ils ne vont pas/ils ne sont pas près d'accepter cela.

– soit leur certitude :

She won't marry me, I know.
Elle ne m'épousera pas, je le sais.
It's going to rain. Il va pleuvoir.

Sens de l'énoncé	Forme utilisée
Prédiction, certitude personnelle	*It **will** never be the same again.*
Prédiction basée sur des repères objectifs	*Watch out for that bus ! You**'re going** to get yourself killed.*
Intention	*We're definitely **going to** do something about it.*
Rappel de faits prévus	*No, because I**'m leaving** tomorrow. Did you forget ?*
Simple information	*I **leave** tomorrow. You had better be ready.*
Immédiateté	*The film **is about** to begin.*
Volonté, refus	*I'**m not about to** do that.*
Annonce de ce qui est prévu ou décidé par le destin	*The DVD of the film **is to** be released tomorrow.*
Commandement	*Thou **shalt** not kill.*
Proposition (remise de la décision dans les mains d'autrui)	***Shall** we help you with all those bags ?* (UK)

• Comme le montre le tableau, les formes qui véhiculent ces valeurs sont très variées mais contiennent toutes un verbe conjugué au présent, car c'est au moment de parole (le présent) que l'intention, la volonté ou la certitude sont exprimées.

• L'action à laquelle il est fait référence, elle, n'existe pas au moment de parole, d'où la forme non conjuguée qui suit les outils linguistiques utilisés (base verbale).

• Référence à l'avenir dans les subordonnées de temps. Les modaux *will* et *shall* ne peuvent être utilisés dans les subordonnées de temps (celles introduites par *when, till/until, as soon as, as long as*, etc.) :

As soon as she arrives I will take my leave.
Aussitôt qu'elle sera là, je prendrai congé.
But I won't leave until she gets here.
Mais je ne partirai pas tant qu'elle ne sera pas là.

• Pour le « futur » dans le passé (action postérieure à une autre action passée ou à un repère passé), les formes « présentes » ci-contre deviennent des formes passées :

He said that he would leave as soon as she arrived.
Il a dit qu'il partirait aussitôt qu'elle arriverait.
He wouldn't leave until she got there.
Il ne partirait pas tant qu'elle ne serait pas là.

8 La voix passive

Emploi/choix de la voix passive

• L'énonciateur qui préfère la voix passive à la voix active veut attirer l'attention du co-énonciateur sur autre chose que l'agent de l'action. Il souhaite attirer cette attention sur :

– l'objet ou la victime de l'action :

She was injured in a road accident.
Elle a été blessée dans un accident de la circulation.

– le bénéficiaire de l'action :

He was awarded a grant to go to college.
On lui a remis/accordé une bourse d'études pour l'université.

Formation de la forme passive

• Comme en français, elle est formée avec *be* + participe passé et c'est *be* qui porte les formes du temps et de l'aspect. L'agent, quand il est mentionné, est introduit par la préposition *by* (= par). Là s'arrêtent les similitudes !

• En français seuls les verbes transitifs directs (accompagnés d'un COD) peuvent être employés à la voix passive. En anglais un complément indirect, d'attribution, voire circonstanciel, peut devenir le sujet d'un verbe passif. La souplesse de l'anglais dans ce cas est bien plus grande que celle du français et pose des problèmes de traduction (voir ci-contre):

Holmes noticed that the bed hadn't been slept in.
(*Bed* est ici le complément circonstanciel de lieu du verbe *sleep* à l'actif).
Holmes remarqua que le lit n'avait pas été défait/que personne n'avait dormi/qu'on n'avait pas dormi dans le lit.

• Comme le montre l'exemple précédent les verbes prépositionnels gardent leur préposition ; celle-ci est renvoyée à la fin de la proposition ou de la phrase :

She didn't like to be stared at.
Elle n'aimait pas qu'on la dévisage.

• On combine assez souvent le passif et la forme continue (*be* + V-*ing*) pour renforcer l'idée que le sujet grammatical est soumis à l'action d'autrui :

She had the strangest feeling that she was being followed.
Elle avait la bizarre impression qu'on la suivait/qu'elle était suivie/d'être suivie/que quelqu'un la suivait.

Traduction du passif anglais en français

• Lorsqu'il est impossible de traduire littéralement un passif anglais, le français a le plus souvent recours à une forme active dont le sujet est le pronom indéfini « on » :

She had the strangest feeling that she was being followed.
Elle avait l'étrange sensation qu'on la suivait.

Mais cette traduction n'est pas la seule possible :

Elle avait l'étrange sensation d'être suivie.

• On a parfois recours à d'autres pronoms indéfinis que « on » :

Holmes noticed that the bed hadn't been slept in.
Holmes remarqua que personne n'avait dormi dans le lit.

Autre traduction possible :

Holmes remarqua que le lit n'avait pas été défait.

• Enfin, le français a parfois recours à l'emploi d'un verbe actif dont le sens est en fait passif :

He was awarded a grant to go to college.
Il reçut une bourse pour aller étudier à l'université./
Il bénéficia d'une bourse...

ou à des expressions intraduisibles mot à mot :

Il se vit remettre une bourse...

Omission du complément d'agent

Dans de nombreux cas, l'énonciateur choisit de ne pas mentionner l'agent de l'action.

• Soit parce qu'il n'est pas important de le mentionner :

The film was released last week.
Le film est sorti la semaine dernière.

• Soit parce qu'il l'ignore ou ne veut pas le mentionner :

She was told to keep away from us.
On lui a dit de se tenir à l'écart de nous.

• Soit parce qu'il serait dangereux ou imprudent de le faire :

I've been informed that....
On m'a informé que...

• Soit parce que l'identité de l'agent est évidente :

When the storm began, the candles were all blown out.
Quand l'orage a éclaté, toutes les bougies ont été soufflées.

9 Les auxiliaires modaux

Caractéristiques

- Ils n'ont que deux formes (comme *do* auxiliaire) : présent et passé (voir tableau récapitulatif ci-dessous).
- *Must* n'a qu'une forme. Ce modal apparaît dans des contextes présents mais aussi, assez souvent, dans des contextes passés surtout dans les cas de discours indirect (voir Le discours WBT n° 14) :

  The doctor said I must stop smoking at once.
  Le médecin a dit que je devais m'arrêter de fumer immédiatement.
- Les modaux ne sont jamais précédés de l'opérateur *to*.
- Leur conjugaison est invariable (pas de « -s » à la troisième personne du singulier).
- Ils ne sont jamais suivis de l'opérateur *to* :

  My five-year old ***can swim****.*
  Mon petit de cinq ans sait nager.
- Ils n'ont pas besoin d'auxiliaire aux formes affirmative, négative ou interro-négative :

  Would you *be so kind as to help me with these bags?*
  Seriez-vous assez aimable pour m'aider à porter ces bagages ?
  You ***can't*** *smoke in here, I'm afraid.*
  J'ai bien peur que vous ne puissiez pas fumer ici.
- Ils servent donc d'auxiliaires à la base verbale du verbe qu'ils accompagnent.

Sens des modaux

Lorsqu'un énonciateur utilise un modal, il exprime son point de vue.

- Il évalue les chances qu'un événement a ou a eu de se produire. On parle dans ce cas de degré de certitude de l'énonciateur (que nous préférons à l'idée de « probabilité ») :

  He must be stuck in the traffic.
  Il doit être coincé dans les embouteillages.
  She may well refuse to marry him.
  Il se peut très bien qu'elle refuse de l'épouser.
- Il essaie d'agir sur le sujet de l'énoncé ou au moins de l'influencer :

  You mustn't tell him anything.
  Tu ne dois rien lui dire.
  They should work a little harder.
  Ils devraient travailler un peu plus dur.
- Il parle des caractéristiques du sujet ou les commente :

  David can't drive! He almost got us killed the other day.
  David ne sait pas conduire! Il a failli nous faire tuer l'autre jour.
  Oh, I know, Mum will always say things like that.
  Oh, je sais, Maman dit toujours des choses de ce genre.

Ce qu'il faut retenir

Un modal peut véhiculer plusieurs des valeurs indiquées ci-dessus. Un modal est le reflet de l'opinion de l'énonciateur (« je ») et de lui seul, il n'est donc pas anormal qu'il ne prennent pas de « -s » à la troisième personne du singulier puisqu'il « appartient » à l'énonciateur et non au sujet grammatical. Dans :

Mary may come after all.
Il se peut que Mary vienne après tout.

Mary est le sujet potentiel de *come*, et *may* représente l'opinion de l'énonciateur. Et comme l'action *come* n'est pas réalisée au moment de parole elle ne comporte aucune trace de conjugaison (base verbale).

Tableau récapitulatif des valeurs des modaux

Modal	Certitude de l'énonciateur	L'énonciateur essaie d'agir sur le sujet	L'énonciateur parle des caractéristiques du sujet
can/could	Logiquement possible *A hurricane can wipe out a city.* *A hurricane could wipe out a city.*	Permission *Can we go out on Friday night?* *They asked whether they could go out on Saturday night.*	Capacité physique ou intellectuelle *Can you swim?* *At the age of five, Mozart could play the violin.*
can't/couldn't	Totalement impossible (à mon avis) *That can't be true.* *I knew it couldn't be true.*	Interdiction *You can't park in front of my driveway.* *He said I couldn't park in front of his driveway.*	Incapacité du sujet *They can't drive.* *At the age of ten, he still couldn't ride a bike.*
will/would won't/wouldn't	Certitude absolue *Someone broke the window. That will be Tom.* *Believe me, she won't do that ever again.* *He knew he would be late.* *I knew he wouldn't come.*		Volonté, intention, habitude *I will come with you, I promise.* *She won't marry me.* *Dad would switch the TV off at ten and send us to bed.* *He wouldn't go to bed himself until 12 a.m.*

Modal	Certitude de l'énonciateur	L'énonciateur essaie d'agir sur le sujet	L'énonciateur parle des caractéristiques du sujet
may/might *may not/might not*	Faible certitude *That may be the right decision after all.* *He may not like that at all.* *She might hate us for doing this.* *She might not appreciate what we are doing.*	Autorisation formelle, refus d'autorisation, suggestion, conseil, concession *May I have some more?* *No, sorry, you may not.* *You may well be my father but that doesn't give you the right to rummage through my things.* *You might try being nice to her.*	
shall/shan't *should/shouldn't*	Cela arrivera inévitablement *MLK said: "We shall overcome!"* *Trust me, I shan't disappoint you.* Risque que cela arrive *If you should meet my parents there...* *That shouldn't be a major problem.*	Proposition, promesse formelle, contrainte *Shall I help you with your math?* *You shall do it whether you like it or not.* Commandement, interdiction, *Your parents you shall honour.* *You shall not kill.* Conseil, reproche *You should keep that in mind.* *You shouldn't talk to your parents like that.*	
must/mustn't	Quasi-certitude *She looks very tired. She must be stressed at work.* *I guess she mustn't be the right woman for me.*	Contrainte, obligation, devoir, interdiction *You must stop to let pedestrians cross the street.* *Hey! You mustn't jump red lights!*	
needn't		Absence de nécessité *You needn't do the housework, we have a maid.*	

- Les formes passées des modaux renvoient souvent à **l'irréel** et à **l'hypothétique** (voir Le groupe verbal 6, Le prétérit modal). Il convient donc de bien analyser l'énoncé et le contexte pour déterminer s'il est question de passé chronologique (narration) ou de passé de type modal.
- Le français emploie soit l'imparfait soit le conditionnel présent pour traduire les formes passées des modaux.

10 Modaux et aspects

Les modaux et l'aspect *have* + participe passé

- Lorsque les idées et concepts véhiculés par les modaux portent sur des faits passés, on les combine avec l'aspect *have* + participe passé :

They can't have done/made that on their own.
Ils n'ont pas pu faire cela tout seuls.
She could have been nicer to her parents.
Elle aurait pu être plus aimable avec ses parents.
I shouldn't have told them.
Je n'aurais pas dû le leur dire.
That must have been a shock.
Ça a dû être un choc.
He would have refused anyway.
Il aurait refusé de toute façon.

Les modaux et l'aspect *be* + V-*ing*

- Lorsque l'énonciateur considère les faits sous l'un des angles décrits plus haut (Le groupe verbal 4 et 5, Valeurs de *be* + V-*ing*) et qu'il combine le modal à cet aspect, les valeurs des modaux restent les mêmes, mais l'énoncé prend l'aspect plus marqué d'un commentaire de ce qui est dit.

I have got to leave you now. I must be getting back to work. Thanks for the meal. (excuse)
Il faut que je vous quitte maintenant. Il faut que je retourne travailler. Merci pour le déjeuner.

11 Les semi-modaux

Souhait et préférence

• L'énonciateur peut les exprimer à l'aide d'expressions qui fonctionnent comme les modaux et qui sont suivies :
– soit de la base verbale du verbe relatif à l'action considérée ;
– soit d'un prétérit modal si le sujet potentiel de l'action en question n'est pas l'énonciateur:

PATIENT : I'd rather leave my bed and go to work. (I'd = I would)
Je préfèrerais quitter mon lit et aller travailler.
DOCTOR : And I would rather you stayed in bed for a couple more days.
Et moi je préfèrerais que vous gardiez le lit encore un jour ou deux.

Conseil ou mise en garde

• L'énonciateur exprime ces concepts avec *had better, need* (nécessité, avoir besoin de) et *dare* (oser).

• *Need* et *dare* fonctionnent tantôt comme des modaux, tantôt comme des verbes lexicaux :

You'd better slow down, there's a radar not far from here.
Tu ferais mieux de lever le pied, il y a un radar pas loin d'ici.
I need to tell you something very important.
J'ai besoin de vous dire/il faut que je vous dise quelque chose d'important.
You needn't have told me, I would have known sooner or later.
Tu n'avais pas besoin de me le dire, je l'aurais appris tôt ou tard.
How dare you speak to me like that?
Comment osez-vous me parler ainsi ?
She didn't dare to speak her mind.
Elle n'osa pas dire ce qu'elle pensait.

Used to ['ju:stʊ] ['ju:stə]

• Cette tournure apparaît uniquement dans des contextes passés et ses formes en anglais moderne ne sont pas toujours nettement fixées. Elle sert à marquer avant tout le caractère révolu des actions ou événements relatés. Elle véhicule parfois la notion d'action passée répétée voire habituelle :

"There used to be a church here. What's happened to it?"
"It was destroyed during the Blitz."
– Il y avait une église ici, autrefois. Que lui est-il arrivé ?
– Elle a été détruite pendant le Blitz.
People used to get up before dawn to go to work on foot.
Autrefois, les gens se levaient avant l'aube pour se rendre à leur travail à pied.
"Did you use to smoke?" "Yes, I used to."
– Est-ce que vous fumiez ? – Oui, (mais plus maintenant)

N.B. Ne pas confondre ce semi-modal avec le passé du verbe *use/used* [ju:zd] = utiliser, ni avec l'adjectif *used* [ju:st] = habitué à, ni avec l'adjectif *used* [ju:zd] = déjà utilisé, d'occasion (*used cars*).

12 Les substituts des modaux

Les auxiliaires modaux ont des « équivalents » aux formes verbales ou ils n'existent pas.

Modaux	Formes dites équivalentes
can/could	*be able to/be allowed to*
will/would	*be about to*
will/shall	*be going to*
will/shall/must	*is to/was to*
may/might	*be allowed to*
must	*have to, be obliged to*
should	*ought to*
would	*used to*

• Les deux types de formes cohabitent au présent et au prétérit, mais avec des nuances de sens.

– L'emploi d'un modal par l'énonciateur indique que celui-ci prend personnellement en charge ce qu'il dit (opinion, volonté, commentaire). On a donc affaire à un énoncé « subjectif » ;

– Le choix d'une forme dite équivalente indique que l'énonciateur se place d'un point de vue « objectif » : il n'appuie pas ce qu'il dit sur sa propre opinion mais sur des circonstances extérieures et constatables par tous. On a alors affaire à un énoncé objectif.

• Les formes équivalentes sont toutes suivies de l'opérateur *to* + BV. Ce *to* ne doit pas être confondu avec la préposition *to* malgré l'origine commune des deux mots :

"Must I really wear this uniform to go to school?"
"Yes, dear, you have to. It's the rule."
(Je n'y suis personnellement pour rien, C'est le règlement qui l'exige).
"Why can't I smoke in my own office?"
"Because people are not allowed to smoke in public places."
(C'est la loi !)
"You should give the poor beggar some money."
"Why is that?"
"Because people ought to be generous to the poor and destitute."

13 Traduction du subjonctif français

• L'anglais n'a pas de mode subjonctif au sens français du mot. Les références à l'irréel s'expriment de diverses façons :

– à l'aide d'une subordonnée infinitive :

I don't want him to join us.
Je ne veux pas qu'il nous rejoigne/qu'il se joigne à nous.

– à l'aide d'un verbe « non conjugué » ou dont on n'utilise que la base verbale quel que soit le temps :

He demanded we arrive before dawn.
Il a exigé que nous soyons là avant l'aube.

– à l'aide d'une forme passée (voir Le groupe verbal 6, Le prétérit modal) :

I'd rather he didn't come.
Je préférerais qu'il ne vienne pas.

– à l'aide d'un des auxiliaires modaux :

Don't tailgate that car lest it should stop abruptly.
Ne colle pas cette voiture de crainte qu'elle ne s'arrête brutalement.

14 Le mode impératif

• L'énonciateur qui donne un ordre direct à un ou plusieurs co-énonciateurs emploie simplement la base verbale du verbe considéré : *Listen and be quiet!*

N.B. au moment où l'ordre est donné, l'action commandée n'est pas exécutée, d'où l'absence de forme de conjugaison sur le verbe.

• Si l'ordre donné porte sur une autre personne que la deuxième, l'énonciateur utilise l'auxiliaire *let* (+ COD + base verbale) (voir La phrase 11, Les structures causatives) :

Let's get out of here! (= let us)
Sortons d'ici !
Let her go!
Qu'elle parte ! (Vire-la ! [dans le contexte de l'entreprise])
Let them be!
Mais qu'on les laisse tranquilles !

• Si l'ordre est négatif, l'énonciateur utilise l'auxiliaire *don't* :

Don't let them escape!
Ne les laissez pas s'échapper !
Don't let him know!
Qu'il ne le sache surtout pas !

• Le cas de *be* :

Don't be so harsh on him.
Ne sois pas si dur(e) avec lui.

15 Traduction de la forme pronominale française

Il existe trois types de formes pronominales en français.

• **La forme pronominale réfléchie** employée lorsque le sujet et l'objet d'une action sont la où les mêmes personnes :

Il se regarde dans la glace.
He's looking at himself in the mirror.

(Voir *GN 16,* les pronoms personnels réfléchis – tableau)

• **La forme pronominale réciproque** employée lorsque plusieurs sujets font la même action les uns sur les autres :

Ils se connaissent.
They know each other/one another.
Ils se battent.
They're fighting each other/(with) one another.

Traditionnellement, on emploie *each other* quand on a affaire à deux sujets, et *one another* quand ils sont plus de deux. Mais cette « règle » est loin d'être systématiquement appliquée.

• **La forme dite « simplement » pronominale** qui ne correspond à aucun des deux cas précédents :

Ils se sont enfuis.
They ran away.
La bougie s'est éteinte.
The candle went out.
Elles se lèvent à 6 heures.
They get up at 6am.

Notez que ces verbes sont le plus souvent traduits par des *phrasal verbs* anglais.

16 Questionnement, négation, réponses courtes et «tags»

Principes

- En anglais, on a besoin d'un auxiliaire pour construire un énoncé interrogatif ou négatif. Seules les questions commençant par un interrogatif sujet – *who*, *what* – échappent à cette règle.
- Il existe deux types de questions.

– Les questions fermées qui n'appellent que des réponses par « oui » ou par « non » :

Did you see him yesterday?
Have you done your homework?
Do you like classical novels?
Can you swim?

– Les questions ouvertes qui commencent par un mot interrogatif et dont la réponse dépend de la circonstance contenue dans ce mot :

How are you doing?
When did you see her?
What should I do now?
How many children do you have?

Mais :

Who told you?
What made you do that?

Réponses courtes

- Les questions fermées appellent la plupart du temps ce qu'on appelle des réponses courtes qui évitent de reprendre l'intégralité de la question et dans lesquelles les auxiliaires employés résument en quelque sorte l'ensemble de la phrase :

"Did you or did you not see the assassin?"
"No, I didn't, your Honor."
"Yes, I did. He was tall and lanky and wore a heavy black coat."

"Will you marry me, Andrew?"
"Yes, I will."
"I would, but I can't. I already have a family."

Les *tags* et le « jeu » des auxiliaires (traduction de « n'est-ce-pas »)

- Un énonciateur qui emploie un *tag* demande confirmation, remet en question, ou commente ce qu'il vient de dire ou d'entendre. La forme verbale du *tag* est l'inverse de celle utilisée dans l'énoncé de départ, ce qui donne la structure : auxiliaire + (*not*) + sujet :

You saw the assassin, didn't you?
Vous avez vu l'assassin, n'est-ce pas ?
Good heavens! You didn't tell them, did you?
Juste ciel ! Tu ne le leur as pas dit, j'espère ?
We should call it a day, shouldn't we?
Nous devrions en rester là pour aujourd'hui, tu ne crois pas ?
They wouldn't refuse this offer, would they?
Ils ne refuseraient pas une offre comme ça, quand même ?

- Certains *tags* « affirmatifs » véhiculent l'ironie ou la moquerie, parfois la menace :

"I told them everything I knew."
"So you told them, did you?
That wasn't too smart of you, was it?"
– Je leur ai dit tout ce que je savais.
– Ah, oui, vraiment ? Ce n'était pas très malin de ta part, tu ne crois pas ?

L'impératif et les *tags*

- Notez bien les structures particulières suivantes :

Let's all go to the beach today, shall we?
Allons tous faire un tour à la plage, qu'en dites-vous ?
Stop arguing with me, will you?
Cesse de me répondre, veux-tu?

17 Prononciation du -s final et du -ed

Principes à retenir

- Lorsque la base verbale du verbe se termine par un son « sonore », sa désinence se prononce de façon sonore (il ne peut d'ailleurs en être autrement).
- Lorsque, au contraire, elle se termine de façon « sourde » la désinence se prononce de façon « sourde ».
- La marque *-s* de la 3e personne du singulier et du pluriel des noms se prononce :

– [z] après une voyelle ou une consonne sonore.
– [s] après les consonnes [p], [t], [k], [f], [θ].
– [ɪz] après [s], [z], [ʒ], [ʃ].

- La marque *-ed* du passé se prononce :

– [d] après une voyelle ou une consonne sonore.
– [t] après les consonnes [p] [t], [k], [f], [θ].
– [ɪd] après [t], [d].

Terminaisons sonores	Toutes voyelles	[b]	[d]	[g]	[v]	[z]	[ð] (th)	[ʒ]	[l], [m], [n], [r]
Terminaisons sourdes		[p]	[t]	[k]	[f]	[s]	[θ] (th)	[ʃ]	

2. LE GROUPE NOMINAL

A. Le nom WBT

B. Les déterminants du nom

Le nom est déterminé par divers mots que l'on appelle souvent « compagnons du nom ».
Il s'agit des articles, des adjectifs démonstratifs, possessifs, numéraux, qualificatifs et indéfinis.

1 Les articles : ø, an, the

L'article ø (zéro)

- On utilise cet article (ou plutôt cette absence d'article) :

– devant un nom singulier pour faire référence à un concept en général :

I don't like ø tennis. Je n'aime pas le tennis.
He's afraid of ø death. Il a peur de la mort.
I love ø summer. J'adore l'été.

– devant un nom pluriel lorsqu'il fait référence de façon générale à un ensemble d'éléments :

I hate ø liars. Je déteste les menteurs.

– devant un nom de titre si celui-ci est suivi du nom propre de celui ou celle qui le détient :

ø King James I, ø President Obama
le roi Jacques Ier, le Président Obama

– devant les noms de pays :

ø France, ø Germany la France, l'Allemagne

N.B. Notez la différence d'emploi entre le français et l'anglais.

L'article *a/an* (dit article indéfini)

- *A* (*an* devant un son voyelle) correspond au français « un/une ».
- L'énonciateur l'utilise avec des noms dénombrables pour extraire un élément d'un tout :

Can I have a cup of tea, please?
Puis-je avoir une tasse de thé, s'il vous plaît ?

ou pour parler d'un élément pour la première fois :

There was a dog running loose in the dark street.
Il y avait un chien errant dans la rue sombre.

- Au pluriel, *a/an* devient ø : l'anglais n'a pas d'article indéfini pluriel (correspondant littéralement au français « des »).
- Le choix entre *a* et *an* dépend du premier son du nom.

Attention, certaines voyelles se prononcent parfois comme des voyelles, parfois comme des consonnes. On dit *an umbrella*, mais *a unicorn* car dans le second cas, le « u » se prononce [ju:] et le son [j] est une consonne.

Ne pas oublier que dans la majorité des cas, « h » est prononcé en anglais ; on dit donc *a house, a horse*, mais *an hour*, ce dernier faisant partie de ceux (rares) dont le « h » n'est pas « soufflé ».

L'article *the* (dit article défini)

- *The* correspond au français « le, la, les ». Cet article est la trace d'un fort degré de détermination, c'est-à-dire que l'énonciateur qui l'utilise présuppose, à tort ou à raison, que le co-énonciateur sait de quoi il lui parle.

The est donc utilisé :

– pour faire référence à un élément aisément identifiable par le co-énonciateur (parce que déjà mentionné) :

I saw a dog running loose in the dark street.
Je vis un chien errant dans la rue sombre.

– pour faire référence à un élément culturellement identifiable par le co-énonciateur :

The dog is a faithful animal. Le chien est un animal fidèle.

Bien faire la différence entre l'énoncé ci-dessus et :

Jane, did you take the dog out?
Jane, as-tu sorti le chien?

– pour donner à l'article un caractère nettement démonstratif :

"Did you like him?"
"No! I hated the man!"
– Est-ce que tu l'aimais?
– Non ! Je détestais cet homme !

2 Les adjectifs possessifs

- Ils indiquent à qui appartient le nom qui les suit.
- Ils sont invariables en genre et en nombre et leur forme ne dépend que de la personne du possesseur.
- Ils correspondent au français « mon, ma, mes », etc.

Personne	Adjectif possessif	Français
1re	*my*	mon, ma, mes
2e	*your*	ton, ta, tes
3e m.	*his*	son, sa, ses
3e f.	*her*	son, sa, ses
3e n.	*its*	son, sa, ses
1re pl.	*our*	notre, nos
2e pl.	*your*	votre, vos
3e pl.	*their*	leur, leurs

3 Les adjectifs indéfinis (1)

- Ils sont généralement répertoriés sous le nom de « quantifieurs ».
- Un certain nombre de quantifieurs sont utilisés indifféremment devant des noms singuliers ou pluriels.
- D'autres dépendent du caractère dénombrable ou indénombrable du nom qu'ils accompagnent.
- Pour obtenir une information relative à la quantité on utilise l'interrogatif *how much/how many*.
- Employés seuls, ces mots deviennent des pronoms indéfinis.

Indéfinis quantifieurs employés indifféremment devant un nom singulier ou pluriel

Quantité	Indéfini	Exemple
zéro	*no, not any*	*I have no money and not any friends either.*
moyenne ou indéterminée	*some*	*I have some money in the bank and some stocks* [actions] *too.*
indéfinie	*any*	*You can get the car in any color you like provided it's black. (Henry Ford)*
grande	*a lot of, plenty of, lots of, etc.*	*I wish you lots of luck!*
suffisante	*enough**	*No thank you, I have enough work as it is.*

* Quand il est adjectif, *enough* se place devant le nom. Quand il est adverbe, il se place après l'adjectif.

Indéfinis quantifieurs employés devant un nom pluriel

Quantité	Indéfini	Exemple
pénurie ou très petite quantité	*few*	*The few friends I had left me when I went bankrupt.*
deux items ensemble	*both*	*Both sisters went to the same school.*
trois items et plus	*several*	*They have several children.*
quantité moyenne	*a few*	*Can you give me a few minutes?*
abondance ou grande quantité	*many**	*Have you seen this film many times? You seem to know it by heart.*
totalité	*all*	*All things come to an end.*

* *Many* est rarement utilisé dans les énonces affirmatifs.

Indéfinis quantifieurs employés devant un nom singulier

Quantité	Indéfini	Exemple
une seule unité	*another, any, each*, either, every*, neither, the other*	*Give me another lemonade, please.* *You can choose any car you like from this list.* *Each car is the same price anyway.* *You can park on either side of the street.* *It's the same old thing every day!* *Neither candidate was selected for the job.* *I talked to him the other day.*
quantité moyenne	*a little*	*Give me a little time to think about it.*
pénurie ou très petite quantité	*little*	*We've got little money left.*
grande quantité ou abondance	*much***	*Did he show much courage?*

* *Each* et *every* veulent tous les deux dire « chaque ». Mais avec *each* l'énonciateur « extrait » les éléments un par un, alors qu'avec *every* il les voit dans leur ensemble ou leur répétition, ce qui fait qu'il est souvent traduit par « tous ».
** *Much* est rarement utilisé dans les énonces affirmatifs.

Remarques sur le trio *some, any, no*

- *Some* n'apparaît pas que dans les contextes affirmatifs :
  She had some time left. Il lui restait du temps.

On le rencontre souvent dans des énoncés interrogatifs, quand l'énonciateur sait ou suppose qu'il existe une certaine quantité de ce dont il parle :
  The waitress asked me if I wanted some coffee.
  (Elle en avait de toute évidence.)

- *Any*, lui, apparaît dans tous les contextes, qu'ils soient affirmatifs, interrogatifs ou négatifs :
  You can choose any car from the list.
  Tu peux choisir n'importe quelle voiture sur cette liste.
  The street was totally empty. I couldn't see any cars.
  La rue était totalement vide. Je ne voyais aucune voiture.
  Did you see any person wearing a black hat?
  As-tu vu quelqu'un qui portait un chapeau noir ?
- *No* ne se rencontre que dans des énoncés affirmatifs :
  He has no money and, guess what, no friends either.
  Il n'a pas d'argent et – surprise – pas d'amis non plus.

Voir les composés de *some, any, no* (Le groupe nominal, Les adjectifs indéfinis WBT n° 5).

4 Degrés de comparaison de l'adjectif : les comparatifs

Principes

- Les formes des comparatifs permettent de comparer deux éléments seulement. Il existe trois types de comparatifs : d'égalité, d'infériorité, de supériorité, auxquels s'ajoute le double comparatif.

Le comparatif d'égalité

- Il se forme à l'aide de la structure *as* + adjectif + *as* :
  He's as good-looking as his older brother.

Le comparatif d'infériorité

- Il prend deux formes possibles :

– celle d'un comparatif d'inégalité *not as* + adjectif + *as* :
  She's not as intelligent as her sister.

– celle de l'infériorité *less* + adjectif + *than* :
  She's less intelligent than her sister.

Notez que *less* est le comparatif irrégulier de *little*.

Le comparatif de supériorité

- Sa forme dépend de la longueur de l'adjectif.

– Si l'adjectif est long (plus de deux syllabes) on utilise « *more* + adjectif + *than* » :
  She's more intelligent than her younger sister.

Notez que *more* est le comparatif irrégulier de *much/many*.

– Si l'adjectif est court (moins de deux syllabes) on utilise la structure « adjectif + *-er* + *than* » :
  She's younger/older than her sister.

- Le comparatif de supériorité de certains adjectifs courts entraîne quelques modifications orthographiques :
  easy → *easier*, *big* → *bigger*

Le double comparatif

- Il est utilisé pour exprimer la notion d'accroissement ou de diminution progressifs :
  The climate is getting warmer and warmer.
  Le climat devient de plus en plus chaud.
  Droughts are more and more widespread and crops less and less abundant.
  Les sécheresses s'étendent de plus en plus et les récoltes sont de moins en moins abondantes.
  The harder you work, the faster you 'll succeed.
  Plus dur tu travaille(ra)s (et) plus vite tu réussiras.
  The less you earn, the less you pay in taxes.
  Moins tu gagnes, moins tu paies d'impôts.
  The less I work the happier I am.
  Moins je travaille, plus je suis heureux.

5 Degrés de comparaison de l'adjectif : le superlatif

Le superlatif permet de comparer un élément à tous les autres.

- Le superlatif d'infériorité se forme avec la structure « *the least* + adjectif » (quelle que soit la longueur de l'adjectif) :
  This is one of the least interesting books I've ever read.
  C'est un des livres les moins intéressants que j'aie jamais lus.
- Le superlatif de supériorité, comme le comparatif, distingue entre les adjectifs longs (*the most* + adjectif) et les adjectifs courts (*the* + adjectif + *-est*) :
  Jane is the most intelligent girl I've ever met.
  Jane est la fille la plus intelligente que j'ai recontrée.
  She's also the smartest.
  C'est aussi la plus élégante.
- Comme pour le comparatif de supériorité, certaines transformations orthographiques accompagnent la mise au superlatif de certains adjectifs courts :
  easy → *easiest* • *funny* → *funniest* • *big* → *biggest*

6 Formes irrégulières de certains comparatifs et superlatifs de supériorité

Adjectif	Comparatif	Superlatif
bad	*worse*	*the worst*
far	*farther* (distance) *further* (figuré)	*the farthest,* *the furthest*
good	*better*	*the best*
late	*later* (plus tard) *latter* (le second mentionné)	*the latest* (le plus récent) *the last* (le dernier)
little	*less*	*the least*
much/many	*more*	*the most*

- Le complément d'un superlatif (quand il est mentionné) n'est pas toujours introduit par la préposition *of* :
  The Sears Tower is the tallest skyscraper in Chicago.
  La Sears Tower est le plus haut gratte-ciel de Chicago.
- Lorsqu'en français le superlatif est utilisé pour ne comparer que deux éléments, l'anglais emploie un mélange de comparatif et de superlatif avec les formes suivantes :
  Edna was the more generous of the two sisters.
  She was also the nicer (one).
  Edna était la plus généreuse des deux sœurs.
  C'était aussi la plus gentille.

7 Autre forme de complémentation du nom : le génitif

Structure prépositionnelle

- Un nom peut être complété par un autre nom introduit par une préposition. Le français utilise la préposition « de ». L'anglais ne se limite pas à l'utilisation de son équivalent *of* :

  une pièce de Shakespeare → *a play by Shakespeare*
  la photo du musée → *the picture of the museum*
  une ville d'Amérique → *a town in America*
  le premier nom de la liste → *the first name on the list*

Structure «N's N»

- Avec le génitif, l'anglais dispose d'une autre construction pour compléter un nom, non pas vers la droite mais vers la gauche grâce à la structure « N's N » :

  Shakespeare's plays → les pièces de Shakespeare
  Mr Brown's black dog → le chien noir de M. Brown
  today's paper → le journal d'aujourd'hui
  the teacher's desk → le bureau du maître
  Mary's sister → la sœur de Marie
  America's First Lady → La première dame d'Amérique

Remarques importantes

- Un génitif n'est jamais suivi d'un article.
- La marque « 's » n'est pas uniquement réservée à la notion de possession comme les exemples ci-dessus le montrent.
- Une tournure en « nom + préposition + nom » n'est pas forcément l'équivalent d'une structure génitive « N's N » :

  1. I've come for the photos of my mother.
  2. I've come for my mother's photos.

Dans le premier cas, la mère est sur les photos, dans le second c'est la mère qui a pris les photos.

- Si le premier nom d'une structure génitive est au pluriel, le « s » disparaît à l'écrit pour ne plus laisser que l'apostrophe :

  the teachers' union = le syndicat des enseignants

Mais si ce nom a un pluriel irrégulier, le « 's » subsiste :

  the children's room

Génitif générique ou génitif spécifique ?

La différence est d'importance pour éviter des contresens.

- Un génitif spécifique apporte une information particulière concernant le second nom :

  The woman's bag was found in the ditch.
  Le sac de la femme a été trouvé dans le fossé.

- Un génitif générique apporte une information qui se rapproche plus de celle exprimée par un adjectif, et concerne les caractéristiques du second nom :

  A woman's bag was found in the ditch.
  Un sac de femme (ayant toutes les caractéristiques d'un sac porté par les femmes) a été trouvé dans le fossé.

Dans le premier exemple, la structure est « *the woman* + *'s* + *bag* », et *the* se rapporte à *woman*. Dans le second, la structure est « *a* + *woman's* + *bag* », et *a* se rapporte à *bag*.

Dans le premier cas, le sac trouvé est celui de la femme mais ce n'est peut-être pas un sac à main, mais un sac de voyage. En tout cas, c'est le sien.

Ainsi, il faut bien faire la différence entre :

  the boys' school
  l'école / le lycée des garçons (là où ils vont en cours)
  a boys' school
  une école de garçons (où les filles ne sont pas admises)

Le génitif « incomplet »

- Lorsque le second mot d'une structure génitive désigne un endroit évident à identifier ou culturellement connu, ce second mot est souvent omis :

  They took him to St John's (hospital).
  Jenny is at the dentist's (surgery).
  Dad went to the chemist's (shop).

- Le second nom est également omis quand il a déjà été dit une première fois :

  First I'm going to hoover our room, then I'll do the boys'. (= the boys' room)
  Je vais passer l'aspirateur d'abord dans notre chambre, ensuite dans celle des garçons.

Whose

- *Whose* est l'interrogatif utilisé pour demander à qui quelque chose appartient. Comme tout génitif, il n'est jamais suivi d'article :

  Whose book is this? It's Mark's.

Voir aussi le relatif *whose* (La phrase 5).

8 Le nom verbal ou gérondif

Caractéristiques

- Il est formé de la base verbale + la désinence « -ing ». Il a donc la même forme que le participe présent : *run* → *running*.
- Il exprime le fait de (faire quelque chose).
- Il a toutes les fonctions du nom :

Running may not be advisable in your case. (sujet)
Courir n'est peut-être pas conseillé dans votre cas.
My favorite sport is horseback riding. (attribut)
Mon sport préféré est l'équitation.
Stop yelling, OK? (COD) Arrête de crier, veux-tu ?

Formes en *-ing*

- Ne pas confondre le nom verbal/gérondif avec les autres formes en « *-ing* ». En particulier :

– le participe présent :
He's washing the car.
– les noms se terminant en « *-ing* » :
the beginning, the evening
– les adjectifs verbaux à sens actif :
an exciting story (voir Le groupe nominal WBT n° 7).

9 Les substituts du nom : les pronoms

Les pronoms relatifs

Voir ci-dessous (La phrase 5 et 6).

Les pronoms démonstratifs

Voir plus haut (GN 5), les démonstratifs *this, that, these, those*.
- Les pronoms démonstratifs fonctionnent seuls selon les mêmes principes de pluriel et de sens que ceux énoncés pour les adjectifs démonstratifs. Ils servent à désigner ou à renvoyer à des éléments annoncés ou déjà mentionnés :

this one = celui/celle-ci
that one = celui/celle-là

– Au pluriel «ceux-ci»/«celles-ci», «ceux-là»/«celles-là» sont traduits par *these* et *those* (sans le pronom indéfini *one*) :
Which do you prefer, this one or that one?/these or those?
– *This* et *that* correspondent à « ceci » et « cela ».

Les pronoms quantifieurs

- Tous les adjectifs quantifieurs étudiés ci-dessus (Le groupe nominal, Adj. indéfinis 3 et Adj. indéfinis WBT n° 5) deviennent des pronoms quand ils sont employés seuls :

"How much money do you have?" "A little."
– Tu as combien d'argent ? – Un peu.
"Did he have any friends?"
"He had many, more than anyone else."
– Est-ce qu'il avait des amis ?
– Il en avait plein, plus que n'importe qui.
"How many countries have you visited?" "Quite a few."
– Tu as visité combien de pays ? – Pas mal.

Les pronoms interrogatifs

- Ils sont l'origine des pronoms relatifs dont nous parlons à la section 9 de La phrase :

What did you say?
Which did you like best?
Who did you tell?

Pronoms personnels /adjectifs et pronoms possessifs

Personne	Pronom sujet	Pronom complément	Pronom réfléchi	Adjectif possessif	Pronom possessif
1sg	*I*	*me*	*myself*	*my*	*mine*
2sg	*you*	*you*	*yourself*	*your*	*yours*
2bis (tu)	*thou* [ðɑ]	*thee* [ði:]	*thyself*	*thy* [ðɑɪ]	*thine*
3m	*he*	*him*	*himself*	*his*	*his*
3f	*she*	*her*	*herself*	*her*	*hers*
3n	*it*	*it*	*itself*	*its*	
1pl	*we*	*us*	*ourselves*	*our*	*ours*
2pl	*you*	*you*	*yourselves*	*your*	*yours*
3pl	*they*	*them*	*themselves*	*their*	*theirs*

Notez la double origine de la formation des pronoms réfléchis : les troisièmes personnes sont formées à partir du pronom personnel complément, les autres à partir de l'adjectif possessif.

3. LA PHRASE ET LE DISCOURS

A. La phrase

1 Les adverbes

Nature, emploi, sens des adverbes

- Il existe des adverbes de manière, de temps, de lieu, etc. : *fast, today, there*…
- L'adverbe porte soit sur un verbe, soit sur un adjectif, soit sur une proposition entière dont il modifie le sens :

  She rarely cried.
  Elle pleurait rarement.
  That was a very good answer.
  C'était une très bonne réponse.
  Luckily, there was no one else on the road that day.
  Par chance, il n'y avait personne d'autre sur la route ce jour-là.

- Certains adverbes ont un sens chronologique (*first, then, finally*…) ; d'autres un sens logique (*so, therefore, thus*…). Enfin, il existe des adverbes qui expriment des idées de répétition, d'opposition, ou de restriction (*again, yet, still, however*…).

Place des adverbes

- La place des adverbes qui portent sur une proposition entière varie dans la phrase. On les trouve en début ou en fin d'énoncé :

  Fortunately I was driving very slowly.
  Heureusement, je conduisais très lentement.
  Yes, I'll tell him afterwards.
  Oui, je le lui dirai plus tard. (= quand ce sera fini).

- La plupart du temps, les adverbes modifiant le sens d'un verbe ou d'un adjectif se trouvent devant le mot complété. C'est surtout le cas des adverbes de temps :

  I often wake up before the alarm rings.
  Je me réveille souvent avant que le réveil sonne.

Formation des adverbes

- Les adverbes dérivés d'adjectifs se terminent en « -ly » :

  happy → happily
  wrong → wrongly
  understandable → understandably

- Mais tous les mots qui se terminent en « -ly » ne sont pas des adverbes :

  lovely charmant (adj.)
  lonely seul, solitaire (adj.)

- Certains mots sont tantôt adjectifs, tantôt adverbes :

	adjectif	adverbe
early	→ *in early summer*	*I get up early*
fast	→ *a fast car*	*you really drive fast*
late	→ *in late summer*	*late in the summer*
hard	→ *that is hard work*	*you really worked hard*

- Certains adverbes, tout comme les adjectifs, peuvent avoir des degrés. Ceux-ci prennent les formes du comparatif et du superlatif :

  good/well → That's the one I like best.
  hard → He's the one who worked the hardest.

2 Les prépositions

Revoir ce qui est dit au GV 1 sur les verbes prépositionnels et les verbes à particule.

À quoi sert une préposition ?

- Une préposition est un mot-outil qui permet d'introduire le complément d'un nom, d'un adjectif ou d'un verbe :

  the roof of the house le toit de la maison
  He was sick of it. Il en avait plus qu'assez.
  I've come for the rent. Je suis venu pour (réclamer) le loyer.

- Les compléments de verbes introduits par des prépositions sont des compléments d'objet indirect, de moyen, d'attribution ou des compléments circonstanciels (lieu, temps, manière, cause, but…) :

  I'm talking to you. (COI)
  C'est à toi que je parle.
  She made it with her own hands. (moyen)
  Elle l'a fait de ses propres mains.
  I did it for you. (attribution) Je l'ai fait pour toi.
  They went to America. (c. circ. de lieu)
  Ils sont allés en Amérique.
  I want this finished by tomorrow. (c. circ. de temps)
  Ceci doit être fini pour demain.
  You did that alone, without help? (c. circ. de manière)
  Tu l'as fait tout seul, sans aide ?
  They went away because of you. (c. circ. de cause)
  Ils sont partis à cause de vous.
  What did you do that for? (c. circ. de but)
  Dans quel but as-tu fait ça ?

Traduction des prépositions

- Les prépositions ne se traduisent pas mot à mot du français à l'anglais, et vice versa.
- Il existe en anglais des prépositions à sens statique (absence de mouvement) et des prépositions à sens dynamique (qui indiquent un mouvement).
- En français la même préposition peut avoir les deux valeurs. Le tableau et les exemples suivants résument la situation (liste non exhaustive).

  They're in/at school. Ils sont à l'école.
  They're going to school. Ils vont à l'école.
  See that cloud above the building?
  Tu vois ce nuage au-dessus de l'immeuble ?
  We're now flying over the Atlantic.
  Nous survolons actuellement l'Atlantique.

The cat's inside the house/in the bedroom.
Le chat est à l'intérieur de la maison/dans la chambre.
The cat ran into the house with the first drops.
Le chat s'est précipité dans la maison aux premières gouttes (de pluie).
The dog's outside the house.
Le chien est à l'extérieur de la maison.
The kids ran out of the school.
Les gamins sortirent de l'école en courant.
The vase is on the table.
Le vase est sur la table.
The cat jumped onto the armchair.
Le chat a sauté sur le fauteuil.

- Certaines prépositions n'ont qu'un sens statique :
  between the door and the curtain
  entre la porte et le rideau
- D'autres ont un sens soit statique, soit dynamique :
  across the street, around the garden...
  de l'autre côté de la rue, autour du jardin...

Les principales prépositions

aboard	*about*	*above*
across	*after*	*against*
ahead of	*along*	*alongside*
among(st)	*around*	*as*
as far as	*at*	*before*
behind	*below*	*beneath*
beside	*between*	*beyond*
by	*down*	*for*
from	*in*	*in front of*
inside	*into*	*like*
near	*of*	*off*
on	*onto, on to*	*on top of*
out of	*outside*	*over*
past	*round*	*through*
to	*toward(s)*	*under*
underneath	*up*	*upon*
with	*within*	*without*

Français	Sens statique (immobilité)	Sens dynamique (mouvement)
à	*at, in*	*to*
au-dessus de	*above*	*over*
dans	*in, inside*	*into*
hors de	*outside*	*out of*
sur	*on*	*onto, on to*

3 Les particules adverbiales (post-positions)

Des prépositions sont aussi des particules adverbiales.

Nature des particules adverbiales

- À la différence des prépositions, les particules adverbiales font partie intégrante du verbe (dont elles changent le sens originel) :
  go : aller • *go away* : s'en aller, s'éloigner
  go out : sortir • *go up* : monter
  go through : traverser, feuilleter rapidement...

Transitivité

- Les verbes à particule peuvent être :

– intransitifs (pas de complément d'objet) :
Get out, this minute!

– transitifs directs (avec COD) :
Look him up in the phonebook.
Cherche son nom dans l'annuaire (du téléphone).

– transitifs indirects ou suivis de compléments circonstanciels introduits par une préposition :
I've always looked up to him. Je l'ai toujours admiré.

N.B. Ne pas confondre les *phrasal verbs* (verbes + particule) avec les verbes prépositionnels :
"How did you get here?" "We flew over."
– Comment êtes-vous venus ? – En avion.
Johnny flew over the handlebars.
Johnny est passé par-dessus le guidon.

Les principales particules adverbiales

- Elles n'entrent pas toutes dans la composition des verbes à particules.

aback	*aboard*	*about*
above	*abroad*	*across*
adrift	*after*	*ahead*
along	*alongside*	*apart*
around	*aside*	*away*
back	*backward(s)*	*before*
behind	*below*	*between*
beyond	*by*	*down*
downhill	*downstairs*	*downtown*
forth	*forward(s)*	*home*
in	*indoors*	*in front*
inside	*near*	*off*
on	*on top*	*out*
outside	*over*	*overboard*
past	*round*	*through*
to	*together*	*under*
underground	*up*	*upstairs*
uptown	*without*	

4 Traduction de «il y a», «pendant», «depuis» : ago, for, since

Ago

- *Ago* est un adverbe de temps qui joue le rôle d'une machine à remonter le temps en ceci qu'il renvoie à un moment précis du passé. Il permet de traduire l'expression française « il y a » suivie d'un complément de temps qui exprime la durée séparant le moment de parole (le présent) du moment où l'action évoquée a eu lieu :

  I think the last time I saw them was six months ago.
  Je crois que la dernière fois que je les ai vus, c'était il y a six mois.

Ago apparaît donc dans des énoncés au prétérit.

For

- *For* est une préposition qui introduit, quel que soit le temps du verbe, un complément indiquant la durée de l'action envisagée :

  I stayed in England for over two years.
  J'ai vécu en Angleterre plus de deux ans.
  I'm going for three weeks.
  Je pars trois semaines.

Since

- *Since* est tantôt une préposition (= « depuis ») tantôt une conjonction (= « depuis que ») suivie d'une information qui marque le début des événements dont il est question.
- Ce mot se trouve donc normalement dans les énoncés exprimant un bilan et contenant le *present perfect* ou le *past perfect* :

  I've been working for this company since I first settled in this city.
  Je travaille pour cette société depuis que je me suis installé(e) dans cette ville.
  We haven't seen them since last week.
  Cela fait une semaine que nous ne les avons pas vus. / Nous ne les avons pas vus depuis la semaine dernière.

5 Les pronoms relatifs

- Les propositions relatives sont introduites par un pronom (parfois un adjectif) relatif ou par ø quand on omet le relatif.

Il existe deux sortes de pronoms relatifs, plus les équivalents de ce que le français appelle « relatifs doubles » (voir La phrase 6).

Les pronoms relatifs en *Wh-* (*Who, whom, whose*)

- Ils renvoient à un antécédent humain : *who* (pronom sujet), *whom* (pronom complément), *whose* (pronom génitif = complément de nom à caractère possessif) :

  He's the king who was beheaded in the Tower of London.
  Il s'agit du roi qui a été décapité à la Tour de Londres.
  Mary is the woman of whom we were talking.
  C'est Marie la femme dont nous parlions.
  The person whose car is parked in front of my driveway had better move it.
  La personne dont la voiture est garée devant l'entrée de mon garage ferait mieux de la déplacer.

- *Which* renvoie à un antécédent non humain :

  The car which won the Monte Carlo rally last year was Japanese.
  C'est une voiture japonaise qui a gagné le Rallye de Monte-Carlo l'année dernière.

- *Where* peut être un relatif lorsqu'il renvoie à un antécédent lié à un lieu :

  That's the place where I'd like to live.
  C'est là que j'aimerais vivre.

- *When* peut être un relatif lorsqu'il renvoie à un antécédent lié à la notion de temps :

  On the day when they finally got married, it was pouring.
  Le jour où ils ont fini par se marier, il pleuvait à seaux.

- *Why* peut être un relatif lorsqu'il renvoie à un antécédent exprimant la cause :

  And that's the reason why Napoleon lost the battle of Waterloo.
  Et voilà pourquoi Napoléon a perdu la bataille de Waterloo.

That

- Il renvoie indifféremment à un antécédent humain ou non :

  That's the first tropical butterfly that I've ever seen.
  C'est le premier papillon tropical que je vois de ma vie.
  He's the man that cleans our offices every morning.
  C'est la personne qui fait le ménage tous les matins dans nos bureaux.

Particularités

- *That* remplace souvent tout un groupe nominal :

  That's the last thing that I want to hear!
  C'est bien la dernière chose que j'aie envie d'entendre.

- *Which* remplace souvent toute une proposition :

  He lied at the trial, which cost him the presidency.
  Il a menti au procès, ce qui lui a coûté la présidence.

- Sauf s'ils sont sujets ou compléments de nom (*whose*), quasiment tous les pronoms relatifs sont couramment omis ; on parle dans ce cas de relatif « zéro » (ø) :

  He died on the day ø his daughter was to get married. [when]
  Il est mort le jour où sa fille devait se marier.
  That's the reason ø the wedding was postponed. [why]
  C'est pourquoi le mariage a été reporté.
  She's the lady ø we met yesterday. Don't you remember? [whom]
  C'est la femme que nous avons rencontrée hier, tu ne te rappelles pas ?
  That's the first thing Ø I want to see. [that]
  C'est la première chose que je veux voir.

10 Structures particulières

L'accroissement ou la diminution parallèles

- Cette notion recouvre des énoncés du type :

  Plus je travaille et plus je paie d'impôts.
  Moins tu travailleras et moins de chances tu auras de réussir.
  Plus je travaille et moins j'ai de temps libre.
  Moins j'en fais et mieux je me porte.

ainsi que des expressions comme :

  Le plus tôt sera le mieux.
  Plus on est de fous, plus on rit.

- Comme on le voit, il s'agit d'acroissement ou de diminution. Le mouvement peut se faire dans le même sens ou en sens inverse, ce que nous symbolisons par le jeu de flèches suivant :

  plus/plus : ↑↑ moins/moins : ↓↓
  plus/moins : ↑↓ moins/plus : ↓↑

Traduction

↑↑ *The more I work, the more taxes I pay.*
Plus je travaille, plus je paie d'impôts.

↓↓ *The less you (will) spend, the fewer friends you will have.*
Moins tu dépenses, moins tu as d'amis.

↑↓ *The more I work the less free time I have.*
Plus je travaille et moins j'ai de temps libre.

↓↑ *The less I do, the better I feel.*
Moins j'en fais, mieux je me porte.

↑↑ *The sooner the better.*
Le plus tôt sera le mieux.

↑↑ *The more the merrier.*
Plus il y a de fous, plus on rit.

11 Les structures dites « causatives »

Let/make someone do something

- Les structures causatives permettent de traduire les expressions françaises « laisser faire » et « faire faire » :

  At Summerhill, our teacher lets us come to school whenever we like. (our teacher = 1, lets = a, us = 2, come = b)
  À Summerhill, notre professeur nous laisse venir en classe quand on veut.
  But once we get to class, she makes us work like slaves! (she = 1, makes = a, us = 2, work = b)
  Mais une fois en classe, elle nous fait travailler comme des esclaves !

Dans les énoncés ci-dessus le sujet 1 agit à l'aide du verbe causatif a sur le sujet 2 et le verbe b indique l'action faite par le sujet 2. Notez que le sujet 2 est en quelque sorte l'objet de l'action du sujet 1, d'où la forme complément prise par le sujet 2. Le sujet 1 est bien la cause de ce que fait (ou ne fait pas) le sujet 2.

- Très souvent, *make* n'est qu'une sorte « d'auxilaire de cause », et n'exprime dans ce cas aucune contrainte :

  He makes me laugh. Il me fait rire.
  That made me think that I'd forgotten all about her birthday.
  Ça m'a fait penser que j'avais totalement oublié son anniversaire.

Have someone do something

- Le choix entre *make* et *have* dépend souvent du degré de contrainte que le sujet 1 applique sur le sujet 2.

  My parents made us learn Greek. We couldn't stand it.
  (Les parents n'ont pas laissé le choix, ils ont forcé les enfants).
  We'll have the gardener rake up the dead leaves.
  (On le lui demandera, c'est son travail.)

Have/get something done

- Le groupe qui suit l'auxiliaire subit l'action indiquée par le participe passé.
- La structure est « sujet + *have/get* + objet de la seconde action + participe passé » :

  We had the car repaired immediately after the accident.
  (C'est la voiture qui a été réparée à notre [*we*] demande, on ne précise pas par qui car cela va sans dire).
  You'd better get that light fixed.
  Tu ferais bien de faire réparer cette lampe.

Attention ! *Let, have* et *make* ne sont pas dans ce cas de « vrais » auxiliaires : ils ont besoin, aux formes négative et interrogative, des mêmes auxiliaires que les verbes lexicaux pour être conjugués :

  Did she make you do that?
  C'est elle qui t'a fait faire ça ?
  Will you have him come earlier?
  Tu le feras venir plus tôt ?
  The neighbours don't let us play with their dog.
  Les voisins ne nous laissent pas jouer avec leur chien.
  We didn't have this house built. We bought it from Mr Harris.
  Ce n'est pas nous qui avons fait construire cette maison. Nous l'avons achetée à M. Harris.

12 Les structures verbales et la traduction de l'infinitif français

Remarques concernant l'infinitif français

- L'infinitif français fonctionne de deux façons :

– soit seul :

Attention, ouvrez vos parapluies, le barde va chanter.

– soit derrière une préposition qui « flèche » le moment où l'action est envisagée (passé ou avenir) :

J'ai encore un rapport à rédiger ce soir.
Je travaille pour obtenir des résultats !
Mais, voyons, je viens de le dire.

- Par rapport au moment de parole (le présent), les actions « rédiger » et « obtenir » ne sont pas encore réalisées.

Par contre, dans le dernier exemple, « dire » est du domaine du déjà accompli.

Dans le premier exemple, c'est le sens du verbe « aller » qui suffit à flécher « chanter » dans l'avenir.

Fonctionnement de l'anglais

- La logique n'est pas foncièrement différente du français.

La forme non conjuguée d'un verbe est celle que l'on trouve dans les dictionnaires anglais, et que nous appelons base verbale. Elle indique que l'action dont il est question n'est pas réalisée mais simplement nommée, envisagée, etc.

Cette base verbale (BV) peut comme l'infinitif français porter des marques de « fléchage » vers le passé ou l'avenir.

- Si l'énonciateur se contente de mentionner une action qui n'a pas lieu au moment où il parle, il a le choix entre la structure « V + BV » (*I can swim* = Je sais nager) ou la structure « V + *to* + BV » (*I still have to write this report.* = J'ai encore ce rapport à rédiger).
- Si l'énonciateur fait référence à une action déjà accomplie, vécue ou même simplement pensée, il a recours à la structure « V + BV + *-ing* » :

You must stop smoking. Il faut vous arrêter de fumer.
(Il faut avoir commencé pour pouvoir s'arrêter de fumer.)

Attention aux « calques »

- Les exemples ci-contre pourraient faire croire que les structures anglaises peuvent être calquées sur celles du français. Si c'est très souvent le cas, cela n'est pas vrai à 100 %. Tout dépend du sémantisme du verbe anglais :

And remember to call your grandparents, OK?
Et n'oublie pas d'appeler tes grands-parents, compris ?
I remember calling him a thousand times and only getting his answering machine.
Je me rappelle l'avoir appelé un millier de fois et être toujours tombé(e) sur son répondeur.

- Ne pas confondre l'opérateur *to* devant les bases verbales et la préposition *to* qui, comme toutes les prépositions, est suivie d'une forme nominale en *-ing* ou d'un simple nom :

I want you to leave immediately.
(On parle ici de proposition infinitive pour le groupe "*you to leave immediately*".)
Je veux que tu partes immédiatement.
I'm not used to getting up so early.
(*used* [adjectif = habitué] + préposition *to*)
Je n'ai pas l'habitude de me lever si tôt.

- Les verbes dits « de perception » (*see, hear, smell, feel, taste*...) peuvent être suivis :

– soit de la structure « verbe + COD + BV » :

I saw him light a cigarette.
Je l'ai vu allumer une cigarette.

– soit de la structure « verbe + COD + BV-*ing* » :

I can smell something burning.
Ça sent le brûlé.

Traditionnellement, la première structure est utilisée quand l'intégralité de l'action a été perçue, et la seconde lorsque ce n'est pas le cas. En fait le choix de « BV-*ing* » indique comment l'énonciateur perçoit l'action et ce qu'elle lui inspire (commentaire, sentiment, etc.).

13 Les cas d'inversion

- On inverse l'ordre normal « sujet verbe » dans les phrases affirmatives dans un certain nombre de cas.

Ces emplois se rencontrent en langue soutenue et quand l'énonciateur souhaite donner de l'emphase à ses propos.

- Ces énoncés avec inversion commencent par un adverbe ou une expression à sens négatif ou restrictif :

Never will I make such a speech!
Jamais je ne ferai un discours pareil !
Hardly had we set out when it started to rain!
Nous étions à peine partis qu'il s'est mis à pleuvoir.
No sooner did she see me than she started to cry.
À peine m'avait-elle vu(e) qu'elle se mit à pleurer.

- La suppression de la conjonction *if* entraine l'inversion :

Had I known what sort of person he was, I would never have gone along with his scheme. (= *If I had known him*...)
Si j'avais su quel genre de personne c'était, jamais je n'aurais marché dans sa combine.
Should you happen to come across this person...
Si jamais tu rencontres/rencontrais cette personne...

- Les reprises affirmatives ou négatives entrainent aussi une inversion :

My mom wouldn't believe me, and neither would my dad.
Ma mère ne voulait pas me croire, mon père non plus.
I jumped for joy at the news, and so did my sister.
J'ai sauté de joie quand j'ai su ça, et ma sœur aussi.
"I do not believe a word he says." "Neither do I."
– Je ne crois pas un mot de ce qu'il raconte. – Moi non plus.

B. Le discours WBT

Verbes irréguliers

Ce sont les verbes irréguliers les plus courants.
Ne figurent pas sur la liste tous les verbes composés (préposition + verbe de base) comme *undo*, *remake*, etc., qui se forment de la même façon que le verbe de base.

Base verbale (BV)	Prétérit	Participe passé	Traduction
arise	arose	arisen	*se lever*
awake	awoke	awoken	*se réveiller*
be	was	been	*être*
bear	bore	borne	*supporter*
beat	beat	beaten	*battre*
become	became	become	*devenir*
begin	began	begun	*commencer*
bend	bent	bent	*(se) courber*
bet	bet	bet	*parier*
bind	bound	bound	*lier*
bite	bit	bitten	*mordre*
bleed	bled	bled	*saigner*
blow	blew	blown	*souffler*
break	broke	broken	*casser*
bring	brought	brought	*apporter, amener*
build	built	built	*construire*
burn	burned/burnt	burned/burnt	*brûler, incendier*
burst	burst	burst	*éclater*
buy	bought	bought	*acheter*
cast	cast	cast	*jeter*
catch	caught	caught	*attraper*
choose	chose	chosen	*choisir*
cling	clung	clung	*s'accrocher*
come	came	come	*venir*
cost	cost	cost	*coûter*
creep	crept	crept	*ramper*
cut	cut	cut	*couper*
deal	dealt [delt]	dealt	*traiter*
dig	dug	dug	*creuser*
do	did	done	*faire*
draw	drew	drawn	*dessiner*
drink	drank	drunk	*boire*
drive	drove	driven	*conduire*
eat	ate [eɪt, et]	eaten	*manger*
fall	fell	fallen	*tomber*
feed	fed	fed	*nourrir*
feel	felt	felt	*(se) sentir*

Base verbale (BV)	Prétérit	Participe passé	Traduction
fight	fought	fought	*se battre, combattre*
find	found	found	*trouver*
fit	fitted/fit	fitted/fit	*être juste, être de la bonne taille*
flee	fled	fled	*fuir*
fling	flung	flung	*jeter*
fly	flew	flown	*voler (= avion)*
forbid	forbade [fəˈbæd]	forbidden	*interdire*
forecast	forecast	forecast	*prédire, prévoir*
forget	forgot	forgotten	*oublier*
forgive	forgave	forgiven	*pardonner*
freeze	froze	frozen	*geler*
get	got	got/gotten	*obtenir, devenir, aller chercher, arriver*
give	gave	given	*donner*
go	went	gone	*aller*
grow	grew	grown	*cultiver*
hang	hung	hung	*suspendre*
have	had	had	*avoir*
hear	heard [hɜːd]	heard	*entendre*
hide	hid	hidden	*(se) cacher*
hit	hit	hit	*frapper*
hold	held	held	*tenir, contenir*
hurt	hurt	hurt	*blesser*
keep	kept	kept	*garder, se conserver*
kneel	kneeled/knelt	kneeled/knelt	*s'agenouiller*
knit	knitted/knit	knitted/knit	*tricoter*
know	knew	known	*connaître, savoir*
lay	laid	laid	*mettre (la table)*
lead	led	led	*mener*
leap	leaped/leapt	leaped/leapt	*sauter*
learn	learned/learnt	learned/learnt	*apprendre*

Base verbale (BV)	Prétérit	Participe passé	Traduction
leave	left	left	*partir, quitter*
lend	lent	lent	*prêter*
let	let	let	*permettre*
lie	lay	lain	*s'allonger*
light	lit/lighted	lit/lighted	*allumer*
lose	lost	lost	*perdre*
make	made	made	*faire*
mean	meant [ment]	meant	*signifier*
meet	met	met	*rencontrer*
pay	paid	paid	*payer*
put	put	put	*mettre, poser*
read [ri:d]	read [red]	read [red]	*lire*
ride	rode	ridden	*monter (à cheval/ à vélo...)*
ring	rang	rung	*sonner*
rise	rose	risen	*se lever, s'élever*
run	ran	run	*courir, gérer*
saw	sawed	sawed/sawn	*scier*
say	said [sed]	said	*dire*
see	saw	seen	*voir*
seek	sought [sɔːt]	sought	*chercher*
sell	sold	sold	*vendre*
send	sent	sent	*envoyer*
set	set	set	*placer, poser*
sew [səʊ]	sewed	sewed/sown	*coudre*
shake	shook	shaken	*secouer*
shine	shone [ʃɒn]	shone	*briller*
shoot	shot	shot	*fusiller, tirer (sur)*
show	showed	shown	*montrer*
shrink	shrank	shrunk	*rétrécir*
shut	shut	shut	*fermer*
sing	sang	sung	*chanter*
sink	sank	sunk	*couler (sous l'eau)*
sit	sat	sat	*s'asseoir*
sleep	slept	slept	*dormir*
slide	slid	slid	*glisser*
smell	smelled/smelt	smelled/smelt	*sentir (à l'odeur)*
speak	spoke	spoken	*parler*
spell	spelled/spelt	spelled/spelt	*épeler*
spend	spent	spent	*dépenser, passer (du temps)*

Base verbale (BV)	Prétérit	Participe passé	Traduction
spill	spilled/spilt	spilled/spilt	*déverser*
spread [spred]	spread	spread	*étendre, étaler*
spring	sprang	sprung	*jaillir*
stand	stood	stood	*être debout*
steal	stole	stolen	*voler (= dérober)*
stick	stuck	stuck	*coller*
strike	struck	struck	*frapper*
swear [sweə]	swore	sworn	*jurer*
sweep	swept	swept	*balayer*
swell	swelled	swelled/ swollen	*gonfler*
swim	swam	swum	*nager*
take	took	taken	*prendre, emporter, emmener*
teach	taught [tɔːt]	taught	*apprendre, enseigner*
tear	tore	torn	*déchirer*
tell	told	told	*dire, raconter*
think	thought [θɔːt]	thought	*croire, penser*
throw	threw	thrown	*jeter*
thrust	thrust	thrust	*enfoncer, plonger*
understand	understood	understood	*comprendre*
upset	upset	upset	*bouleverser, renverser*
wake	woke	woken	*(se) réveiller*
wear	wore	worn	*porter (un vêtement)*
weave	wove	woven	*tisser*
win	won [wʌn]	won	*gagner (un prix, etc.)*
wind [waɪnd]	wound [waʊnd]	wound	*enrouler, serpenter*
withstand	withstood	withstood	*supporter*
write	wrote	written	*écrire*

Crédits photographiques

Couverture :

Gandhi Corbis/Bettman Premium • *Ayers Rock* Photo12.com/Alamy • Times Square © iStock/Andreykrav • *Children of Lir* Bridgeman Giraudon/Private Collection • *Étudiants* Corbis/Blend Images/Jon Feingersh • Thinkstock/Stockbyte •

Chapitre 1 p. 10 Corbis/DPA/Nicolas Armer • p. 11h Photo12/Alamy • p. 11b Corbis/UNHCR • p. 12 Photo12/Alamy • p. 13 Réa/The New-York Times-Redux/Philip Greenberg • p. 14h www.bookcrossing.com • p. 14b www.swap-able.com p. 14m www.homeforswap.com • p. 15 Getty Images/Steven Puetzer • p. 16hg Réa/The New-Yok Times/STF • p. 16hd Gamma Rapho/Camerapress/Guardian/Theane Smith • p. 16b CartoonStock.com • p. 17 AFP/Fred Tanneau • p. 18h Photo12.com/Alamy • p. 18m Gamma Rapho/David Lefranc • p. 18b Réa/Zuma/Robin Nelson • p. 19h Getty Images/Superstock • p. 19m AFP/Karen Bleier • p. 19b Reuters/Larry Downing • p. 20 Cagle Cartoons/Mike Keefe • p. 21 The Cartoon Bank/The New-Yorker Collection/Harley L. Schwadren • p. 22 Photo12.com/Alamy • p. 23h Age Fotostock/Russellkord.com • p. 23b Age Fotostock/Blickwinkell/S Sailer/A Sailer •p. 25 www.etdp.org. • **Chapitre 2** p. 26 Getty Images/Mark Edward Atkinson • p. 27 Photo12.com/Alamy • p. 28 Photo12.com/Alamy • p. 29 CartoonStock.com •p. 30h CartoonStock.com • p. 31h Thinstock/iStock/Sven Hoppe (drapeaux) • p. 31m Thinkstock/Collection Hemera/Christopher Futcher (étudiants) • p. 31b Thinsktock/iStock/PaulMcArdleUK • p. 32 Guernsey Post • p. 33 Getty Images/Superstock • p. 34hg Roger-Viollet/Ullstein Bild • p. 34hd Prod DB ©MGM-Seveb Arts/DR • p. 34bg Gamma Rapho Keystone • p. 34bd Prod DB © Columbia Pictures/DR • p. 35hg Corbis/Bettmann• p. 35hm Prod DB © MK2 Production/DR • p. 35hd Picture Desk/The Kobal Collection/Universal Pictures/Miramax Films • p. 35m Getty Images/Elizaberth Lippman • p. 35bg Picture Desk/The Kobal Collection/Merchant Ivory/Columbia • p. 35bd Sipa/ddaa-zob/wenn.com • p. 36 Punch Limited • p. 37 Punch Limited • p. 38 Cartoonstock.com • p. 40h Sipa/Rex Features/Tony Kyriacou • p. 40m Photo12.com/Alamy • p. 40b Photo12.com/Alamy • **Chapitre 3** p. 42 Getty Images/Apic • p. 43h Fricaar.com/Droits réservés • p. 43b Sipa/Rex Features/Tony Kyriacou • p. 44 Photo12.com/Alamy • p. 45 Reuters/Mike Blake • p. 46hg Corbis/Andrew Aitchinson • p. 46hd Droits réservés • p. 46b José Cabezas/Droits réservés • p. 48h Corbis/Ashley Cooper • p. 48b Canadian Labour Congress • p. 49 Sipa/AP/Jacquelyn Martin • p. 50hg Akg-images/SPL • p. 50hd Prod DB © First National Pictures/DR • p. 50mg Corbis/ Bettmann • p. 50md Reuters/Gus Ruelas • p. 50bg Prod DB © MGM/DR • p. 50bd Corbis/Kenneth James • p. 51hg Leemage/Photo-Re-Pubblic • p. 51hd AFP/Adrian Dennis • p. 51mg La Collection/Interfoto • p. 51md Akg-images • p. 51b Corbis/Lothar Heidtmann • p. 52 Cartoonist Group/Steve Kelley • p. 53 CartoonStock.com • p. 54 Photononstop/PhotoAlto/Michèle Constantini • p. 55hg Dreamstime.com/RobWilson39 • p. 55hd Photo12.com/Alamy • p. 55b Thinkstock/iStock/Thorsten Schmitt • p. 59 Corbis/Sygma/Hervé Collart • p. 60 Corbis/Bettmann • **Chapitre 4** p. 62 Getty Images/Popperfoto • p. 63h Getty Images/The Life Images Collection/Don Cravens • p. 63b Abaca Press/PA Wire/Jonathan Brady/PA •p. 64hg Akg-images/Archiv Peter Rühe/GandhiServe •p. 64hd Corbis/David Pollack •p. 64mg Corbis/dpa/Ton Köln •p. 64bg Corbis/Sygma/JP Laffont • p. 64bd AFP/Gerry Penny • p. 65hg Getty Images/ Thomas Monaster/NY Daily News Archive • p. 65hm AFP/Getty Images/Sean Gallup • p. 65hd Corbis/Bettmann • p. 65bg • Corbis/Bettmann • p. 65bm AFP/The Guardian/EyePress • p. 65bd Sipa/AP • p. 66h Reuters/Luke MacGregor • p. 66b Coll. part. p. 67 Getty Images/Earmonn M. MacCormack • p. 68h US AirForce • p. 68bg Akg-images/IAM • p. 68bd Photo12.com/Alamy • p. 69h Getty Images/New-York Daily News • p. 69b Akg-images • p. 70h Prod DB © Geffen Pictures-Warner Bros/DR •p. 70m Prod DB © N. Dove-Calamity Films/DR •p. 70b Prod DB © Walt Disney Pictures-Mayhem Pictures-Who's Nuts Productions/DR • p. 71hg Prod DB © The Weinstein Company- Laura Ziskin Productions/DR • p. 71hd Prod DB © Plan B-Regency Enterprises-Fox-Searchlight Pictures-River-Road-Film4/DR • p. 71md Prod DB © Imagine Entertainement/DR • p. 71bg Prod DB © Paramount-Red Granite Pictures-Sikelia Productions-Appian Way/DR • p. 72 Randy Glasbergen/Glasbergen.com • p. 73 CartoonStock.com • p. 74h Bridgeman Images © Wilbertforce House, Hull City Museums and Art Galleries • p. 74mg Thinkstock/iStock/Britt Mc Tammany • p. 74md Bridgeman Images/The Royal Mint Museum, Liantrissant • p. 74bg Corbis/Stocktrek Images • p. 74bd US Mint • p. 75 Archant Norfolk • **Chapitre 5** p. 78h Reuters/Shaun Best • p. 78b Coll. part • p. 79h Reuters/Stringer/George Frey • p. 79b Sipa/AP/Paul Hurschman • p. 80h Akg-images/SPL • p. 80m Apple • p. 80b Prod DB © Black Beard Pictures-Bristol Automotive/DR • p. 81 La Collection/Artothek • p. 82h Reuters/Shannon Stapleton • p. 82b Droits réservés • p. 83 Dirck Halstead • p. 84h www.6sqft.com • p 85 Projects A Broad • p. 86hg Photo12.com/Alamy • p. 86hd Photo12.com/Alamy • p. 86b Photo12.com/Alamy • p. 87h Age Fotostock/Superstock • p. 87bg Photo12.com/Alamy • p. 87bd Photo12.com/Alamy • p. 88 CartoonStock.com • p. 89 Marshall Ramsey/Daveramsey.com • p. 90h Thinkstock/iStock/G-Stockstudio • p. 90b Akg-images /Interfoto/Friedrich • p. 91hg www.nysut.org p. 91m Sipa/Rex Features/Stuart Clarke • p. 91d GetStock.com/Rick Westhead • p. 91b Corbis/Demotix/Gagan Thapa Thapa • p. 93 Sipa/AP/Tetsuya Kikumasa • **Chapitre 6** p. 94 Bridgeman Images © Tarker • p. 95h Morar, submitted Gheorghita 19 March 2012 Cosmin/KPMG/Contrapunto BBDO Moscow • p. 95b Finola Finlay et Robert Harris • p. 96g Akg-images/Sotheby's • p. 96d Prod DB © BBC-Shine/DR • p. 97 Prod DN © Warner/DR • p. 98h Leemage/Costa • p. 98b Age Fotostock/Image Broker/Markus Keller • p. 99 Photo12.com/Alamy • p. 100 Age Fotostock/Christian Goupi • p. 101h Bridgeman Giraudon/Private Collection • p. 101b Mary Evans Picture Library • p. 102h Corbis/The Print Collector • p. 102b Akg-images/Erich Lessing • p. 103hg Coll. part • p. 103hd Bridgeman Images/© Look and Learn/Coll.part. • p. 103b Corbis/GraphicaArtis • p. 104 The Cartoon Bank/The New Yorker Collection/Mick Stevens • p. 105 CartoonStock.com • p. 106 AFP/Getty IMages/Patrick Aventurier • p. 107hg Art: jasonedmiston.com <http://jasonedmiston.com> Mars Attacks © of The Topps Company Inc. • p. 107hd Getty Images /The Life Picture Collection/Peter Stackpole • p. 107b Prod DB © 20th Century Fox Television/DR • p. 111 Prod DB © Fox 2000 Pictures-Studio Babelsberg/DR • p. 112 Prod DB © Walt Disney/DR • **Chapitre 7** p. 114 © Robert Graves and Didier Madoc-Jones, aerial photograph by Jason Hawkes. www.postcardsfromthefuture.com <http://www.postcardsfromthefuture.com> @futurepostcards • p. 115h The Seasteading Institute/Floating City Project • p. 115b AFP/Getty Images/David McNew • p. 116 Cagle Cartoons/Dave Granlund • p. 117 Naturimages/Alain Bidart • p. 118 Getty Images/Andy Rouse • p. 119 Nasa/Trent Schindler and Matt Rodel • p. 120 Tangram 3DS/Solent • p. 121h Shimizu Corporation • p. 121b AFP/Shimizu Corporation • p. 122h Akg-images/Les Arts décoratifs, Paris/Jean Tholance • p. 122b Age Fotostock/Mark Edward Smith • p. 123h Dreamstime/Anthony Aneese Totah Jr. • p. 123m Age Fotostock/EasyFotostock/Tono Balaguer • p.123b hemis.fr/Jon Arnold • p. 124 Stuart Carlson • p. 125h Chris Madden • p. 125b Prod DB © Centropolis Entertainement/DR • p. 126 Réa/Laif/Zénit/Paul Langrock • p. 127 Songdo Landmark City/Rex Agency • **Chapitre 8** p. 130 AFP/Getty Images/Phil Cole • p. 131h Sipa/Rex/Steve Bell • p. 131b Instagram • p. 132h Cagle Cartoons/Gary Varvel • p. 132m Fotolia/Stephen VanHorn • p. 132b Google Chrome • p. 133 Bridgeman Images/Christie's Images/Coll. part. • p. 134h Thinkstock/iStock/Prudkov • p. 134bg Funny Times/Matt Wueker • p. 134bd Corbis/Norman Rockwell, *Freedom from want*, The Saturday Evening Post © 1943 Curtis Publishing Company • p. 135hg Thinkstock/iStock/Anankkml • p. 135hd © Apple • p. 136h © Apple • p. 136b Sipa/Rex/Rinspeed • p. 138h Bridgeman Images/The Higgins Art Gallery and Museum, Bedford,U.K. • p. 138b Bridgeman Images/Yale Center for British Art, Paul Mellon Coll. USA • p. 139h Bridgeman Images/Private coll. • p. 139md Akg-images/Erich Lessing © Estate of Roy Lichtenstein, New-York/Adagp Paris, 2015 • p. 139bg Bridgeman images/Cauer Collection, Germany • p. 140 CartoonStock.com • p. 141 CartoonStock.com p. 142 Thinkstock/iStock/PeterHermesFurian • p. 143h Thinkstock/iStock/Scanrail • p. 143b Thinkstock/iStock/Alexander Bryljaev • p. 145 AFP/Ria-Novosti/Sergey Guineev • **Chapitre 9** p. 146 Getty Images/fStop images-Caspar Benson • p. 147h Droits réservés • p. 147b Getty Images/Dr Grounds • p. 148h Corbis/Matthias Kulka • p. 148b Prod DB ©Universal/DT • p. 149 Laura Zalenga • p. 150 AFP/Mike Sargent • p. 151 Prod DB © Fox Searchlight Pictures-DNA Films-Film 4/DR • p. 152h Novapix/Nasa • p. 152b Sipa/AP/Ringo H. W. Chiu • p. 153 Prod DB © DNA Films-IM Global/DR • p. 154hg Prod DB © MGM/DR • p. 154hd Prod DB © Warner Bros-Esperanto Filmoj-Heyday Films/DR • p. 154bg Prod DB © Warner Bros-Village Roadshow Pictures-The Aaron Sims Company/DR • p. 154bd Prod DB © 20th Century Fox-Scott Free Productions/DR • p. 155hg Collection Agence Martienne • p. 155hd Coll. part. • p. 155bg Coll. part. • p. 155bd Coll. part • p. 156 Punch Limited • p. 157 Gary Markstein • p. 158 Novapix/Nasa • p. 159 Novapix/Don Dixon • p. 163 Reuters/Ben Weller • p. 164 Collection Christophel/Rosen • **Chapitre 10** p. 166 AFP/Gewel Samad • p. 167h Sipa/AP/Invision for Ubisoft/John Shearer • p. 167b Getty Images/Stephen Webster • p. 169 Collection Christophe L • p. 170 Which? 2015 • p. 172h Thinkstock/iStock/Ljupco • p. 172b Thinkstock/iStock Creatista • p. 173h Photo12.com/Alamy • p. 173b Bridgeman Images/Peter Jackson Collection © Look and Learn • p. 174hg Bridgeman Images/Woburn Abbey, Bedordshire, UK • p. 174md Picture Desk/The Kobal Collection/William, Craig/Universal/Studio Canal/Working Title • p. 174bg Reuters/Roy Letkey • p. 175hg Akg-images • p. 175hd Brian Pike, based on Cutherland 's portrait • p. 175b Picture Desk/Dagli Orti/Pulver Pictures • p. 176 Punch Limited • p. 177 Punch Limited • p. 178 Thinkstock/Otmar Winter Leitner • p. 179hg Reuters/Stephen Lam • p. 179hd AFP/Saeed Khan • p. 179mg Reuters/Kevin Lamarque • p. 179md AFP/Stan Honda • p. 179bg AFP/Getty Images for Vanity Fair/Kimberley White • p. 179bm Reuters/Kevin Lamarque • p. 179bd AFP/Getty Images/Elsa • **Chapitre 11** p. 182 Getty Images/Nathalie Lagneau/Catwalking • p. 183h Sipa/AP/Marcio José Sanchez • p. 183b Photo12.com/Alamy • p. 184g Picture Desk/The Kobal Collection/Wetcher, Barry/20th Century Fox • p. 184d Picture Desk/The Kobal Collection/20th Century Fox • p. 185 Getty Images for IMG/Stephen Lovekin • p. 186h Randy Glasbergen • p. 186b CagleCartoons/Brian Fairrington • p. 187 Cyber Bulling Facts • p. 188h Don Addis/Droits réservés • p. 189 The Sun/News Syndication • p. 190h Library of Congress, Washington • p. 190b BBC/Droits réservés •p. 191hg Getty Images/New York Daily News Archives • p. 191hd The Sun/News Syndication • p. 191bg Twitter/Brutus Maximus • p. 192 CartoonStock.com • p. 193h Droits réservés • p. 193b John Kudelka • p. 195h Thinkstock/iStock/Lucadp • p. 195b Thinkstock/iStock/Rommma • p. 197 AFP/Adem Attan • **Chapitre 12** p. 198 Corbis/Onoky/Fabrice Lerouge • p. 199h Thinkstock/Photodisc/Keith Brofsky • p. 199b Sipa/AP/Denis Farrell • p. 200h AAP Image/Tracey Nearmy • p. 200b Reuters/Mike Hutchings • p. 201 Prod DB © DreamWorks Pictures-Reliance Big Entertainement/DR • p. 202h Sipa/AP/Keystone/Jean-Christophe Bott • p. 202m Reuters/Danny Moloshok • p. 202b Corbis/Sygma/Henri Bureau • p. 203 AFP/Getty Images for Fortune/Paul Morigi • p. 204h Zits is used with the permission of the Zits Partnership, King Features Syndicate and the Cartoonist Group. All rights reserved • p. 204b Advertisising Archives • p. 205 Prod DB © Fox-Warner Bros Television/DR • p. 206hg Reuters/Mark Blinch • p. 206md Corbis/Bettmann • p. 206bg Corbis/EPA/Niall Carson • p. 207hd Photononstop/AGF/Laurence Simon • p. 207mg Réa-Report Digital/Jess Hurd • p. 207bd Réa/Zuma/Gail Orenstein • p. 208h CagleCartoons/Hartford Courant • p. 208b CartoonStock.com • p. 209 CartoonStock.com./ Jantoo Cartoons/Harley Schwadron • p. 210 AFP/Damien Meill • p. 211h Reuters/Roberto Jayme • p. 211m Getty Images/Win MacNamee • p. 211b Reuters/Carlo Allegri • p. 215 Corbis/ Bettmann • p. 216 Fotolia/Aleksey Mnogosmyslov

IMPRIM'VERT®

Imprimé en France par Pollina S.A. – 85400 Luçon
N° d'imprimeur : L11434 - Dépôt légal : Avril 2015
N° d'édition : 70119274-01